Essays on the
Representational and
Derivational Nature of
Grammar

To Stan and Phyllis.

I hope you will not be bored
by the technicalities.
Phyllis, I could have used
your talent.
Thank you for your
friendship.
with my Best wishes.

Linguistic Inquiry Monographs
Samuel Jay Keyser, general editor

Essays on the Representational and Derivational Nature of Grammar

The Diversity of *Wh*-Constructions

Joseph Aoun and
Yen-hui Audrey Li

The MIT Press
Cambridge, Massachusetts
London, England

This book was set in Times New Roman on 3B2 by Asco Typesetters, Hong Kong.
Printed and bound in the United States of America.

Library of Congress Cataloging-in-Publication Data

Aoun, Joseph.
 Essays on the representational and derivational nature of grammar : the diversity of *Wh*-constructions / Joseph Aoun and Yen-hui Audrey Li.
   p.   cm. — (Linguistic inquiry monographs ; 40)
 Includes bibliographical references and index.
 ISBN 0-262-01200-6 (hc. : alk. paper) — ISBN 0-262-51132-0 (pbk. : alk. paper)
   1. Grammar, Comparative and general—Interrogative. 2. Grammar, Comparative and general—Relative clauses. 3. Grammar, Comparative and general—Syntax. 4. Generative grammar. I. Li, Yen-hui Audrey, 1954– II. Title. III. Series.
 P299.I57 A58   2003
 415—dc21   2002043163

10 9 8 7 6 5 4 3 2 1

Contents

Series Foreword

We are pleased to present the fortieth in the series *Linguistic Inquiry Monographs*. These monographs present new and original research beyond the scope of the article. We hope they will benefit our field by bringing to it perspectives that will stimulate further research and insight.

Originally published in limited edition, the *Linguistic Inquiry Monographs* are now more widely available. This change is due to the great interest engendered by the series and by the needs of a growing readership. The editors thank the readers for their support and welcome suggestions about future directions for the series.

Samuel Jay Keyser
for the Editorial Board

Acknowledgments

Our book has benefited from the input of many friends and colleagues. We would like to thank especially Margy Avery, Elabbas Benmamoun, Hagit Borer, Lina Choueiri, Francesca Del Gobbo, Tom Ernst, Bella Feng, Naoki Fukui, Hajime Hoji, James Huang, Yuki Kuroda, Mina Lee, Yafei Li, Yan Li, Bingfu Lu, Anoop Mahajan, Anne Mark, David Pesetsky, Barry Schein, Patricia Schneider-Zioga, Jing Shao, Andrew Simpson, Dominique Sportiche, Tim Stowell, Jean-Roger Vergnaud, Zoe Wu, Shenglan Zhang, Maria Luisa Zubizarreta, our colleagues at the University of Southern California, and the students and guests attending our seminars. In addition, we would like to acknowledge the intellectual impact of Noam Chomsky, Norbert Hornstein, and Jamal Ouhalla on this work.

Introduction

Consider some of the diagnostics for movement rules, as discussed in the Extended Standard Theory (see Chomsky 1977a):

(1) a. Movement leaves a gap.
   b. It observes the Complex NP Constraint.
   c. It observes the Adjunct Island Constraint.
   d. It observes the Subject Island Constraint.

Within this model, it is easy to ascertain that a distinction needs to be made between a construction where the *wh*-element leaves a gap and a construction where it leaves a "resumptive" pronoun, as in the following examples from Lebanese Arabic (LA):

• *Gap strategy:* The *wh*-phrase occurs at the beginning of a clause and is related to a gap.

(2) ʔayya mmasil šəft   bə-l-matʕam
    which actor   saw.2MS in-the-restaurant
    'Which actor did you see in the restaurant?'

• *Resumptive strategy:* The *wh*-phrase occurs at the beginning of a clause and is related to a resumptive pronoun.

(3) ʔayya mmasil šəft-uu   bə-l-matʕam
    which actor   saw.2MS-him in-the-restaurant
    'Which actor did you see (him) in the restaurant?'

The necessity of making this distinction arises from their different behavior with respect to island constraints. *Wh*-constructions with a gap observe island constraints, but *wh*-constructions with a resumptive pronoun do not (Ross 1967). Examples illustrating these distinct behaviors in LA are to be found in chapters 1 and 2 and the references cited therein.

The principles-and-parameters framework incorporated reconstruction as an additional diagnostic of movement (Chomsky 1981).[1]

(4) a. Movement constructions display reconstruction.

b. Nonmovement constructions do not display reconstruction.

With the incorporation of reconstruction as a diagnostic for movement, linguists were able to both question the standard and prevalent approach to resumption and deepen their understanding of this phenomenon. Indeed, consider the following two representations:

(5) *No island boundary between an antecedent and the resumptive pronoun*
[antecedent ... resumption]

(6) *Island boundary between an antecedent and the resumptive pronoun*
[antecedent ... [$_{island}$ ... resumption ...]]

In the first representation (5), the antecedent and the resumptive element are not separated by an island and in the second (6), they are. Within the Extended Standard Theory, it suffices to show that the antecedent-resumptive relation is well formed across islands in order to conclude that it is never generated by movement. This conclusion can no longer be drawn once reconstruction is incorporated as a diagnostic for movement. Instead, one has to show that movement is not available in (5) *and* in (6) to conclude that resumption is not generated by movement. It turns out, as discussed in Aoun and Benmamoun 1998, Aoun and Choueiri 2000, and Aoun, Choueiri, and Hornstein 2001, that in LA reconstruction is available in (5) but not in (6). The following conclusion becomes inevitable: resumption can be generated by movement when no island intervenes between the antecedent and the resumptive as in (5), and it is not so generated when an island intervenes between the two as assumed in the references mentioned above. A distinction thus can be made between "true" resumption as in (6), which does not involve movement, and "apparent" resumption as in (5), which can be derived by movement.

Obviously, one could introduce a distinction between two types of movement rules. The first one (call it *standard movement*) displays reconstruction; the second one (call it *illicit movement*) applies across islands and does not display reconstruction. However, within a minimalist framework, this option is not available since "islandhood" or minimality is part of the definition of Move (see Chomsky 1995, chap. 4).

Assume, then, that true resumption is *not* generated by Move, and consider phenomena that have been associated with movement such as superiority effects.

(7) miin ʔannaʕto   yzuur   miin
    who persuaded.2P 3MS.visit who
    'Who did you persuade to visit whom?'

(8) *miin ʔannaʕto   miin yzuur
    who persuaded.2P who 3MS.visit
    '*Who did you persuade whom to visit?'

As originally stated by Kuno and Robinson (1972), superiority effects are a property of *wh*-movement and they prevent a *wh*-word from being pre-posed, crossing over another *wh*. Within the Minimalist Program, this original insight, which related superiority effects to movement, is maintained. Superiority effects are subsumed under the notion Attract Closest, which allows an element α to raise and target K only if there is no legitimate operation Move β targeting K, when β is closer to K (Chomsky 1995, 296), *closer* being defined in terms of c-command.

With this in mind, let us revisit multiple *wh*-constructions involving true resumption. Since it cannot be generated by movement, true resumption is expected not to display superiority effects. As we will show, however, it *is* sensitive to such effects.

One way this result can be incorporated into the grammatical framework is to view it as corroborating the existence of two types of movement: standard movement and the illicit movement that applies across islands, as discussed above (also see Boeckx 2001). Superiority then would be viewed as a true characteristic of all types of movement, whereas reconstruction would be characteristic of only one type (see Boeckx 2001, chap. 4, for relevant discussion). Alternatively, one can divorce Superiority from movement and provide an account of superiority effects without making reference to extraction.[2]

The second approach is the one adopted in chapters 2 and 3. We argue that chains can be generated either derivationally or representationally. The derivational process is at work when Move applies. The "moved" element forms a chain with its trace(s) (copies). The representational process is needed when Move is not at work, as in cases involving true pronouns: when an operator is directly generated in the Spec of Comp, it needs to seek an element to bind that could count as a variable; otherwise, vacuous quantification ensues. The derivational process of chain formation is a bottom-up process, whereas the representational one, call it *Match*, is a top-down process (see Sauerland 1998).[3] We further argue that minimality constrains all chains. That is, minimality constrains not only Move but also Match. Minimality constraining Move is the familiar Minimal Link Condition (see Chomsky 1995, 311), whereas the Minimal Match Condition formulated in (9) constrains Match.[4]

(9) *Minimal Match Condition (MMC)*
An operator must form a chain with the closest XP that it c-commands that contains the same relevant features.

The MMC is checked at the end of each cycle and thus is a condition on the output (i.e., on representation). The MMC accounts for Superiority violations in movement as well as nonmovement structures—with true resumption, for instance.

The MMC, we argue, accounts for Superiority violations and is more desirable than an account based on Attract Closest or an account that takes superiority effects to be a property of two distinct types of movement (standard and illicit, as mentioned above). It also extends to cases exhibiting superiority effects that have been overlooked in the relevant literature. Some of these cases do not involve "crossing" or "c-command." Consider the following representations:

(10) *$[_{CP}$ wh_1 ... $[_{IP}$ ... $[_{island}$ ... resumptive pronoun$_1$ ...] ... wh_2 ...]]

(11) *$[_{CP}$ wh_1 ... $[_{IP}$ ... $[_{island}$ ... wh_2 ...] ... x_1 ...]]

In (10), the resumptive pronoun and the *wh*-in-situ (wh_2) do not c-command each other, and in (11), the *wh*-in-situ (wh_2) and the trace of the extracted *wh*-element (x_1) do not c-command each other. Both (10) and (11) are instances of Superiority violations in LA. Like other cases of Superiority violations, (10) and (11) improve if the *wh*-element in situ, wh_2, is a 'which' phrase instead of a non-'which' phrase, such as 'who' in LA. Obviously, the standard account for superiority effects in terms of crossing cannot apply in (10). Similarly, Attract Closest is not violated in (11): there is no legitimate operation Move β (wh_2) that could target K (Spec of Comp), where β is closer to K than x_1, because wh_2 does not c-command x_1.[5] The MMC, on the other hand, accounts for such Superiority violations under the assumption that, when c-command does not obtain between the resumptive element or variable and the *wh*-in-situ, neither element is closer to the *wh*-element in the Spec of Comp (see section 2.2 for a detailed analysis).

Assuming that the grammar needs to incorporate a principle such as the MMC, certain analytical and theoretical consequences follow. The absence of superiority effects with so-called D-linked *wh*-phrases such as 'which' phrases is no longer to be related to the absence of movement. Rather, in LA, the adequate distinction is between morphologically simplex (e.g., 'who') and morphologically complex (e.g., 'which' phrase) *wh*-elements. Only the latter escape Superiority (see also Uriagereka 1998).

As for the theoretical consequences, chains can be formed derivationally (via Move) or representationally (via Match). That the MMC applies to representations entails that a grammar has to incorporate representational mechanisms and constraints alongside derivational ones (cf. Brody 1995—also see Lappin, Levine, and Johnson 2000a; the summary and response in Roberts 2000; and the further response in Lappin, Levine, and Johnson 2000b). Superiority, as such, is not to be accounted for by a movement-based approach, nor is it to be subsumed under an interpretive-based approach, Weak Crossover, as in Watanabe 1995 and Hornstein 1995. The discussion of interpretive-based accounts of Superiority leads us to investigate the interpretation of multiple *wh*-interrogative constructions. We demonstrate that *three* different types of interpretation need to be distinguished:

(12) a. a *pair-list* interpretation in constructions containing a *wh*-interrogative phrase interacting with another *wh*-interrogative,

   b. a *distributive* interpretation in constructions containing a *wh*-interrogative phrase interacting with a quantificational phrase (QP), and

   c. a *functional* interpretation in constructions containing a *wh*-interrogative phrase interacting with a QP.

This conclusion differs from standard analyses, which do not distinguish (12a) from (12b) (and for some linguists, all three readings are the same; see section 3.2.3 for detailed discussion and references). The three types of interpretation are each shown to be subject to distinct locality requirements. The distinctions in (12) allow us to account for certain cross-linguistic variations affecting them. A comparison between Chinese and LA reveals that the variations are to be traced back to morphological differences in the composition of *wh*-expressions between these two languages (chapter 3).

In part I of the book, on superiority and interpretation, reconstruction is crucially used to establish the existence of extraction and to draw a distinction between "apparent" and "true" resumption. In part II, reconstruction also plays a significant role, helping to determine the structural properties of relative constructions that are usually assumed to involve *wh*-operators (Chomsky 1977b).

Starting with the study of Head-initial relative constructions,[6] we argue in chapter 4 that both the promotion analysis of Brame (1968), Schachter (1973), Vergnaud (1994), and Kayne (1994) and the standard *wh*-operator movement analysis of Chomsky (1977b) have to be at work in the derivation of relative constructions. Reconstruction, once again, provides the crucial evidence. We show that in LA and English, relative constructions that involve a *wh*-operator in the peripheral position of a relative clause relating to a gap inside the relative clause do not allow reconstruction.[7] Reconstruction is available only when no *wh*-operator is present. Such a contrast indicates (1) that the Head of a relative construction can be raised to its surface position when reconstruction is available (promotion analysis) and (2) that the Head is directly generated in its surface position when reconstruction is not available (*wh*-operator movement analysis). In the first instance, a DP is raised; in the second, an operator is involved.

When we consider Head-final relative constructions in chapter 5, Chinese adds a new twist: reconstruction of the Head of a relative construction in this language is available for binding purposes (anaphors, bound pronouns) but is not available for relative scope. What is raised and thus allowed to reconstruct in Chinese is an NP, not a DP, the nonavailability of DP raising following from the morphosyntactic structures of quantificational expressions.

Another difference between Head-initial and Head-final relative constructions considered in this book has to do with the representation of the relative clause per se. When the Head precedes the relative clause as in English and LA, this clause is also selected by (a complement of) a determiner D: [$_{DP}$ D CP]. However, when the Head follows the relative clause as in Chinese, this relative clause behaves like an adjunct and not like a complement: [$_{NP}$ CP NP]. This provides support for allowing left-adjunction (chapters 5–6; see Kayne's (1994) Antisymmetry approach to word order and phrase structure).

The different results concerning relative constructions are brought together in chapter 7. With respect to reconstruction, relative constructions exhibit the following behavior:

(13) a. The Head can be fully reconstructed with respect to binding and scope. (English and LA)

    b. The Head can be partially reconstructed with respect to binding but not scope. (Chinese)

    c. The Head cannot be reconstructed.

(14) Full reconstruction indicates DP movement and partial reconstruction, NP movement. No reconstruction obtains when no movement applies or when operators only are moved. Full reconstruction and partial reconstruction are at work in English/LA and Chinese relative constructions, respectively. In the former, a relative clause is to be analyzed as a complement of a determiner, and in the latter, it is to be analyzed as an adjunct to an NP.

Relative constructions in the grammar, then, do not necessarily have the same phrase structure (complementation or adjunction), nor are they derived by the same strategy (movement of DP, NP, or operator, or no movement). These variations, however, are not random. They are determined by the general properties of phrase structures and by morpho-syntactic properties of nominal expressions in individual languages.

PART I

Wh-Interrogatives:
Superiority and
Interpretation

Chapter 1

Superiority and Movement

As originally stated by Kuno and Robinson (1972, 474), Superiority constrains *wh*-preposing in the following way:

(1) A *wh*-word cannot be preposed, crossing over another *wh*.

This generalization embodies the following three claims:

(2) a. Superiority applies to *wh*-words.
b. Superiority is a property of movement.
c. Superiority involves crossing.

The statement in (1) captures the ill-formedness of (3b), where the *wh*-object is preposed and crosses over the *wh*-subject.

(3) a. I wonder who bought what.
b. *I wonder what who bought.

Since superiority effects were observed and formulated as in (1), additional data have been discovered and various proposals have been made to accurately locate Superiority within the general theory of grammar. Throughout the development of this line of research, the essence of superiority has generally been analyzed as a condition on the movement of *wh*-phrases,[1] and *wh*-phrases not displaying superiority effects have generally been analyzed as not undergoing movement. For instance, it has been pointed out that not all *wh*-words exhibit the effect of superiority: specifically, *which*-phrases do not exhibit this effect. The link between superiority and movement has naturally led to proposals to distinguish the two types of *wh*-phrases in terms of movement: according to this approach, D(iscourse)-linked *which* phrases, which do not exhibit superiority effects, do not undergo movement, whereas non-*which* phrases do exhibit superiority effects and therefore must move (see, e.g., Pesetsky

1987). In this chapter, we will demonstrate not only that the claim in (2a) is empirically inadequate, but also, contra (2b), that superiority effects are exhibited in structures that are not derived by movement and, contra (2c), that they do not involve crossing.

1.1 Superiority as a Condition on Movement

Working within the principles-and-parameters framework (Chomsky 1981),[2] many researchers have adopted the assumption that *wh*-phrases must undergo movement and have suggested some version of the Empty Category Principle (ECP) or other well-formedness conditions on empty categories to derive Superiority as stated in (1) and illustrated in (3). Representative formulations are Kayne's (1983) Connectedness; May's (1985) and Pesetsky's (1982) Path Containment Conditions; Huang's (1982), Lasnik and Saito's (1984), and Rizzi's (1990) head and antecedent government; and Aoun's (1985, 1986) Generalized Binding in place of the antecedent government clause of the ECP.[3] Indeed, under an ECP approach, the superiority effect exhibited in (3b) was used in turn to argue for the existence of LF movement. The overt movement of *what* in (3b) makes the empty category left by the LF movement of the subject, *who*, ill formed, whereas the trace left by the covert movement of the direct object, *what*, in (3a) is well formed. The contrast between (3a) and (3b) is reduced to the well-formedness of the traces generated by movement of the in-situ *wh*-phrases at LF.

In fact, ECP-based accounts have proven to be not quite adequate empirically. First, it was observed that Superiority is not a condition on D-linked *wh*-expressions. (The examples in (4) are from Hornstein 1995, 130–132; those in (5)–(6) are from Pesetsky 2000, 16.)

(4) a. Which man reviewed which book?
    b. Which book did which man review?

(5) a. Which person ____ bought which book?
    b. Which book did which person buy ____?

(6) a. Which person did John talk to ____ about which topic?
    b. Which topic did John talk to which person about ____?

Second, an ECP approach essentially reduces the subject/object asymmetry to a left branch effect or argument/adjunct asymmetry. This is, however, not completely accurate. As Hornstein notes (1995, 124):

[T]here are well-known empirical puzzles.... For example, Hendrick and Roche-mont (1982) note that sentences like [(7b)] display superiority effects without either of the *wh*-words being in subject position. The Superiority Condition can capture these cases straightforwardly as *who* is superior to *what*. However, an ECP-style analysis has to postulate that *who* in such cases is actually a kind of subject or adjunct and this is what prevents its LF movement. Though it is possi-ble to elaborate such an ECP-style theory, it lacks naturalness.[4]

(7) a.   Who did you persuade to buy what?
    b. *What did you persuade who to buy?

Moreover, as Kayne (1983) notes, in sentences like (8a–b) with three or more *wh*-phrases, Superiority is no longer relevant, a fact that is difficult to capture under an ECP-based approach.[5] (The following examples are from Pesetsky 2000, 17.)

(8) a. *What did who give _____ to Mary?   (detectable superiority effect)
    b.   What did who give _____ to whom?   (no detectable superiority effect)

ECP-based approaches thus have been replaced by approaches such as those based on Connectedness or the Path Containment Condition. Despite these adjustments, it remains the case that superiority effects are considered a property of movement structures.

This line of pursuit—relating superiority effects to movement—has been incorporated into the latest theoretical development, the Minimalist Program. Within this framework, superiority effects have been subsumed primarily under the notion of Attract Closest (Chomsky 1995, 296).

(9) α can raise to target K only if there is no legitimate operation Move β targeting K, where β is closer to K.[6]

In a structure such as (10), C^0 has a strong *wh*-feature that requires checking by a *wh*-element.

(10) $[C^0 [_{IP}$ who saw what$]]$

Either *who* or *what* can satisfy this requirement. Movement of *who* is preferred since the distance it must travel is shorter than the distance *what* would need to travel in order to check the same feature. This captures the contrast found in the following pair of sentences:

(11) a.   Who saw what?
     b. *What did who see?

We will return to the details of this type of analysis in section 1.3. For present purposes, it suffices to point out that a very prominent line of research historically has been to subsume superiority effects under general conditions on movement structures.[7]

1.2   Superiority in Nonmovement Structures

Though superiority effects have often been related to movement our investigation of Lebanese Arabic (LA) demonstrates that such effects occur in nonmovement as well as movement structures.

In LA, a *wh*-element can remain in situ, be moved to the Spec of Comp, or be directly generated in the Spec of Comp. When it is directly generated in the Spec of Comp, the *wh*-interrogative is related to a resumptive pronoun in argument position. Questions containing two *wh*-phrases, which have the potential to display superiority effects, may be generated in any of the following ways:

(12) a. One *wh*-phrase undergoes *wh*-movement, leaving a gap in the position from which it is raised; the other stays in situ.

   b. One *wh*-phrase occurs at the beginning of a sentence and is related to a resumptive pronoun in the sentence; the other stays in situ.

   c. Both *wh*-phrases stay in situ.

There is evidence, to be discussed shortly, indicating that the (12b)-type construction cannot be derived by movement when the resumptive pronoun is within an island. Significantly, not only the (12a)-type but also the (12b)-type of *wh*-construction displays superiority effects. This fact shows that superiority effects do not arise from movement alone. We elaborate on this point by first discussing in detail the types of *wh*-interrogatives in LA and then demonstrating the relevance of Superiority to nonmovement structures.

1.2.1   *Wh*-Interrogatives in Lebanese Arabic
In LA, three different strategies, illustrated in (13)–(15), can be used to generate *wh*-interrogative constructions.

• *Gap strategy:* The *wh*-phrase occurs at the beginning of a clause and is related to a gap.

(13) ʔayya mmasil šəft   bə-l-matʕam
     which actor   saw.2MS in-the-restaurant
     'Which actor did you see in the restaurant?'

• *Resumptive strategy:* The *wh*-phrase occurs at the beginning of a clause and is related to a resumptive pronoun.

(14) ʔayya mmasil šəft-uu   bə-l-matʕam
     which actor   saw.2MS-him in-the-restaurant
     'Which actor did you see (him) in the restaurant?'

• *In-situ strategy:* The *wh*-phrase remains in situ.

(15) šəft   ʔayya mmasil bə-l-matʕam
     saw.2MS which actor   in-the-restaurant
     'Which actor did you see in the restaurant?'

As established in Aoun and Benmamoun 1998, Aoun and Choueiri 1997, 1999, and Aoun, Choueiri, and Hornstein 2001, the gap strategy is generated by movement. The resumptive strategy is also generated by movement when the *wh*-element and the resumptive pronoun are not separated by an island; otherwise, it is base-generated. Finally, movement does not play a role at all for the in-situ strategy. Evidence for the above distinctions comes from the relevance of island conditions to the various strategies and the possibility of reconstruction. Below, we briefly sketch some of the syntactic differences among the three strategies. (For details and examples, see the works mentioned above.)

Wh-elements related to gaps are sensitive to islands: a gap cannot be separated by an island from the *wh*-phrase it is related to. Moreover, a *wh*-phrase related to a gap displays reconstruction effects: the *wh*-phrase behaves as if it were in the gap position with respect to binding, for instance. In sentence (16), which illustrates a reconstruction effect, the pronoun contained in the fronted *wh*-element can be bound by a quantifier that c-commands the gap position, but the fronted *wh*-element itself cannot.

(16) ʔayya ṭaalib   min   ṭulaab-a   fakkarto   ʔənno kəll
     which student among students-her thought.2P that   every
     mʕallme   ħatnaʔe
     teacher.FS will.3FS.choose
     'Which of her$_i$ students did you think that every teacher$_i$ would choose?'

Such diagnostics lead to the conclusion that the gap strategy is generated by movement: a *wh*-phrase is moved from the gap position to the beginning of a sentence—the Spec of Comp.

The resumptive strategy is not a unified strategy; reconstruction facts indicate that two different types of constructions with resumptive pronouns need to be distinguished. Reconstruction is possible when the *wh*-phrase and the resumptive pronoun are not separated by an island; it is not possible when the *wh*-phrase and the resumptive pronoun are separated by an island. In sentence (17) (no islands involved), but not sentence (18) (an island involved), the pronoun contained within the *wh*-element can be bound by the quantifier.

(17) ?ayya ṭaalib min   ṭulaab-a   fakkarto   ?ənno kəll
     which student among students-her thought.2P that   every
     mʕallme ħatna?-ii
     teacher.FS will.3FS.choose-him
     'Which of her₍ᵢ₎ students did you think that every teacher₍ᵢ₎ would
     choose?'

(18) ?ayya ṭaalib min   ṭulaab-a   ?ənbasaṭṭo la?inno kəll
     which student among students-her pleased.2P because every
     mʕallme ħatna?-ii
     teacher.FS will.3FS.choose-him
     '*Which of her₍ᵢ₎ students were you pleased because every teacher₍ᵢ₎
     would choose him?'

Assuming with Chomsky (1995, 71–74) that reconstruction is a diagnostic for movement, Aoun and Benmamoun (1998), Aoun and Choueiri (1997, 1999), and Aoun, Choueiri, and Hornstein (2001) argue that resumption can and in fact must be generated by movement when the *wh*-element and the resumptive pronoun are not separated by an island. Resumption is base-generated otherwise: when separated by an island, the *wh*-phrase and the resumptive pronoun are generated in the Spec of Comp and the argument position, respectively. In other words, a distinction can be made between "true" resumption in cases not allowing reconstruction and "apparent" resumption in cases allowing reconstruction.

In brief, the following generalizations regarding *wh*-interrogatives with resumption can be advanced:

(19) a. A *wh*-phrase is generated by movement when it is not separated
        from its resumptive pronoun by an island (an "apparent"
        resumptive pronoun).

    b. A *wh*-phrase is not generated by movement when it is separated from its resumptive pronoun by an island (a "true" resumptive pronoun).

The following generalization applies to in-situ *wh*-interrogatives, as will be illustrated:

(20) In-situ constructions allow a *wh*-phrase in situ to occur within an island and have interrogative scope outside the island.

Consider the following sentence:

(21) Ɂənbasaṭṭo laɁinno raaħit minduun-ma tɁarrif   miin Ɂala
     pleased.2P because left.3FS without   3FS.introduce who to
     saami
     Sami
     'lit. You were pleased because she left without introducing whom to Sami?'
     'Who were you pleased because she left without introducing to Sami?'

This sentence is interpreted as a direct question; the *wh*-in-situ in the adjunct clause can take matrix scope. With Aoun and Choueiri (1999), we assume that the interpretation of this *wh*-in-situ in LA is not generated by (overt or covert) movement to the Spec of Comp (see, e.g., Chomsky 1995, 68–70; Watanabe 1992; Aoun and Li 1993b).[8]

    Given the three strategies available for *wh*-interrogatives (13)–(15), a sentence containing two *wh*-phrases may be generated as follows:

(22) a. One *wh*-phrase undergoes *wh*-movement to the Spec of Comp, leaving a gap in the position from which it is raised; the other stays in situ.
    b. One *wh*-phrase is directly generated in the Spec of Comp and is related to a resumptive pronoun in the sentence; the other stays in situ.
    c. Both *wh*-phrases stay in situ.

What will prove significant is that superiority effects arise in both of the first two patterns and not in the third, as we discuss in the following section.

1.2.2 Superiority in *Wh*-Interrogatives

It is not surprising that the pattern in (22a), which involves movement of a *wh*-phrase, exhibits superiority effects: a lower *wh*-phrase cannot be moved across a higher *wh*-phrase.

(23) miin ?anna\Sto   yzuur   miin
     who persuaded.2P 3MS.visit who
     'Who did you persuade to visit whom?'

(24) *miin ?anna\Sto   miin yzuur
     who persuaded.2P who 3MS.visit
     '*Who did you persuade whom to visit?'

Schematically, these configurations, involving Superiority, can be represented as follows (t is the trace left by *wh*-movement; irrelevant details are omitted):

(25) a. $[_{CP}\ wh_1\ [_{IP} \ldots t_1 \ldots wh_2 \ldots]]$ (t_1 c-commands wh_2)
     b. $*[_{CP}\ wh_2\ [_{IP} \ldots wh_1 \ldots t_2 \ldots]]$ (wh_1 c-commands t_2)

Furthermore, as is generally true with Superiority violations, replacing 'who' with a 'which' NP renders (24b) grammatical.

(26) ?ayya walad ?anna\Sto   ?ayya m\Sallme tzuur
     which boy   persuaded.2P which teacher.FS 3FS.visit
     'Which boy did you persuade which teacher to visit?'

   Next, consider the resumptive strategy discussed in (22b). Recall that two types of resumptive structures must be recognized in LA. One is derived by movement; in this case, no island intervenes between the *wh*-phrase and the resumptive pronoun. The other is base-generated; in this case, an island intervenes between the *wh*-phrase and the resumptive pronoun. Interestingly, superiority effects occur in both types of resumptive constructions: the one that is derived by movement and the one that is not. In (27a–b), the *wh*-element in the Spec of Comp is not separated from the resumptive pronoun by an island and Superiority must be respected, as illustrated by the ungrammaticality of (27b). In (28a–d), an island intervenes between the *wh*-element and the resumptive pronoun and Superiority is also respected, as indicated by the ungrammaticality of (28b,d).

(27) a.   miin ?anna\St-u   yzuur   miin
          who persuaded.2P-him 3MS.visit who
          'Who did you persuade (him) to visit whom?'
     b. *miin ?anna\Sto   miin yzuur-u
          who persuaded.2P who 3MS.visit-him
          'Who did you persuade whom to visit (him)?'

(28) a. miin ʔənbasaṭṭo laʔinno saami ʕarraf-o   ʕa-miin
      who pleased.2P because Sami introduced.3MS-him to-whom
      'Who$_i$ were you pleased because Sami introduced him$_i$ to whom?'

    b. *miin ʔənbasaṭṭo laʔinno saami ʕarraf   miin ʕəl-e
      who pleased.2P because Sami introduced.3MS who to-him
      'Who$_i$ were you pleased because Sami introduced whom to him$_i$?'

    c. miin hannayt-u   laʔinno saami zaar   miin
      who congratulated.2P-him because Sami visited.3MS who
      'Who$_i$ did you congratulate (him$_i$) because Sami visited whom?'

    d. *miin hannayto   miin   laʔinno saami zaar-o
      who congratulated.2P whom because Sami visited-him
      'Who$_i$ did you congratulate whom because Sami visited him$_i$?'

Sentences (27a–b) are schematically represented in (29a–b), and sentences (28a–d) are schematically represented in (30a–b) (*RP* stands for *resumptive pronoun*; irrelevant details omitted).

(29) a. $[_{CP} \, wh_1 \, [_{IP} \ldots RP_1 \ldots wh_2 \ldots]]$ (RP$_1$ c-commands wh_2)

    b. *$[_{CP} \, wh_2 \, [_{IP} \ldots wh_1 \ldots RP_2 \ldots]]$ (wh_1 c-commands RP$_2$)

(30) a. $[_{CP} \, wh_1 \, [_{IP} \ldots [_{island} \ldots RP_1 \ldots wh_2 \ldots] \ldots]]$ (RP$_1$ c-commands wh_2)

    b. *$[_{CP} \, wh_2 \, [_{IP} \ldots [_{island} \ldots wh_1 \ldots RP_2 \ldots] \ldots]]$ (wh_1 c-commands RP$_2$)

    c. $[_{CP} \, wh_1 \, [_{IP} \ldots RP_1 \ldots [_{island} \ldots wh_2 \ldots] \ldots]]$ (RP$_1$ c-commands wh_2)

    d. *$[_{CP} \, wh_2 \, [_{IP} \ldots wh_1 \ldots [_{island} \ldots RP_2 \ldots] \ldots]]$ (wh_1 c-commands RP$_2$)

Again, the unacceptable sentences in (27b) and (28b,d) become acceptable when 'who' is replaced with a 'which' phrase.

(31) a. ʔayya walad ʔannaʕto   ʔayya bint tzuur-o
      which boy persuaded.2P which girl 3FS.visit-him
      'Which boy$_i$ did you persuade which girl to visit him$_i$?'

    b. ʔayya walad ʔənbasaṭṭo laʔinno saami ʕarraf   ʔayya
      which boy pleased.2P because Sami introduced.3MS which
      bənt ʕəl-e
      girl to-him

'Which boy$_i$ were you pleased because Sami introduced which girl to him$_i$?'

c. ʔayya walad hannayto   ʔayya bənt laʔinno saami
    which boy   congratulated.2P which girl   because Sami
    zaar-o
    visited.3MS-him
    'Which boy$_i$ did you congratulate which girl because Sami visited him$_i$?'

In the ill-formed cases (27b) and (28b,d), the intervening *wh*-in-situ c-commands the RP. Now, consider sentences in which c-command does not obtain between the *wh*-in-situ and the resumptive pronoun. These sentences are also unacceptable.

(32) a. *miin fakkarto   laʔinno l-mʕallme   ħikət   maʕ-o
      who thought.2P because the-teacher.FS spoke.3FS with-him
      ʔənno l-mudiira   ħa-təšħaṭ   miin
      that   the-principal.FS will-3FS.expel who
      'Who$_i$ did you think because the teacher spoke with him$_i$ that the principal would expel whom?'

b. *miin fakkarto   laʔinno l-mʕallme   ħikət   maʕ miin
     who thought.2P because the-teacher.FS spoke.3FS with who
     ʔənno l-mudiira   ħa-təšħaṭ-o
     that   the-principal.FS will-3FS.expel-him
     'Who$_i$ did you think because the teacher spoke with whom that the principal would expel him$_i$?'

c. *miin fakkarto   laʔinno l-mʕallme   ħikət   maʕ-o
     who thought.2P because the-teacher.FS spoke.3FS with-him
     ʔənno l-mudiira   ħa-truuħ   minduun-ma təšħaṭ   miin
     that   the-principal.FS will-3FS.leave without   3FS.expel who
     'Who$_i$ did you think because the teacher spoke with him$_i$ that the principal would leave without expelling whom?'

d. *miin fakkarto   laʔinno l-mʕallme   ħikət   maʕ miin
     who thought.2P because the-teacher.FS spoke.3FS with who
     ʔənno l-mudiira   ħa-truuħ   minduun-ma təšħaṭ-o
     that   the-principal.FS will-3FS.leave without   3FS.expel-him
     'Who$_i$ did you think because the teacher spoke with whom that the principal would leave without expelling him$_i$?'

Once again, as is true of Superiority violations, the sentences in (32) become acceptable just in case the in-situ 'who' is replaced with a 'which' NP.

(33) a. miin fakkarto   laʔinno l-mˤallme   ħikət   maʕ-o
       who thought.2P because the-teacher.FS spoke.3FS with-him
       ʔənno l-mudiira   ha-təšhaṭ   ʔayya walad
       that   the-principal.FS will-3FS.expel which boy
       'Who$_i$ did you think because the teacher spoke with him$_i$ that
       the principal would expel which boy?'

    b. miin fakkarto   laʔinno l-mˤallme   ħikət   maʕ ʔayya
       who thought.2P because the-teacher.FS spoke.3FS with which
       walad ʔənno l-mudiira   ha-təšhaṭ-o
       boy   that   the-principal.FS will-3FS.expel-him
       'Who$_i$ did you think because the teacher spoke with which boy
       that the principal would expel him$_i$?'

    c. miin fakkarto   laʔinno l-mˤallme   ħikət   maʕ-o
       who thought.2P because the-teacher.FS spoke.3FS with-him
       ʔənno l-mudiira   ha-truuħ   minduun-ma təšhaṭ
       that   the-principal.FS will-3FS.leave without   3FS.expel
       ʔayya walad
       which boy
       'Who$_i$ did you think because the teacher spoke with him$_i$ that
       the principal would leave without expelling which boy?'

    d. miin fakkarto   laʔinno l-mˤallme   ħikət   maʕ ʔayya
       who thought.2P because the-teacher.FS spoke.3FS with which
       walad ʔənno l-mudiira   ha-truuħ   minduun-ma
       boy   that   the-principal.FS will-3FS.leave without
       təšhaṭ-o
       3FS.expel-him
       'Who$_i$ did you think because the teacher spoke with which boy
       that the principal would leave without expelling him$_i$?'

The sentences in (32) are schematically represented in (34).

(34) a. *$[_{CP} wh_1 [_{IP} \ldots [_{island} \ldots RP_1 \ldots] \ldots wh_2 \ldots]]$
    b. *$[_{CP} wh_2 [_{IP} \ldots [_{island} \ldots wh_1 \ldots] \ldots RP_2 \ldots]]$[9]
    c. *$[_{CP} wh_1 [_{IP} \ldots [_{island} \ldots RP_1 \ldots] \ldots [_{island} \ldots wh_2 \ldots] \ldots]]$
    d. *$[_{CP} wh_2 [_{IP} \ldots [_{island} \ldots wh_1 \ldots] \ldots [_{island} \ldots RP_2 \ldots] \ldots]]$

The unacceptability of (34a,c) is especially significant in light of the formulation of Superiority in (1)–(2). Note that in these two patterns,
RP_1 does not cross another wh-phrase to be related to the wh-phrase in the
Spec of Comp, with "crossing" interpreted either linearly or hierarchically.

This fact indicates that crossing is not an intrinsic property of superiority effects.

Finally, let us consider constructions in which both *wh*-phrases remain in situ.

(35) a. ʔannaʕto   miin yzuur   miin
        persuaded.2P who 3MS.visit who
        'Lit. You persuaded whom to visit whom?'
        'Who did you persuade to visit whom?'

   b. ʔənbasaṭto laʔinno saami ʕarraf   miin ʕala miin
        pleased.2P because Sami introduced.3MS who to   who
        'Lit. You were pleased because Sami introduced whom to whom?'
        'Who were you pleased because Sami introduced ____ to whom?'

   c. hannayto   miin laʔinno saami zaar   miin
        congratulated.2P who because Sami visited.3MS who
        'Lit. You congratulated whom because Sami visited whom?'
        'Who did you congratulate because Sami visited whom?'

   d. fakkarto   laʔinno l-mʕallme   ḥikət   maʕ miin ʔənno
        thought.2P because the-teacher.FS spoke.3FS with who that
        l-mudiira   ḥa-təšḥaṭ   miin
        the-principal.FS will-3FS.expel who
        'Lit. You thought because the teacher spoke with whom that the principal would expel whom?'

   e. fakkarto   laʔinno l-mʕallme   ḥikət   maʕ miin ʔənno
        thought.2P because the-teacher.FS spoke.3FS with who that
        l-mudiira   ḥa-truuḥ   minduun-ma təšḥaṭ   miin
        the-principal.FS will-3FS.leave without   3FS.expel who
        'Lit. You thought because the teacher spoke with whom that the principal would leave without expelling whom?'

The sentences in (35a–e), schematically represented as (36a–e), are all acceptable; no Superiority violation occurs.

(36) a. ... wh_1 ... wh_2 ...
   b. ... [island ... wh_1 ... wh_2 ...] ...
   c. ... wh_1 ... [island ... wh_2 ...] ...
   d. ... [island ... wh_1 ...] ... wh_2 ...
   e. ... [island ... wh_1 ...] ... [island ... wh_2 ...] ...

1.3   Superiority and Movement

The facts presented so far not only pose problems for the generalizations in (1)–(2) but also challenge any movement approach to Superiority. Such approaches are best represented by the recent work of Pesetsky (2000—also see Oka 1993; Bošković 1998, 1999), which presents quite a refined movement (Attract Closest) analysis for Superiority. We show below that even such a refined movement analysis does not account for superiority effects in LA. We first briefly describe Pesetsky's (2000) analysis and then show what challenges the LA data pose.

1.3.1   Pesetsky's (2000) Approach to Superiority

Pesetsky (2000) refines the movement approach to superiority effects based on Attract Closest (AC; see (9)) and offers a comprehensive account that accommodates various types of counterexamples to the standard superiority effects.[10] He argues that superiority effects are accounted for by AC and some special requirement on how the Spec of Comp should be filled. English, for example, has a rule like (37), which requires the Spec of Comp to be filled in the overt syntax by more than one *wh*-phrase ($C_{m\text{-spec}}$ = multispecifier complementizer).

(37) *Specifier potential of* $C_{m\text{-spec}}$
      $C_{m\text{-spec}}$ requires more than one *wh*-specifier.

The fact that English requires multiple *wh*-specifiers in $C_{m\text{-spec}}$ is not obvious from superficial inspection of a string because the following language-specific pronunciation rule operates in English:

(38) *Pronunciation rule (English)*[11]
      a. The first instance of *wh*-phrase movement to C is overt, in that *wh* is pronounced in its new position and unpronounced in its trace positions.
      b. Secondary instances of *wh*-phrase movement to C are covert, in that *wh* is pronounced in its trace position and unpronounced in its new position.

Superiority in English is, then, accounted for by AC and the multiple Spec requirement in (37), tempered by the pronunciation rule in (38).

   A *wh*-element can undergo either phrasal movement or feature movement. In sentences with two *wh*-expressions, such as (39a), AC requires the higher *wh* (in (39a), *who*) to move first. *What* also undergoes movement to satisfy (37), whose effect is not detectable by surface inspection because of the pronunciation rule in (38). (39a) is therefore well formed. (39b), however, violates either AC or the multiple Spec requirement (37). (39b) violates AC if *what* is moved first to the Spec of Comp. However, AC can still be satisfied if feature (as opposed to phrasal) movement applies first to *who*—that is, if only the [+*wh*] feature of *who* is moved first. *What* could then legitimately undergo phrasal movement to the Spec of Comp, which would be overt according to the pronunciation rule. However, this derivation violates (37), which requires the Spec of Comp to be filled by more than one *wh*-phrase. Feature movement of *who* cannot satisfy (37), and thus there is no well-formed derivation of (39b).

(39) a. Who saw what?
     b. *What did who see?

Apparent violations of Superiority involving three *wh*-elements, such as the grammatical example in (40), are accounted for by AC, Richards's (1997) Principle of Minimal Compliance (PMC) (41), and the specific English pronunciation rule in (38).

(40) What did who persuade whom to buy _____?

(41) *Principle of Minimal Compliance (PMC; Richards 1998, 601)*
     For any dependency D that obeys constraint C, any elements that
     are relevant for determining whether D obeys C can be ignored for
     the rest of the derivation for purposes of determining whether any
     other dependency D' obeys C.
         An element X is *relevant* to determining whether a dependency D
     with head A and tail B obeys constraint C iff
     a. X is along the path of D (that is, X = A, X = B, or A
     c-commands X and X c-commands B), and
     b. X is a member of the class of elements to which C makes
     reference.

The PMC allows AC to be met only once. Once AC is satisfied, subsequent movement does not also need to satisfy AC. The derivation of sentence (40) is as follows:

(42) a. *Input to* wh-*movement*
         $C_{\text{m-spec}}$ [who persuaded whom to buy what]
     b. *Step 1*
         C attracts the [+*wh*] feature of *who* (H), pays "AC tax."
         F_i-C [F_i-who persuade whom to buy what]

c. *Step 2*
C attracts either of the remaining *wh*-phrases, since the PMC no longer requires obedience to AC.
what F_i-C [F_i-who persuade whom to buy ____]

d. *Step 3*
C attracts the other *wh*-phrase(s).
what whom F_i-C [F_i-who persuade ____ to buy ____]

e. *Pronounced result*
What did who persuade whom to buy?

As for the fact that *which*-phrases escape superiority effects as in (4)–(6) and (43), Pesetsky suggests that for sentences containing *which* phrases, there is no requirement that at least two *wh*-phrases must be attracted by $C_{m\text{-}spec}$. That is, the multiple Spec requirement in (37) does not apply in cases involving *which* phrases. In (43), for instance, the *wh*-phrase *which person* can undergo feature movement first, thus satisfying AC, and the multiple Spec requirement in (37) is suspended. The step-by-step derivation is given in (44).

(43) Which book did which person buy?

(44) a. *Input to* wh-*movement*
$C_{m\text{-}spec}$ [which person bought which book]

b. *Step 1*
$C_{m\text{-}spec}$ attracts the [$+wh$] feature of *which person*.
F_i-C [F_i-which person bought which book]

c. *Step 2*
$C_{m\text{-}spec}$ attracts the *wh*-phrase *which book*.
which book F_i-C [F_i-which person bought ____]

d. *Pronounced result*
Which book did which person buy?

Recall that feature movement of the first *wh*-phrase is not possible in (39b) because of the multiple Spec requirement in (37). The contrast between (39b) and (43) is the consequence of different requirements on the number of *wh*-phrases in the Spec of Comp: (37) does not apply to *which* phrases.

The existence of feature movement, Pesetsky argues, is supported by contrasts like the following (É. Kiss 1986; Hornstein 1995):[12]

(45) a. Which person did not read which book?
b. Which person didn't read which book?

    c.   Which book did which person not read?

    d.   *Which book didn't which person read?

(45d) is unacceptable.[13] The unacceptability of this sentence is captured by the requirement of AC together with the blocking effect of negation. To satisfy AC, the subject *which person* needs to undergo movement first—feature movement in this case. However, feature movement is blocked by negation in C. In contrast, (45a) and (45b) are acceptable because the object *which book* can undergo phrasal movement, after *which person* undergoes phrasal movement. Negation does not block phrasal movement. (45c) is grammatical because negation is not in Comp, therefore does not intervene between the subject and the Spec of Comp, and therefore does not intercept feature movement of the subject.

1.3.2 Attract Closest in Lebanese Arabic

An immediate difficulty in extending an AC approach to the LA data is the relevance of superiority effects in nonmovement structures involving resumption, such as those involving islands, discussed earlier and repeated here:

(46) a. $[_{CP}$ wh_1 $[_{IP}$ ... $[_{island}$ ... RP_1 ... wh_2 ...] ...]]   (RP_1 c-commands wh_2)

     b. *$[_{CP}$ wh_2 $[_{IP}$ ... $[_{island}$ ... wh_1 ... RP_2 ...] ...]]   (wh_1 c-commands RP_2)

     c. $[_{CP}$ wh_1 $[_{IP}$ ... RP_1 ... $[_{island}$ ... wh_2 ...] ...]]   (RP_1 c-commands wh_2)

     d. *$[_{CP}$ wh_2 $[_{IP}$ ... wh_1 ... $[_{island}$ ... RP_2 ...] ...]]   (wh_1 c-commands RP_2)

(47) a. *$[_{CP}$ wh_1 $[_{IP}$ ... $[_{island}$ ... RP_1 ...] ... wh_2 ...]]   (neither RP_1 nor wh_2 c-commands the other)

     b. *$[_{CP}$ wh_2 $[_{IP}$ ... $[_{island}$ ... wh_1 ...] ... RP_2 ...]]   (neither wh_1 nor RP_2 c-commands the other)

     c. *$[_{CP}$ wh_1 $[_{IP}$ ... $[_{island}$ ... RP_1 ...] ... $[_{island}$ ... wh_2 ...] ...]]   (neither RP_1 nor wh_2 c-commands the other)

     d. *$[_{CP}$ wh_2 $[_{IP}$ ... $[_{island}$ ... wh_1 ...] ... $[_{island}$ ... RP_2 ...] ...]] (neither wh_1 nor RP_2 c-commands the other)

We have argued that these patterns cannot be derived by movement because of a lack of reconstruction. As a result, AC is not relevant and the contrast found in (46) and (47) cannot be captured by a movement approach.[14]

Suppose we weaken a movement approach by proposing that, despite standard assumptions, movement is possible from within islands and that the lack of reconstruction is due to other factors.[15] Even an approach based on such a weakening of grammatical theory would still fail for empirical reasons. Recall that resumption in LA is sensitive to Superiority but in-situ *wh*-phrases are not, as illustrated by the contrast in (46) and (47) and the cases with all *wh*-phrases in situ as in (48).

(48) a. ... wh_1 ... wh_2 ...
　　 b. ... [... wh_1 ... wh_2 ...]
　　 c. ... wh_1 ... [... wh_2 ...] ...
　　 d. ... [... wh_1 ...] ... wh_2 ...
　　 e. ... [... wh_1 ...] ... [... wh_2 ...] ...

According to Pesetsky's analysis, all *wh*-phrases undergo movement (feature movement or phrasal movement). They appear in different positions—peripheral or argument positions—because of a difference in pronunciation rules: *wh*-phrases appearing in peripheral positions are generated by spelling out the head of the chain; in-situ *wh*-phrases are generated by spelling out the tail of the chain. Under such an approach, it is not clear, for instance, why the corresponding pairs of patterns in (47a–d) and (48d–e) differ in acceptability.[16]

In brief, the LA data cannot be satisfactorily accommodated by an AC approach to Superiority. Superiority in LA is at play in nonmovement structures and does not apply to constructions involving only *wh*-in-situ as in (48). The intervention effects are not responsible for Superiority violations. They are relevant for pair-list interpretations but not single-pair interpretations.

Even if illicit movement is made to apply to those cases with *wh*-phrases in situ or resumptive pronouns within islands, a movement approach to superiority effects cannot adequately capture the differences in acceptability exhibited in (46)–(48).

1.4 Summary

In this chapter, we investigated the behavior of the three types of LA *wh*-interrogative constructions listed in (22a–c), repeated here, with respect to superiority effects. We showed that, when an island separates a resumptive pronoun in a (b)-type structure from the *wh*-phrase in the Spec of Comp, the structure cannot be derived by movement. Nonetheless, (b)-type structures as well as (a)-type structures exhibit superiority effects.

(22) a. One *wh*-phrase undergoes *wh*-movement to the Spec of Comp, leaving a gap in the position from which it is raised; the other stays in situ.

    b. One *wh*-phrase is directly generated in the Spec of Comp and is related to a resumptive pronoun in the sentence; the other stays in situ.

    c. Both *wh*-phrases stay in situ.

In view of the prominent, decades-old line of research that subsumes Superiority under movement relations, the data we have discussed so far are significant. They present a novel and interesting picture: Superiority is relevant even in certain nonmovement structures such as those involving a resumptive pronoun separated from its *wh*-antecedent by an island, as in (46) and (47). These facts indicate that Superiority violations are not restricted to constructions involving movement. We further showed that cases involving *which* phrases do not exhibit Superiority, thus confirming that we are indeed dealing with superiority effects in LA. Moreover, we established that Superiority violations do not necessarily involve crossing. This argues that the view of Superiority as originally formulated in (1), consisting of the three subclaims in (2a–c), is not adequate empirically. A movement approach fails to capture the contrasts found in (46)–(48), even if movement is made to apply more broadly (allowing illicit movement) and the movement theory greatly weakened. Consequently, Superiority must be approached from a new perspective—an important focus of the next chapter.

Chapter 2

Superiority and the Minimal Match Condition

The facts presented in chapter 1 force us to search for an account of superiority effects that accommodates their occurrence in movement and nonmovement, crossing and noncrossing structures. In this chapter, we argue that superiority effects can be accounted for by a minimality condition on chain formation. We argue that chains can be generated derivationally via Move (or Agree, as in Chomsky 1995, 44, 182, 201–202) or representationally via a process we refer to as *Match*. Move is a bottom-up process that merges copies of lexical items while building up tree structures. Match is a top-down process that governs the relations between elements that need to be interpreted. We further argue, in the spirit of Chomsky 1995 (especially pp. 89–90, 204–297, 311), that minimality constrains all chains; that is, minimality constrains not only Move but also Match. Minimality constraining Move is the Minimal Link Condition (Shortest Move; Chomsky 1995, 267–268, 311). Minimality constraining Match is formulated as follows:

(1) *Minimal Match Condition (MMC)*
    An operator must form a chain with the closest XP it c-commands that contains the same relevant features.[1]

The MMC, we argue, accounts for Superiority violations adequately and is more desirable than an account that subsumes Superiority under Attract Closest or an account that takes superiority effects to be a property of two distinct types of movement (standard licit movement and illicit movement). Indeed, we show in this chapter that the MMC adequately captures the superiority effects exhibited in all the patterns discussed in chapter 1. We first determine what elements enter into the formation of operator-variable chains (section 2.1) and illustrate how the MMC accounts for superiority effects (section 2.2). Because Superiority applies to representations derived by movement as well as nonmovement, the absence of superiority effects with so-called D-linked *wh*-phrases such as *which* phrases can no longer be accounted for in terms of absence of movement. Rather, in LA the adequate distinction is between morphologically simplex and morphologically complex *wh*-phrases (section 2.3).

We then discuss the workings of the MMC and its relation to other conditions that have been suggested in the literature (section 2.4). Specifically, we consider the relation between the MMC and the Minimal Link Condition (MLC), which applies to movement structures during derivations, and the relation between the MMC and the Minimal Binding Requirement (MBR) in Aoun and Li 1989, 1993a. The distinction between the MLC and the MMC lies in what chain formation is relevant: the former applies to chain formation during derivations and the latter to representations. The MBR requires a variable to be bound by the closest operator, a requirement quite close to the spirit of the MMC. Since these conditions all express some notion of minimality, are they perhaps all the same condition and should they therefore be collapsed? Or are they different, independently relevant conditions? We show in section 2.4.1 that the MLC and the MMC are both necessary, a result that has important implications for the derivational and representational nature of grammar. In section 2.4.2, we show that the MBR can be reduced to the MMC.

2.1 Distinguishing Resumptive Pronouns from Bound Pronouns

Before we can develop the analysis further, we need to introduce a distinction between resumptive pronouns and bound pronouns. First, consider constructions involving only *wh*-in-situ. We assume that an in-situ *wh*-phrase is interpreted with respect to an appropriate Comp that dominates a question complementizer (see, e.g., Baker 1970; Pesetsky 1987; Aoun and Li 1993b). More than one in-situ *wh*-phrase can be licensed by a question complementizer (Qu).

(2) Qu [... wh_1 ... wh_2 ...]   (wh_1, wh_2 licensed by Qu)

Now, consider *wh*-phrases that appear in the Spec of Comp. A *wh*-phrase can undergo overt *wh*-movement to the Spec of Comp or can be base-generated in that position. A *wh*-phrase in the Spec of Comp is an operator and needs to bind a variable for proper interpretation. Under the copy-and-merge theory of movement (see Chomsky 1995, chap. 4), the variable bound by a moved *wh*-operator is the copy in argument position. This copy is not spelled out and surfaces as a gap (see, e.g., Nunes 1995). Clearly, a resumptive pronoun should be interpreted as a variable as well; otherwise, the *wh*-operator in the Spec of Comp would bind no variable and vacuous quantification would ensue (see Sells 1984, chap. 1, for the claim that operator-bound resumptive pronouns are variables). For instance, in the LA sentence (3), it must be that the resumptive pronoun serves as a variable for the *wh*-phrase in the Spec of Comp.

(3) miin raaḥit   saamia minduun-ma tšuuf-o
    who left.3FS Samia without   3FS.see-him
    'Who$_i$ did Samia leave without seeing him$_i$?'

In the following discussion, we will establish that not all pronouns coindexed with a *wh*-operator are alike and not all such pronouns are interpreted as variables. They should be distinguished according to two criteria: Superiority and Weak Crossover (WCO). Because of their different behavior with respect to these two criteria, we should at least recognize the distinction between resumptive pronouns and bound pronouns.

In *wh*-constructions involving more than one coindexed pronoun, at most one of the two pronouns is interpreted as a variable. Consider the following ungrammatical sentence:

(4) *ʔayya təlmiiz min   tlamiið-a   xabbarto ʔəmm-o
    which student among students-her told.2P   mother-his
    ʔənno kəll mʕalme ḥa-təḥke   maʕ-o
    that   every teacher.FS will-3FS.speak with-him
    '[Which of her$_i$ students]$_j$ did you tell his$_j$ mother that every teacher$_i$ will speak with him$_j$?'

The unacceptability of this sentence can be captured as follows. For the pronoun 'her' to be bound by 'every teacher' in (4), the *wh*-phrase in the Spec of Comp 'which student among her students' must be reconstructed to 'him', given the standard assumption that a bound pronoun needs to be c-commanded by its quantificational antecedent (Chomsky 1976; Higginbotham 1980). Therefore, 'him' must be analyzed as a variable bound by the *wh*-phrase in the Spec of Comp. However, there is a pronoun to the left of this variable; thus, a WCO violation occurs.

Now, consider the following acceptable sentence:

(5) ʔayya təlmiiz min   tlamiiz   saamia xabbarto ʔəmm-o
    which student among students Samia told.2P   mother-his
    ʔənno kəll mʕallme ḥa-təḥki   maʕ-o
    that   every teacher.FS will-3FS.speak with-him
    '[Which of Samia's students]$_j$ did you tell his$_j$ mother that every teacher would speak with him$_j$?'

This sentence is well formed because the first pronoun can be interpreted as a resumptive pronoun, or variable, whereas the second pronoun can be interpreted as a bound pronoun. The well-formedness of this sentence indicates that a bound pronoun is unaffected by the occurrence of a pronoun bearing the same index to its left. This contrasts with the behavior of resumptive pronouns, which cannot have such a pronoun to their left, as demonstrated in (3).

Bound pronouns are also distinct from resumptive pronouns with respect to Superiority: only resumptive pronouns display superiority effects. Observe the contrast between (6a) and (6b).

(6) a. *miin$_i$ xabbarto saami ?ənno miin$_j$ ħa-yexd-o$_i$
        who told.2P   Sami   that   who   will-3MS.take-him
        ʕa-l-maṭaar
        to-the-airport
        'Who$_i$ did you tell Sami that who$_j$ would take him$_i$ to the
        airport?'

    b. miin$_i$ xabbart-u$_i$?ənno miin$_j$ ħa-yexd-o$_i$ ʕa-l-maṭaar
        who told.2P-him that   who   will-3MS.take-him to-the-airport
        'Who$_i$ did you tell him$_i$ that who$_j$ would take him$_i$ to the
        airport?'

In (6a), the pronoun in the embedded clause must be interpreted as a resumptive pronoun; otherwise, the 'who' in the matrix clause would not bind a variable. This configuration violates Superiority. In (6b), however, the pronoun in the matrix clause can serve as a resumptive pronoun. Therefore, the pronoun in the embedded clause must be a bound pronoun, not a resumptive pronoun. The sentence is well formed; no Superiority violation occurs.

In brief, the following distinction exists between resumptive pronouns (or variables) and bound pronouns:

(7) A resumptive pronoun, but not a bound pronoun, is sensitive to superiority and WCO effects.

How is the distinction between resumptive and bound pronouns syntactically encoded, given that both take the form of a pronoun and both are coindexed with the *wh*-phrase?

The linking mechanism introduced by Higginbotham (1983, 1985) can be used to encode the relevant distinction: a pronoun linked to a (*wh*-)operator is a *resumptive pronoun* and a pronoun linked to a resumptive pronoun is a *bound pronoun*.[2] The partial representations for (4) and (5) are (8a) and (8b), respectively. (For simplicity, the representations use only the English gloss.)

(8) a. [which of her$_i$ students]$_j$ ... his$_j$ mother ... every teacher$_i$ ... him$_j$

b. [which of Samia's students]$_j$ ... his$_j$ mother ... every teacher ... him$_j$

Another option available in a framework that incorporates illicit movement is to characterize a resumptive pronoun, in contrast to a bound pronoun, as the residue of an illicit movement. However, such an approach is not possible within minimalism because illicit movement (e.g., movement across islands) is not allowed in that framework.[3]

A more radical possibility, more compatible with a minimalist approach like that in Chomsky 1995, chap. 4, is to represent resumptive pronouns somewhat like variables generated by movement (see McCloskey 1990, to appear, and Sells 1984, identifying RPs as syntactic variables). We have mentioned that a variable bound by a *wh*-phrase is a copy of the *wh*-phrase. In similar fashion, we would like to suggest that a resumptive pronoun in a *wh*-construction, which counts as a variable to be bound by a *wh*-phrase, has a [+*wh*] feature associated with it. This characterization of resumptive pronouns may be better understood by assuming the distinction between Move and Bind introduced by Aoun, Choueiri, and Hornstein (ACH) (2001). ACH distinguish Move and Bind because illicit movement is not available within minimalism. They assume that a *wh*-element in the Spec of Comp can be related to the element that serves as a variable by Move (Copy and Merge) or by Bind. The first strategy, Move, is used in (9), where a gap appears in the argument position.

(9) miin šəft
    who saw.2s
    'Who$_i$ did you see t$_i$?'

The other strategy, Bind, is used in sentences like (10) where, owing to island effects, movement is not available.

(10) miin ʔənbasaṭṭo laʔinno l-mʕallme   hannet-o
     who pleased2P because the-teacher.FS congratulated.3FS-him
     'Who$_i$ were you pleased because the teacher congratulated him$_i$?'

Recall that in the following sentence, the relation between the pronoun and the *wh*-element can be generated by movement, as evidenced by the reconstruction effects previously discussed:

(11) miin šəft-o
       who saw.2s-him
       'Who$_i$ did you see him$_i$?'

In fact, ACH argue that in a sentence such as (11), the relation between the pronoun and the *wh*-element must be generated by movement in order to account for a variety of disjointness effects, the details of which need not concern us here. They argue that Bind is more costly than Move and is used as a last resort only when Move is not available. In (11), Move is available and therefore is the required strategy.

Why is Bind more costly than Move? The reason is that it involves more operations than Move. Move is Copy and Merge. Bind is argued to involve Copy, Merge, Demerge, and Merge again. Demerge is an operation whereby a lexical item is removed from the syntactic object and returned to the array. We illustrate with the following examples (for convenience, only the English gloss is used in (12)–(14)):

(12) you were pleased because the teacher congratulated who + him

The derivation proceeds as follows. The *wh*-element is first merged with the pronoun that occurs within the island. However, because of the island boundary, the *wh*-element cannot be copied and merged in the matrix Spec of Comp. In order for this *wh*-element to end up in the matrix position, it is demerged (placed back in the array) and remerged with the matrix Comp, thus generating the following representation:

(13) who [you were pleased [because the teacher congratulated him]]

For present purposes, we can assume that Demerge leaves a copy of the ɸ-features of the demerged element in the original position from which it was demerged. These ɸ-features include the [+*wh*] feature of the demerged *wh*-element:

(14) who [you were pleased [because the teacher congratulated
       [*wh* + him]]]

Still another available option relies on neither Bind, nor illicit movement, nor Higginbotham's linking to characterize a resumptive pronoun: it is possible to simply assume that a resumptive pronoun is generated by merging a [+*wh*] feature with a pronominal, [+*wh* + *him*], in contrast to a bound or referential pronoun, which does not have a [+*wh*] feature.

No matter which option is chosen, a distinction must be made between resumptive and bound pronouns (see (7)). Fundamentally, a resumptive pronoun has a [+*wh*] feature; a bound pronoun does not.

In brief, it is necessary to distinguish between resumptive pronouns and bound pronouns for empirical reasons: the former but not the latter display superiority and WCO effects. This distinction can be captured via linking, the notion of illicit movement, Bind, or simply the merging of a [+*wh*] feature with a pronominal. For concreteness, we adopt this final option, assuming that a resumptive element is a pronominal merged with a [+*wh*] feature, in contrast to a bound pronoun, which is not merged with a [+*wh*] feature. A *wh*-operator has to bind a *wh*-variable. An element qualifies as a variable for a *wh*-operator if it has a [+*wh*] feature and the same categorial specification as the *wh*-operator, in addition to the widely accepted requirement that a variable is c-commanded by an operator. In other words, the *wh*-operator and the variable it binds agree with respect to the [+*wh*] feature and categorial specification.[4]

When Move applies, the variable is a full copy of the *wh*-operator. Therefore, it obviously has a [+*wh*] feature. When Move does not apply, the variable, which surfaces as a resumptive pronoun, is a pronominal with a [+*wh*] feature. Schematically, the operator-variable relation may be represented in a unified way in movement and nonmovement contexts.

(15) a. $[_{CP} wh_i [_{IP} \ldots wh_i \ldots]]$

     b. $[_{CP} wh_i [_{IP} \ldots [_{island} \ldots wh_i \ldots]]]$

2.2 The Minimal Match Condition

In the previous discussion, it was necessary to distinguish resumptive pronouns from bound pronouns because only the former display superiority effects. With this distinction clarified, we can now offer an account for these effects. The empirical discussion has established that variables generated by movement as well as resumptive elements are subject to Superiority. Superiority therefore cannot be restricted to movement configurations.

A *wh*-operator in the Spec of Comp must bind a variable; otherwise, vacuous quantification arises. In terms of the notions "chain" and "form chain" in Chomsky 1995, chap. 1, a *wh*-operator in the Spec of Comp needs to form a chain with a variable. Importantly, the operator-variable relation is not necessarily established by movement. It has to be established representationally—for instance, in the cases involving "true" resumptive pronouns where movement cannot apply. We refer to the representational process of chain formation as *Match* and argue in the spirit of the Minimal Link Condition (Chomsky 1995, 311) that Match is subject to a minimality condition: the *Minimal Match Condition*. The MMC accounts for all cases of Superiority.

Restricting ourselves to cases containing *wh*-operators,[5] we may define the MMC as follows:

(16) *Minimal Match Condition (MMC) (narrowly defined)*
     A *wh*-operator must form a chain with the closest XP with a [+*wh*] feature that it c-commands.[6] (Closeness is defined in the generally accepted hierarchical way, namely, in terms of c-command.)

The MMC applying to representations accounts for the Superiority violations discussed in chapter 1. We first schematically summarize the patterns discussed earlier and then demonstrate how the MMC accounts for these patterns.

(17) a. $[_{CP}\ wh_1\ [_{IP}\ \ldots\ t_1\ \ldots\ wh_2\ \ldots]]$ (t_1 c-commands wh_2)
     b. $*[_{CP}\ wh_2\ [_{IP}\ \ldots\ wh_1\ \ldots\ t_2\ \ldots]]$ (wh_1 c-commands t_2)

(18) a. $[_{CP}\ wh_1\ [_{IP}\ \ldots\ RP_1\ \ldots\ wh_2\ \ldots]]$ (RP_1 c-commands wh_2)
     b. $*[_{CP}\ wh_2\ [_{IP}\ \ldots\ wh_1\ \ldots\ RP_2\ \ldots]]$ (wh_1 c-commands RP_2)

(19) a. $[_{CP}\ wh_1\ [_{IP}\ \ldots\ [_{island}\ \ldots\ RP_1\ \ldots\ wh_2\ \ldots]\ \ldots]]$ (RP_1 c-commands wh_2)
     b. $*[_{CP}\ wh_2\ [_{IP}\ \ldots\ [_{island}\ \ldots\ wh_1\ \ldots\ RP_2\ \ldots]\ \ldots]]$ (wh_1 c-commands RP_2)
     c. $[_{CP}\ wh_1\ [_{IP}\ \ldots\ RP_1\ \ldots\ [_{island}\ \ldots\ wh_2\ \ldots]\ \ldots]]$ (RP_1 c-commands wh_2)
     d. $*[_{CP}\ wh_2\ [_{IP}\ \ldots\ wh_1\ \ldots\ [_{island}\ \ldots\ RP_2\ \ldots]\ \ldots]]$ (wh_1 c-commands RP_2)

(20) a. $*[_{CP}\ wh_1\ [_{IP}\ \ldots\ [_{island}\ \ldots\ RP_1\ \ldots]\ \ldots\ wh_2\ \ldots]]$ (neither RP_1 nor wh_2 c-commands the other)
     b. $*[_{CP}\ wh_2\ [_{IP}\ \ldots\ [_{island}\ \ldots\ wh_1\ \ldots]\ \ldots\ RP_2\ \ldots]]$ (neither wh_1 nor RP_2 c-commands the other)
     c. $*[_{CP}\ wh_1\ [_{IP}\ \ldots\ [_{island}\ \ldots\ RP_1\ \ldots]\ \ldots\ [_{island}\ \ldots\ wh_2\ \ldots]$ $\ldots]]$ (neither RP_1 nor wh_2 c-commands the other)
     d. $*[_{CP}\ wh_2\ [_{IP}\ \ldots\ [_{island}\ \ldots\ wh_1\ \ldots]\ \ldots\ [_{island}\ \ldots\ RP_2\ \ldots]$ $\ldots]]$ (neither wh_1 nor RP_2 c-commands the other)

(21) a. ... wh_1 ... wh_2 ...   (both wh-elements are in situ)
   b. ... [$_{island}$ ... wh_1 ... wh_2 ...] ...   (same)
   c. ... wh_1 ... [$_{island}$ ... wh_2 ...] ...   (same)
   d. ... [$_{island}$ ... wh_1 ...] ... wh_2 ...   (same)
   e. ... [$_{island}$ ... wh_1 ...] ... [$_{island}$ ... wh_2 ...] ...   (same)

Consider the patterns in (17), repeated here with their LF representations in (22).

(17) a. [$_{CP}$ wh_1 [$_{IP}$ ... t_1 ... wh_2 ...]]   (t_1 c-commands wh_2)
   b. *[$_{CP}$ wh_2 [$_{IP}$ ... wh_1 ... t_2 ...]]   (wh_1 c-commands t_2)

(22) a. [$_{CP}$ wh_1 [$_{IP}$ ... wh_1 ... wh_2 ...]]
   b. *[$_{CP}$ wh_2 [$_{IP}$ ... wh_1 ... wh_2 ...]]

(17a) is a multiple interrogative pattern with one wh-phrase moved to the Spec of Comp and the other in situ. That is, the LF representation of (17a) is (22a), where the trace of wh-movement is represented by a wh-copy. (22a) has a wh-phrase in the Spec of Comp. This fronted wh-element is an operator and must form a chain with the closest XP with a [$+wh$] feature that it c-commands. There are two candidates within the clause: both t_1 and wh_2 have a [$+wh$] feature. In (22a), wh_1 c-commands wh_2, so wh_1 is closer to the wh in the Spec of Comp than wh_2. The operator therefore forms a chain with wh_1 and takes it as its variable.

(17b), represented in (22b), is a typical Superiority violation. Again, the wh-operator in the Spec of Comp must form a chain with the closest c-commanding XP with a [$+wh$] feature.[7] Wh_1 is closer to the wh-operator than wh_2. According to the MMC, wh_1 should be the variable forming a chain with the wh-operator in the Spec of Comp. In other words, wh_1 should form a chain with wh_2 in the Spec of Comp and the indexing of 1 should be identical to 2. When $1 = 2$, wh_2 will end up bound by wh_1,[8] resulting in a Strong Crossover configuration. (17b) therefore is unacceptable.

Thus, the Superiority violation in (17b) is captured by the MMC and other general principles of the grammar such as the one accounting for Strong Crossover.[9]

The other contrasts discussed earlier follow straightforwardly from the MMC. Consider (18a–b), repeated here.

(18) a. [$_{CP}$ wh_1 [$_{IP}$ ... RP_1 ... wh_2 ...]]   (RP_1 c-commands wh_2)
   b. *[$_{CP}$ wh_2 [$_{IP}$ ... wh_1 ... RP_2 ...]]   (wh_1 c-commands RP_2)

As mentioned earlier, a resumptive pronoun is also represented as an element with a $[+wh]$ feature. At the end of the derivation, the representations of (18a–b) are (23a–b) respectively.

(23) a. $[_{CP} \, wh_1 \, [_{IP} \ldots wh_1 \ldots wh_2 \ldots]]$
     b. $*[_{CP} \, wh_2 \, [_{IP} \ldots wh_1 \ldots wh_2 \ldots]]$

The MMC is violated in (23b), because the *wh*-operator in the Spec of Comp does not form a chain with the closest XP with a $[+wh]$ feature. In contrast, the MMC is not violated in (23a), where the closest *wh*-element forms a chain with the *wh*-operator in the Spec of Comp. (18b) is therefore unacceptable.

Next, we turn to (19a–d), repeated here, which involve islands, and to their representations in (24).

(19) a. $[_{CP} \, wh_1 \, [_{IP} \ldots [_{island} \ldots RP_1 \ldots wh_2 \ldots] \ldots]]$ $(RP_1$ c-commands $wh_2)$
     b. $*[_{CP} \, wh_2 \, [_{IP} \ldots [_{island} \ldots wh_1 \ldots RP_2 \ldots] \ldots]]$ $(wh_1$ c-commands $RP_2)$
     c. $[_{CP} \, wh_1 \, [_{IP} \ldots RP_1 \ldots [_{island} \ldots wh_2 \ldots] \ldots]]$ $(RP_1$ c-commands $wh_2)$
     d. $*[_{CP} \, wh_2 \, [_{IP} \ldots wh_1 \ldots [_{island} \ldots RP_2 \ldots] \ldots]]$ $(wh_1$ c-commands $RP_2)$

(24) a. $[_{CP} \, wh_1 \, [_{IP} \ldots [_{island} \ldots wh_1 \ldots wh_2 \ldots] \ldots]]$
     b. $*[_{CP} \, wh_2 \, [_{IP} \ldots [_{island} \ldots wh_1 \ldots wh_2 \ldots] \ldots]]$
     c. $[_{CP} \, wh_1 \, [_{IP} \ldots wh_1 \ldots [_{island} \ldots wh_2 \ldots] \ldots]]$
     d. $*[_{CP} \, wh_2 \, [_{IP} \ldots wh_1 \ldots [_{island} \ldots wh_2 \ldots] \ldots]]$

The representation for (19a) is (24a). Here, a *wh*-operator in the Spec of Comp (wh_1 in the Spec of Comp) needs to form a chain with the closest XP with a $[+wh]$ feature. It properly binds wh_1 (the first in-situ *wh* within the island), thus satisfying the MMC. In contrast, the ungrammatical (19b) has the representation in (24b), which violates the MMC. Similarly, the contrast between (19c) and (19d), with the representations in (24c) and (24d), respectively, follows straightforwardly from our account.

The patterns in (20a–d), repeated here, with their representations (25a–d), differ from those discussed so far because neither of the two *wh*-elements in argument position c-commands the other.

(20) a. $*[_{CP} \, wh_1 \, [_{IP} \ldots [_{island} \ldots RP_1 \ldots] \ldots wh_2 \ldots]]$ (neither RP_1 nor wh_2 c-commands the other)

b. *$[_{CP}$ wh_2 $[_{IP}$ ... $[_{island}$ ... wh_1 ...] ... RP_2 ...]]   (neither wh_1 nor RP_2 c-commands the other)

c. *$[_{CP}$ wh_1 $[_{IP}$ ... $[_{island}$ ... RP_1 ...] ... $[_{island}$ ... wh_2 ...] ...]]   (neither RP_1 nor wh_2 c-commands the other)

d. *$[_{CP}$ wh_2 $[_{IP}$ ... $[_{island}$ ... wh_1 ...] ... $[_{island}$ ... RP_2 ...] ...]]   (neither wh_1 nor RP_2 c-commands the other)

(25) a. *$[_{CP}$ wh_1 $[_{IP}$ ... $[_{island}$ ... wh_1 ...] ... wh_2 ...]]

b. *$[_{CP}$ wh_2 $[_{IP}$ ... $[_{island}$ ... wh_1 ...] ... wh_2 ...]]

c. *$[_{CP}$ wh_1 $[_{IP}$ ... $[_{island}$ ... wh_1 ...] ... $[_{island}$ ... wh_2 ...] ...]]

d. *$[_{CP}$ wh_2 $[_{IP}$ ... $[_{island}$ ... wh_1 ...] ... $[_{island}$ ... wh_2 ...] ...]]

Consider for instance the representation (25a) for (20a). Because neither wh_1 nor wh_2 c-commands the other, wh_1 and wh_2 are equidistant with respect to the wh-operator in the Spec of Comp. As a result, the wh-operator forms a chain with both wh-elements and takes them as variables because both are equally close. Again as a result, the wh-operator establishes an operator-variable relation with two variables in the case of (25a): wh_1 and wh_2. However, this is ruled out by the Bijection Principle, according to which an operator may bind one and only one variable (Koopman and Sportiche 1982). In short, the wh-operator in (25a) fails to uniquely identify a variable. The unacceptability of (20a) thus follows from the MMC and the Bijection Principle.[10] (20b–d), represented in (25b–d), respectively, are accounted for in exactly the same manner: neither wh_1 nor wh_2 c-commands the other, so there is no uniquely identified variable. The MMC in combination with the Bijection Principle rules out these structures.[11]

In brief, we have shown that the contrast between the acceptable and unacceptable structures in the patterns in (17)–(20) follows from the MMC together with other independently needed principles of the grammar. The MMC requires a wh-operator in the Spec of Comp to form a chain with an XP with a $[+wh]$ feature (a variable) that is closest to it. Application of the MMC may or may not yield well-formed operator-variable pairs, a result that captures the superiority effects discussed so far. An MMC approach predicts that, if there is no operator in the Spec of Comp, the MMC will be satisfied vacuously. A multiple wh-question without a wh-operator in the Spec of Comp therefore should not be ruled out by the MMC. This prediction is indeed accurate, as illustrated in (21a–e) by the sentences with all wh-phrases in situ, repeated here.

(21) a. ... wh_1 ... wh_2 ...
      b. ... [$_{island}$ ... wh_1 ... wh_2 ...] ...
      c. ... wh_1 ... [$_{island}$ ... wh_2 ...] ...
      d. ... [$_{island}$ ... wh_1 ...] ... wh_2 ...
      e. ... [$_{island}$ ... wh_1 ...] ... [$_{island}$ ... wh_2 ...] ...

We have mentioned that such instances require only that the in-situ *wh*-phrases be licensed by a question complementizer in the appropriate Comp. For instance, both *wh*-phrases in (21a) may be identified by a question complementizer in the matrix Comp, yielding multiple direct questions. The licensing of the two in-situ *wh*-phrases, in contrast to operator-variable binding relations, does not entail that they have the same referential index as the licenser and therefore they share the same referential index.[12] Indeed, it is plausible to assume that a question complementizer does not even have a referential index.[13] Furthermore, a question complementizer can license multiple *wh*-phrases while a *wh*-operator can bind only one variable, according to the Bijection Principle. As a result, in sentences containing only *wh*-elements in situ, there is no *wh*-operator in the Spec of Comp searching for a variable to bind.[14] The patterns in (21a–e) therefore do not violate the MMC or any other principle of the grammar.[15]

Summarizing, Superiority violations arise when the MMC and other independently needed principles of the grammar, such as the Bijection Principle or Strong Crossover, are violated. The success of this approach relies on the application of the MMC to representations that cannot have been derived by movement, such as those in (19)–(20).

2.3   Superiority and 'Which' Phrases in Lebanese Arabic

We now discuss the absence of Superiority violations with *ʔayya* 'which' phrases in LA. According to the MMC, a *wh*-operator in the Spec of Comp must seek the closest XP with a [+*wh*] feature that it c-commands and forms a chain with. A variable has a [+*wh*] feature and the same categorial specification as the *wh*-operator in the Spec of Comp. The *wh*-operator in Comp is an XP category, and the variable it binds must also be an XP category.

In the configuration [$_{CP}$ *wh* [$_{IP}$ ... 'who$_1$' ... 'who$_2$']], the *wh* in the Spec of Comp must form a chain with the closest *wh*-element, which is 'who$_1$'— an XP category. Similarly, in the configuration [$_{CP}$ *wh$_2$* [$_{IP}$ ... 'which' NP ... wh$_2$]], all the *wh*-elements can be analyzed as XP categories. In this case, we expect a Superiority violation to arise. However, such cases do not exhibit superiority effects. As we will show, this can be traced to the categorial properties of 'which'. Note that a 'which' phrase (e.g., 'which man') can also be factored into a *wh*-element ('which') and a restriction (the nominal element 'man').

There is evidence that in LA, 'which' is a head, an X^0 category. Consider the following. Clitics in LA are attached to the head that governs them. Complements of verbs, prepositions, and nouns are cliticized onto verbs, prepositions, and nouns, respectively, as in (26a–c). Cliticization is a local phenomenon in LA and there is no process of clitic climbing (see Aoun 1999). In this respect, 'which' behaves like a head governing its restriction (26d).

(26) a. *V + clitic*
       l-mudiira   ħa-təšħat̩-u
       the-principal.FS will-3FS.expel-him
       'The principal will expel him.'
    b. *P + clitic*
       ħekina   maʕ-o
       spoke.1P with-him
       'We spoke with him.'
    c. *N + clitic*
       šəfna   ʔəmm-o
       saw.1P mother-his
       'We saw his mother.'
    d. *'which' + clitic*
       ʔayye-hun   seefar
       which-them travel.3MS
       'Which one of them has traveled?'

In contrast, *miin* 'who' does not behave like a head: it cannot be generated with a clitic.

A second difference between 'which' and 'who' is that the 'which' phrase can be modified by a relative clause, but 'who' cannot.

(27) a. ʕazamto ʔayya walad šəft-uu   mbeeriħ
       invited.2P which boy   saw.2P-him yesterday
       'You invited which boy you saw yesterday?'
    b. *ʕazamto miin šəft-uu   mbeeriħ
       invited.2P who saw.2P-him yesterday
       'You invited who you saw yesterday?'

The relative clause modifies the NP occurring with 'which' and not the whole DP ['which' + NP]. As evidence for this, consider the following. As Kayne (1975) has pointed out, a clitic cannot be modified by a relative clause; when the NP in the complex ['which' + NP] is a clitic, relativization is no longer possible, as in (28). Since relativization is directly sensitive to the clitic/nonclitic status of the NP, this indicates that the relative clause modifies the NP and not the whole DP ['which' + NP].

(28) *ʕazamto ʔayye   šəft-uu   mbeeriħ
     invited.2P which-him saw.2P-him yesterday

A third difference is that, in contrast to 'which', the interrogative pronoun 'who' can be morphosyntactically characterized as an interrogative strong pronoun. In Standard Arabic (SA) and LA, proximate pronouns can be factored into two morphemes: a (strong) pronominal morpheme *ha* and a $+/-$ proximate marker.

	Pronoun	Proximate	
(29)			
SA	haa	ðaa	→ haaðaa 'this'
LA	hay	da	→ hayda 'this'

In SA, *man* 'who' can merge with the proximate morpheme *ðaa* (*manðaa* 'who + proximate morpheme') but not with the strong pronoun and the proximate morpheme (**man haaðaa* 'who + strong pronoun + proximate morpheme').[16] In other words, 'who' is in complementary distribution with the strong pronoun in SA. The complementarity of the strong pronoun and 'who' can be taken to indicate that the two elements compete for the same position or that the interrogative pronoun itself is an interrogative *strong* pronoun (see Ouhalla 1996).[17] That is, 'who' is the morphological spell-out of [*wh* + strong pronoun].[18] In this respect, it is interesting to note that a strong pronoun, parallel to *miin* 'who', also cannot be modified by a relative pronoun in LA.

(30) a. *ʕazamt   huwwe yalli   raaħ
        invited.1s him   REL.PRON left.3MS
     b. *fakkarto ʔanno huwwe yalli   šəft-uu   mbeeriħ
        thought.2P that he   REL.PRON saw.2P-him yesterday
        raaħ
        left.3MS

In Aoun and Choueiri 1997 and in Aoun, Choueiri, and Hornstein 2001, it is argued that weak pronouns or clitics are generated as heads, whereas (as schematized in (31)) strong pronouns are maximal projections generated as Specs of a DP that get their gender and number features from D or the Agr(eement)/Num(ber) Phrase projection (see, e.g., Carstens 1991; Ritter 1991, 1995; Valois 1991).[19]

(31) *Strong pronoun*

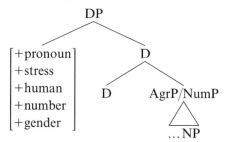

Characterizing *miin* 'who' as an interrogative strong pronoun [*wh* + strong pronoun] leads us to locate it in the Spec of DP, as in (32). In (32), the [+*wh*] feature in D is merged with the strong pronoun (irrelevant details omitted).

(32)

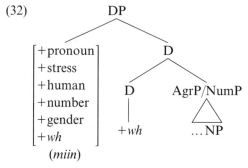

Structurally, then, the contrast between *ʔayya* 'which' and *miin* 'who' may be understood as this: 'which' is in D and 'who' is in the Spec of DP. It may further be understood in the following manner. 'Who' has the combination of features [+*wh*, +human, ...]. It may be generated in the Spec of NP to check the [+human] feature in N,[20] then move through the Spec of NumP/AgrP to check the appropriate number and agreement features, and then move to the Spec of D to check the [+*wh*] feature in D. In contrast, 'which' is simply the [+*wh*] feature in D. In other words, the lexical item 'which' is in D but the lexical item 'who' is in the Spec of DP.

In brief, we are analyzing 'which' as a head (X^0 category) and 'who' as a maximal projection (XP category).

With this in mind, consider the configuration [wh_2 [... 'which' NP ... wh_2]]: the whole in-situ phrase ['which' NP] or the head by itself 'which' can be analyzed as the *wh*-element. When only 'which' is analyzed as the *wh*-element, it does not qualify as a possible variable for the *wh*-phrase in the Spec of Comp because it is an X^0 category. This is why Superiority violations do not arise with 'which' phrases.

In contrast, in the ill-formed configuration [*'which' NP [... 'who$_1$' ... 'which' NP]], the *wh*-phrase in the Spec of Comp ['which' + NP] is an XP category (the entire XP has been pied-piped to the Spec of Comp). It, in turn, needs to bind the closest available XP *wh*-phrase, according to the MMC. 'Who$_1$' qualifies; it is an XP category.

In brief, an in-situ 'which' phrase does not necessarily prevent a *wh*-operator in the Spec of Comp from forming a chain with a lower *wh*-element. However, a 'who' phrase always does because it can be analyzed only as an XP category. Only in-situ 'which' phrases can escape Superiority violations.

(33) a. [$_{CP}$ 'who$_2$' [$_{IP}$ ... 'which' NP$_1$ ... 'who$_2$']]
    b. [$_{CP}$ 'which' NP$_2$ [$_{IP}$ ... 'which' NP$_1$ ... 'which' NP$_2$]]
    c. *[$_{CP}$ 'which' NP$_2$ [$_{IP}$ ... 'who$_1$' ... 'which' NP$_2$]]

The following examples illustrate the patterns in (33a–c), showing the predicted (un)acceptability.

(34) a. miin ṭlabto   min ?ayya bənt ti?zəm   (o)
         who asked.2P from which girl 3FS.invite (him)
         'Who did you ask which girl to invite?'
    b. ?ayya walad ṭlabto   min ?ayya bənt ti?zəm   (o)
         which boy   asked.2P from which girl 3FS.invite (him)
         'Which boy did you ask which girl to invite?'
    c. *?ayya walad ṭlabto   min miin yi?zəm   (o)
         which boy   asked.2P from who 3MS.invite (him)
         '*Which boy did you ask whom to invite?'

As noted in section 1.2.2, Superiority violations disappear when the 'who' phrases are replaced by 'which' phrases. We repeat the relevant examples here.

(35) ?ayya walad ?anna?to   ?ayya m?allme tzuur
     which boy persuaded.2P which teacher.FS 3FS.visit
     'Which boy did you persuade which teacher to visit?'

(36) a. ʔayya walad ʔannaʕto   ʔayya bənt tzuur-o
     which boy   persuaded.2P which girl 3FS.visit-him
     'Which boy$_i$ did you persuade which girl to visit him$_i$?'

   b. ʔayya walad ʔənbasaṭṭo laʔinno saami ʕarraf
     which boy   pleased.2P because Sami introduced.3MS
     ʔayya bənt ʕəl-e
     which girl to-him
     'Which boy$_i$ were you pleased because Sami introduced which
     girl to him$_i$?'

   c. ʔayya walad hannayto   ʔayya bənt laʔinno saami
     which boy   congratulated.2P which girl because Sami
     zaar-o
     visited.3MS-him
     'Which boy$_i$ did you congratulate which girl because Sami
     visited him$_i$?'

In the non-c-commanding cases, such as those repeated in (37), the fact
that 'which' is an X^0 category makes it possible for the *wh*-phrase in the
Spec of Comp to uniquely identify a variable.

(37) a. miin fakkarto   laʔinno l-mʕallme   ħikət   maʕ-o
     who thought.2P because the-teacher.FS spoke.3FS with-him
     ʔənno l-mudiira   ħa-tašħaṭ   ʔayya walad
     that the-principal-FS will-3FS.expel which boy
     'Who$_i$ did you think because the teacher spoke with him$_i$ that
     the principal would expel which boy?'

   b. miin fakkarto   laʔinno l-mʕallme   ħikət   maʕ ʔayya
     who thought.2P because the-teacher.FS spoke.3FS with which
     walad ʔənno l-mudiira   ħa-tašħaṭ-o
     boy   that the-principal-FS will-3FS.expel-him
     'Who$_i$ did you think because the teacher spoke with which boy
     that the principal would expel him$_i$?'

   c. miin fakkarto   laʔinno l-mʕallme   ħikət   maʕ-o
     who thought.2P because the-teacher.FS spoke-3FS with-him
     ʔənno l-mudiira   ħa-truuħ   minduun-ma tašħaṭ
     that the-principal.FS will-3FS.leave without   3FS.expel
     ʔayya walad
     which boy
     'Who$_i$ did you think because the teacher spoke with him$_i$ that
     the principal would leave without expelling which boy?'

d. miin fakkarto   laʔinno l-mʕallme   ħikət   maʕ ʔayya
   who thought.2P because the-teacher.FS spoke.3FS with which
   walad ʔənno l-mudiira   ħa-truuħ   minduun-ma
   boy   that   the-principal.FS will-3FS.leave without
   təšħaṭ-o
   3FS.expel-him
   'Who_i did you think because the teacher spoke with which boy
   that the principal would leave without expelling him_i?'

The contrast between 'which' phrases and 'who' phrases with respect to
Superiority is thus accounted for.

Before concluding this chapter, we briefly compare our account of the
distinction between 'which' phrases and 'who' phrases regarding Superiority with the analysis prevalent in the literature.[21] Our analysis relies
on the morphosyntactic difference between ʔayya 'which' phrases and
non-ʔayya phrases such as miin 'who' (X^0 vs. XP category) in LA. In
contrast, the prevalent analysis relates Superiority to D-linking (see, e.g.,
Bolinger 1978; Pesetsky 1987; Hornstein 1995; Comorovski 1996), and
relies on the pragmatic context to determine whether or not a wh-phrase
is D-linked. The two analyses thus differ in their empirical coverage: ours
claims that 'which' phrases are the only true cases that do not exhibit
superiority effects, whereas the contextual analysis allows non-'which'
phrases such as 'who' to avoid superiority effects in D-linked contexts.

Additional facts suggest that our morphosyntactic approach to Superiority may be on the right track for LA. An in-situ wh-phrase in LA, either
'which' or non-'which', must be D-linked as indicated in Aoun and
Choueiri 1999.[22] In the context where there is a group of boys, each of
whom was to be invited by someone, the in-situ wh-elements are clearly
D-linked. Nonetheless, (38), involving 'who', is not an acceptable question; (39), involving 'which' instead of 'who', must be used instead.

(38) *miin ṭlabṭo   min miin min-un yiʕzəm
      who asked.2P from who of-them 3FS.invite
      'Who did you ask whom among them to invite?'

(39) ʔayya walad ṭalabṭo   min ʔayya bənt tiʕzum
     which boy   asked.2P from which girl 3FS.invite
     'Which boy did you ask which girl to invite?'

The contrast between (38) and (39) is mysterious if we simply say that a
D-linked wh-phrase can avoid Superiority violations.[23]

2.4 The Minimal Match Condition and Other Minimality Conditions

We have shown so far that the facts concerning superiority effects can be adequately accounted for by the MMC, a minimality condition on chain formation applying to representations. We would now like to explore the workings of the MMC in more detail, by considering the relation between the MMC and similar conditions suggested in the literature: specifically, the relation between the MMC and the Minimal Link Condition (MLC) (Chomsky 1995, chap. 4), which applies derivationally, and the relation between the MMC and the Minimal Binding Requirement (MBR) (Aoun and Li 1989, 1993a). The MLC applies to derivations, and the MMC to representations. As for the MBR, it requires a variable to be bound by the closest operator, a requirement quite close to the spirit of the MMC. These conditions all express some notion of minimality, raising the question of whether they are all the same condition and therefore should be reduced to one or whether they are different, independently relevant conditions and therefore should all be retained. We show in the following subsections that the MLC and the MMC are both necessary, a result that has important implications for the derivational and representational nature of grammar. On the other hand, we show that the MBR can be reduced to the MMC.

2.4.1 Move and Match
We first would like to clarify the workings of the MMC by considering the relation between Move/MLC and Match/MMC. Chains can be generated by Move and Match. Does Match apply only to elements that could not have been generated by Move? It turns out that Match has to apply more exhaustively to all elements, even those that are in a chain generated by Move.

Consider the representation in (41) of the ungrammatical LA sentence (40).

(40) *miin fakkarit   l-bənt   yalli ʕazamit   miin ʔənno faadi
      who thought.3F the-girl that invited.3FS who that   Fadi
      ħa-yiʕzum
      will-invite.3MS
      'Lit. Who did the girl that invited whom think that Fadi would invite?'

(41) *$[wh_1 \ldots [_{\text{island}} \ldots wh_2 \ldots] \ldots x_1 \ldots]$

In the ungrammatical representation (41), the *wh*-in-situ (*wh*$_2$) is inside an island, and *wh*$_1$ in the Spec of Comp has been moved from x_1. Note that the movement of *wh*$_1$ from x_1 does not violate minimality—the MLC. On the other hand, in our account of superiority effects in section 2.2, we claimed that (41) violates the MMC. For the MMC to rule out (41), it has to be able to reexamine chains that have already been formed by Move. That is, we are led to the following conclusion: Match applies to all *wh*-elements in Ā-positions, even those that are part of a chain generated by Move.[24]

As a concrete execution of this view, one can assume that elements end up subscripted as a consequence of Move, and superscripted as a consequence of Match. Minimality constrains all processes of chain formation (Move and Match). Consider the representation of (41) given in (42).

(42) $[wh^i_{1i} \ldots [_{island} \ldots wh^i_2 \ldots] \ldots x_{1i} \ldots]$

Wh$_1$ forms a chain and is coindexed with x_1 via Move (indicated by subscripting); minimality applying to Move, the MLC, is satisfied. Match requires *wh*$_1$ to be superscripted with *wh*$_2$; if it is not, minimality applying to Match, the MMC, is violated. A Superiority violation ensues.

The evidence also indicates that the MMC operates cyclically (at the end of each phase; see Chomsky 2000, 2001). Consider the following sentence:

(43) miin badtkun taʕrifo   miin šeef-o
     who want.2P know.2P who saw.3MS-him
     'Who$_j$ do you want to know who$_i$ t$_i$ saw him$_j$?'

How does (43) obey minimality—the MMC? Assume that Match operates cyclically (see, e.g., Chomsky 1995, 2000, 2001, for cyclic applications of Shortest Attract or Attract Closest), and consider (44).

(44) ['who^j' ... ['who^i_i' [... t^i_i ... 'him^j' ...]]]

On the lowest cycle, 'who$_i$' in the embedded Spec of Comp needs to form a chain (be superscripted) with the closest XP with a [+*wh*] feature: t$_i$ is the XP with a [+*wh*] feature that is the closest to the *wh*-operator. On the next cycle, the matrix clause, 'who' in the matrix Spec of Comp also needs to form a chain with an XP with a [+*wh*] feature. There is now only one *wh*-element left in the structure because t$_i$ has already been characterized as the variable superscripted with the lower 'who$_i$' (the lower 'who$_i$' and t$_i$ have already formed a chain that satisfies the MMC; that is,

they have already been superscripted).[25] The one with a [+*wh*] feature left
is the resumptive 'him'. The sentence in (43), therefore, is acceptable
according to the MMC.

Now, consider the following sentence, which minimally contrasts with
(43):

(45) *miin badtkun taʕrifo   miin šeef
     who want.2P know.2P who saw.3MS
     '?*Who$_j$ do you want to know who$_i$ t$_i$ saw t$_j$?'

In the same way that (43) is acceptable, (45) should also be acceptable
with respect to the MMC.

(46) $[wh_j^j \ldots [wh_i^i [\ldots x_i^i \ldots x_j^j \ldots]]]$

The only difference between the two sentences is that the [+*wh*] XP in the
embedded clause is a resumptive pronoun 'him$_j$' in (43) and t$_j$ in (45):
Match and the MMC do not distinguish between the two sentences. On
the other hand, Move and the MLC distinguish them: the movement of
'who$_j$' from the trace t$_j$ position violates the MLC. (43) does not violate
the MLC; 'who$_j$' is base-generated in the matrix Spec of Comp. Thus, the
contrast between (43) and (45) can be accounted for if a distinction is
made between Move and Match and if minimality constrains both processes of chain formation.[26]

In brief, there are two processes of chain formation, Move (or Agree)
and Match; minimality constrains both processes. The fact that both
Move and Match are needed suggests that neither movement nor representation can be reduced to the other in the grammar. This conclusion
has implications for the ongoing debate in the generative literature on
whether syntax should be exclusively derivational or exclusively representational (see Roberts 2000 for a brief summary). For instance, it
unfortunately goes against Brody's (1995) claim that derivations and
properties of LF representations duplicate each other and that a parsi-
monious theory of syntax should dispense either with representations or
with derivations. Grammar seems to contain redundancies.

2.4.2 The Minimal Match Condition and the Minimal Binding
Requirement

Recall that the MMC is a condition that governs the identification of a
variable forming a chain with a *wh*-operator: a *wh*-operator forms a chain
with the closest XP with a [+*wh*] feature (variable). The *wh*-operator is

the anchor and searches for a variable to form a chain with.[27] To account for the range of facts concerning the interaction of quantifier scope, we have argued elsewhere (Aoun and Li 1989, 1993a) that a variable must be bound by the closest c-commanding operator (Ā-binder)—the MBR. In this account, the MBR takes the variable as the anchor that searches for a c-commanding operator. The MMC can be thought of as a top-down condition and the MBR as a bottom-up condition. However, both the MMC and the MBR are well-formedness conditions on operator-variable relations, if we generalize the MMC to accommodate cases containing non-*wh*-expressions, such as QPs. The two conditions, then, seem redundant. It would be desirable to eliminate this redundancy and reduce one to the other. Note that, so far, we have narrowly formulated the MMC as applying to cases containing *wh*-phrases only. If the redundancy is to be eliminated, we need to generalize it to accommodate the non-*wh* cases. We, thus, eliminate the specification of the feature as [+*wh*] and generalize the condition to accommodate non-[+*wh*] features.

(47) *The Minimal Match Condition (generalized)*
     An operator must form a chain with the closest XP it c-commands that contains the same relevant features.

(47) is based on the notion that a variable is a copy of the related operator.[28] Before we demonstrate how (47) also accommodates non-*wh* cases, we should clarify what features are relevant to the cases in question. So far, we have concentrated on the [+*wh*] feature (interrogation) when considering *wh*-phrases. However, with respect to interpretation, *wh*-phrases not only characterize clauses as interrogative but also enter scope relations with other quantificational expressions.

Fiengo et al. (1988) argue that a question expression such as *how many* is to be factored into an operator and a quantificational element: it has a [+*wh*] operator ranging over numbers (e.g., $1, \ldots, n$), and a [−*wh*] existential quantifier ranging over individual students.

That the two operators should be distinguished is motivated by the fact that they may have distinct scope properties. The [+*wh*] operator may have wider scope than the subject *every professor* [as in (i)] while at the same time the [−*wh*] existential quantifier may have narrower scope than the latter. So, if '95' is the answer to (i), the interrogator may most naturally understand every professor to have taught 95 students, but not necessarily the same 95 students that another professor has taught. (p. 87)

(i) How many students has every professor taught t?

According to Chomsky (1964, 1995), Katz and Postal (1964), Klima (1964), Kuroda (1965), Nishigauchi (1990), and Kim (1991), question phrases "share semantic and distributional properties of quantifier phrases, and might be composed of an indefinite quantifier, a *wh*-feature, and the restriction on the quantifier" (Chomsky 1995, 70). In other words, it is possible to claim that an interrogative consists of three parts: Question, Quantification, and Restriction. Pertinent to this discussion, it is possible to claim that a *wh*-phrase not only has a [+*wh*] feature (Question) but also a [+quantification] feature. In other words, *wh*-phrases share with QPs the feature [+quantification].

We now turn to the question of how the MBR can be reduced to the generalized MMC as formulated in (47).

The MBR captures the following generalizations concerning QP/QP interaction:

(48) *QP/QP interaction*
    a. $QP_1 \ldots t_1 \ldots QP_2 \ldots t_2$
    b.   *$QP_1 \ldots QP_2 \ldots t_1 \ldots t_2$
    c.   *$QP_2 \ldots QP_1 \ldots t_1 \ldots t_2$

According to (48a–c), a QP cannot be raised across another QP. The MBR also captures the following generalizations concerning QP/*wh* interaction:

(49) *QP*/wh *interaction*
    a. $[wh_1 \ldots t_1 \ldots QP_2 \ldots t_2]$
    b.   *$[wh_1 \ldots QP_2 \ldots t_1 \ldots t_2]$
    c. $[wh_2 \ldots QP_1 \ldots t_1 \ldots t_2]$

According to (49a–c), a QP cannot be raised across a *wh*-element, but a *wh*-element can be raised across a QP. This difference is responsible for the contrast between (50a), where the scope interaction between the *wh*-operator and QP is unambiguous, and (50b), where it is ambiguous (see May 1985).

(50) a. Who saw everything? (unambiguous)
      b. What did everyone see? (ambiguous)

Generalizations (48a–c) follow straightforwardly from the generalized MMC. In (48a), QP_1 and QP_2 each form a chain with the closest XP that bears the same [+quantification] feature: t_1 and t_2, respectively.[29] Therefore, (48a) does not violate the MMC. (48b–c), on the other hand, do violate the MMC: both QP_1 and QP_2 need to look for the closest available XP with a [+quantification] feature, which is t_1 for both. Proper operator-variable relations are not established.

Generalizations (49a–c) also follow from the generalized MMC. According to (47), a *wh*-operator must form a chain with an XP with a [+*wh*] feature (an XP carrying a [+*wh*] feature realized as a gap or a resumptive pronoun after spell-out), as well as a [+quantification] feature, as just noted. A QP, on the other hand, forms a chain with an element with a [+quantification] feature, which is carried by both the copy derived by *wh*-movement and the copy derived by QR. Accordingly, only t_1 in (49a) and (49b) and t_2 in (49c) are elements that contain a [+*wh*] feature and can serve as variables forming a chain with a *wh*-operator. The paradigm in (49a–c) follows. No MMC violation occurs in (49a): wh_1 properly forms a chain with t_1, which is a [+*wh*] XP, and QP_2 properly forms a chain with t_2. In (49b), both wh_1 and QP_2 need to form a chain with the closest XP with a [+quantification] feature, which is t_1. Proper operator-variable relations are not established and the representation is ruled out. In (49c), wh_2 needs to form a chain with the closest *wh*-element, which is t_2 because t_1 does not have a [+*wh*] feature. QP_1 forms a chain with the first available [+quantification] element, which is t_1. Both operators properly form a chain with their variables.[30]

In brief, the MBR can be subsumed under the MMC as stated in (47). This formulation of the MMC is adequate to account for superiority effects as well as other cases accounted for by the MBR.

Alternatively, one might wonder about adopting the other logical possibility: subsuming the MMC under the MBR. This alternative would require additional stipulations. An important difference between the MBR and the MMC is that the former embodies a bottom-up approach and the latter, a top-down approach. The MMC starts from the operator and dictates that an operator must form a chain with an XP with similar features (to establish an operator-variable relation). The MBR starts from the variable and requires a variable to be bound by an operator. The problem is how to decide if the MBR applies. This problem can be illustrated by the following two configurations:

(51) [Qu [wh_1 ... wh_2 ...]]

(52) *[wh_1 ... [wh_2 ... wh_1]]

The configuration in (51) contains two in-situ *wh*-phrases; (52) contains one *wh*-phrase in the Spec of Comp and one in situ. In (51), the in-situ *wh*-phrases are licensed by a question marker in the complementizer position (an X^0 category), which is not subject to the MMC because it does not form a chain with an XP containing a $[+wh]$ feature (the complementizer is a licenser, not possessing a referential index for binding purposes), as discussed earlier. In (52), the *wh*-phrase (an XP with a referential index for binding purposes) in the Spec of Comp needs to bind a variable. The MMC can apply to rule out (52) but is irrelevant in the case of (51). An MBR approach, however, starts from the *wh*-phrase. If any XP with a $[+wh]$ feature is potentially a variable, all the *wh*-copies in (51) and (52) must be subject to the MBR. In (51), however, there is no binder for the in-situ *wh*-phrases. The MBR can only be made to work by adding the stipulation that a variable must be bound by the closest operator *if there is one*.

2.5 Summary

In this chapter, we established that superiority effects manifested in movement as well as nonmovement structures can be captured by the MMC, repeated here.

(16) *Minimal Match Condition (MMC) (narrowly defined)*
     A *wh*-operator must form a chain with the closest XP with a $[+wh]$
     feature that it c-commands.

Together with the morphological distinction between 'which' and 'who' phrases in LA described in (53) and the distinction between resumptive pronouns and bound pronouns described in (54), the MMC captures the generalizations in (55).

(53) Whereas 'who' is morphologically complex and is always an XP
     category, 'which' is an X^0 category and combines with an NP to
     make an XP category.

(54) Resumptive pronouns but not bound pronouns display superiority
     and WCO effects. The two types of pronouns are distinguished
     representationally by the presence versus absence of a $[+wh]$ feature.

(55) a. Interrogative constructions containing a *wh*-element that has
        been preposed to the Spec of Comp display superiority effects.
        The MMC is relevant because a *wh*-element in the Spec of
        Comp is a *wh*-operator that needs to form a chain with the
        closest XP containing a $[+wh]$ feature.

b. Interrogative constructions containing a *wh*-element in the Spec
   of Comp coindexed with a resumptive pronoun display
   superiority effects. The MMC is relevant because a *wh*-element
   in the Spec of Comp is a *wh*-operator that needs to form a chain
   with the closest XP containing a [+*wh*] feature.
c. Interrogative constructions containing only in-situ *wh*-phrases do
   not display superiority effects. In-situ *wh*-phrases are licensed by
   a question complementizer; the MMC is irrelevant.
d. 'Which' phrases in LA do not display superiority effects. The
   reason is that 'which' can be analyzed as a head (only 'which' is
   analyzed).
e. Non-'which' phrases in LA display superiority effects even when
   they are D-linked.

The patterns accounted for by the MMC include not only movement
and nonmovement structures but also cases where c-command or crossing
does not hold. The cases not involving c-command or crossing have generally been overlooked. Such instances provide important support favoring an MMC account over other alternatives. Take the following two
patterns, for instance:

(56) *[$_{CP}$ wh_1 [$_{IP}$ ... [$_{island}$ ... resumptive pronoun$_1$ ...] ... wh_2 ...]]

(57) *[$_{CP}$ wh_1 [$_{IP}$ ... [$_{island}$ ... wh_2 ...] ... x_1 ...]]

In (56), the resumptive pronoun and the *wh*-in-situ (wh_2) do not c-
command each other, and in (57), the *wh*-in-situ (wh_2) and the trace of the
extracted *wh*-element (x_1) do not c-command each other either. Both (56)
and (57) are instances of Superiority violations in LA. Like other cases of
Superiority violations, (56) and (57) improve if the *wh*-element in-situ wh_2
is a 'which' phrase instead of a non-'which' phrase, such as 'who'. Obviously, the standard account for superiority effects in terms of crossing
does not apply in (56). Similarly, neither Attract Closest nor the MLC is
violated in (57): there is no legitimate operation Move β (wh_2) that could
target K (Spec of Comp), where β is closer to K than x_1 (higher than
or c-commanding x_1), because wh_2 does not c-command x_1. The MMC,
on the other hand, accounts for such Superiority violations under the
assumption that, when c-command does not obtain between the resumptive element or variable and the *wh*-in-situ, neither element is closer to the
wh-element in the Spec of Comp and the MMC is not violated.

In brief, the fact that nonmovement structures exhibit superiority
effects, including those not involving a c-command or crossing relation

such as (56) and (57), is not accommodated by an approach to superiority effects based on movement (Attract Closest, the MLC) or crossing. A nonmovement solution has to be pursued. We propose that chains are formed not only by Move but also between operators and variables on representations where operator-variable relations are established and interpreted (referred to as Match). Chains formed on representations are constrained by the Minimal Match Condition. The MMC adequately accounts for superiority effects. So far, we have discussed movement accounts for Superiority and have argued that the MMC is more adequate. However, other accounts link Superiority to interpretation and subsume it under Weak Crossover. We discuss these accounts and the interpretation of multiple *wh*-interrogatives in the next chapter.

Chapter 3

Superiority and Interpretation

At this point, we have examined the distribution of multiple *wh*-interrogative phrases and shown that a movement approach to Superiority is inadequate. Instead, an approach incorporating the MMC, which applies to representations, more adequately accounts for the phenomenon. In this chapter, we first discuss analyses that account for Superiority in terms of Weak Crossover (WCO). These analyses are to be found in Watanabe 1995 and Hornstein 1995, which build on Engdahl 1985 and Chierchia 1991, 1993.

A WCO approach to Superiority, such as the one proposed by Hornstein (1995), requires multiple *wh*-interrogatives to always be functionally interpreted—that is, to have a pair-list interpretation. Superiority is violated when WCO prevents multiple *wh*-interrogatives from having this interpretation. However, a pair-list interpretation is not always required for multiple *wh*-interrogatives in LA. In LA, a pair-list interpretation is available only when two *wh*-phrases are "close enough" to each other (a domain requirement on the relevant *wh*-phrases). More importantly, contrary to standard assumptions, three different types of interpretation need to be distinguished:

(1) a. a *pair-list* interpretation in constructions containing a *wh*-interrogative phrase interacting with another *wh*-interrogative,

    b. a *distributive* interpretation (which has also been termed "pair-list" in the literature) in cases containing a QP interacting with a *wh*-interrogative phrase, and

    c. a *functional* interpretation in cases of QP/*wh* interaction.[1]

A pair-list interpretation is sensitive to both an intervention effect and a domain requirement; a distributive interpretation is sensitive only to an intervention effect; and a functional interpretation is sensitive to neither.

The above distinctions allow us to capture interesting crosslinguistic variations affecting them. For instance, in contrast to LA, Chinese does not exhibit a domain requirement or an intervention requirement with respect to pair-list and distributive interpretations. Such variations, we argue, can be attributed to the difference in the morphological composition of *wh*-expressions in the languages under discussion.

3.1 Superiority and Weak Crossover

The linking of Superiority to interpretation is essentially based on the assumption that multiple *wh*-interrogatives must be interpreted functionally and that a functional interpretation is subsumed under a "binding" relation, which is sensitive to WCO effects. Such an approach is put forward in Hornstein 1995, which builds on Chierchia 1991.

3.1.1 Superiority and Interpretation (Hornstein 1995)

Hornstein (1995) argues that the superiority effect exhibited in *wh*-constructions can be subsumed under WCO, a condition on the relative position of pronouns and variables coindexed with the same operator. His approach relates Superiority violations to the obligatoriness of a functional or pair-list interpretation in multiple *wh*-interrogatives. If a pair-list interpretation is not available in a given sentence because of a WCO violation, the sentence is not acceptable—it violates Superiority.[2]

More precisely, according to Hornstein, the relation between multiple *wh*-phrases is assimilated to the one between quantifiers and bound pronouns. *Wh*-expressions can be functionally interpreted. In particular, *wh*-expressions that are not in the Spec of Comp at LF are functionally interpreted. Such *wh*-expressions are to be distinguished from those in the Spec of CP. A *wh*-expression in the Spec of CP is a *generator*, which provides a *domain* (Chierchia 1991). "Retrieving a domain, Chierchia proposes, is crucial for generating a list" (Hornstein 1995, 114).[3] A pair-list reading depends on the availability of a generator, and the functionally interpreted *wh*-expressions are "cashed out at LF in terms of '[pro N]' structure" (p. 128) (see further discussion in section 3.3.2). For instance, in *Who bought what?*, *what* is functionally interpreted and is represented as containing a pronominal part and a nominal restrictor. The dependent pro is bound by the *who* in the Spec of Comp, which is a generator (providing a domain and enabling generation of a list).

(2) a. Who bought what?

    b. [$_{CP}$ who$_i$ [$_{IP}$ t$_i$ bought [pro$_i$ thing](=what)]]

Superiority violations are assimilated to WCO violations in the follow-ing way. A sentence such as (3a) has the LF representation in (3b), where *who* is represented as [pro N] and pro is coindexed with the generator *what* in the Spec of Comp.

(3) a. What did who buy?

    b. [$_{CP}$ what$_i$ [$_{IP}$ [pro$_i$ person](=who) buy t$_i$]]

In this representation, the pro$_i$ is coindexed with a variable t$_i$ on its right. This is a typical configuration in which WCO violations arise. Hornstein adopts a linking account of WCO (see Higginbotham 1983, 1985).[4]

(4) *Weak Crossover*

    A pronoun cannot be linked to a variable on its right.

    *Q ... pronoun ... variable ...

In brief, the contrast between (2) and (3) is due to the fact that one of the two *wh*-phrases must be interpreted as dependent on the other *wh*-phrase (which is the generator), yielding a functional (pair-list) interpre-tation. A dependent *wh*-phrase contains a pro. Whenever the pro is in a WCO configuration, a Superiority violation arises. Superiority thus asserts itself whenever a pair-list interpretation is not available.

The absence of Superiority violations with *which* phrases in (5a) is due to the fact that a *which* phrase in Comp can be deleted; that is, a *which* phrase need not be in the Spec of CP to act as a generator. The copy of *which song* in the Spec of CP (5b) can be deleted because the in-situ *which man* can be a generator, yielding the representation in (5c).[5]

(5) a. Which song did which man sing?

    b. [$_{CP}$ which song$_i$ [$_{IP}$ which man sing which song$_i$]]

    c. [$_{CP}$ [$_{IP}$ which man sing [pro song] (=which song)]]

Furthermore, to account for the unacceptability of sentences such as (6),

(6) *Which song didn't which man sing?

Hornstein (1995, 124–163, 194) assumes that a *wh*-operator outside an island (in this case, a negative island) can licitly bind a trace within that island if and only if the trace is interpreted as a variable ranging over in-dividuals. That is, the representation in (7a) is licit, but the one in (7b) is not.

(7) a. $[_{CP}\ wh_i\ [_{IP}\ \ldots\ [_{island}\ \ldots\ t_i\ \ldots]\ \ldots]]$

   b. $[_{CP}\ wh_i\ [_{IP}\ \ldots\ [_{island}\ \ldots\ [pro\ t]_i\ \ldots]\ \ldots]]$

A sentence like (6) cannot be represented as in (8a), with the higher copy of *which song* deleted, because negation creates an island. It has to be represented as in (8b), which violates WCO.

(8) a. [which man$_j$ Neg sing [pro$_j$ song]$_i$]

   b. [which song$_i$ [[pro$_i$ man] Neg sing t$_i$]]

Hornstein marks all sentences with *wh*-phrases separated by an island as unacceptable, the assumption being that a multiple *wh*-interrogative can only have a functional interpretation. When the functional interpretation is not available, the sentence is not acceptable. A WCO approach to superiority effects requires the presence of a (bound) pronoun whose purpose is to represent a functional interpretation. Such an approach to superiority effects requires that a multiple *wh*-interrogative be interpreted functionally. When a functional interpretation (pair-list reading) is not available, the multiple *wh*-interrogative is not acceptable.

   (9) summarizes the major points of this approach:

(9) a. A multiple *wh*-interrogative always has a *wh*-phrase interpreted functionally.

   b. One of the *wh*-phrases in a multiple interrogative is represented as [pro N], with the pro bound by a generator that is the other *wh*-phrase in the Spec of Comp or a *which* phrase. The existence of a pro yields a functional interpretation. A functional interpretation is a pair-list interpretation in multiple *wh*-interrogatives.[6]

   c. Functional binding of a pro by a generator is not possible across islands.

   d. Superiority is an instance of WCO.

3.1.2 Obligatory Functional/Pair-List Interpretation?

The WCO approach to Superiority requires multiple *wh*-interrogatives to always be functionally interpreted, that is, to have a pair-list reading. However, a pair-list interpretation is not always required for multiple *wh*-interrogatives in LA. Recall that, with respect to Superiority, LA has the following acceptable and unacceptable patterns:

(10) a. $[_{CP}\ wh_1\ [_{IP}\ \ldots\ t_1\ \ldots\ wh_2\ \ldots]]$ (t$_1$ c-commands wh_2)

   b. *$[_{CP}\ wh_2\ [_{IP}\ \ldots\ wh_1\ \ldots\ t_2\ \ldots]]$ (wh_1 c-commands t$_2$)

(11) a. $[_{CP}$ wh_1 $[_{IP}$ ... $[_{island}$ ... RP_1 ... wh_2 ...] ...]] (RP_1 c-commands wh_2)

   b. *$[_{CP}$ wh_2 $[_{IP}$ ... $[_{island}$ ... wh_1 ... RP_2 ...] ...]] (wh_1 c-commands RP_2)

   c. $[_{CP}$ wh_1 $[_{IP}$ ... RP_1 ... $[_{island}$ ... wh_2 ...] ...]] (RP_1 c-commands wh_2)

   d. *$[_{CP}$ wh_2 $[_{IP}$ ... wh_1 ... $[_{island}$ ... RP_2 ...] ...]] (wh_1 c-commands RP_2)

(12) a. *$[_{CP}$ wh_1 $[_{IP}$ ... $[_{island}$ ... RP_1 ...] ... wh_2 ...]] (neither RP_1 nor wh_2 c-commands the other)

   b. *$[_{CP}$ wh_2 $[_{IP}$ ... $[_{island}$ ... wh_1 ...] ... RP_2 ...]] (neither wh_1 nor RP_2 c-commands the other)

   c. *$[_{CP}$ wh_1 $[_{IP}$ ... $[_{island}$ ... RP_1 ...] ... $[_{island}$ ... wh_2 ...] ...]] (neither RP_1 nor wh_2 c-commands the other)

   d. *$[_{CP}$ wh_2 $[_{IP}$ ... $[_{island}$ ... wh_1 ...] ... $[_{island}$ ... RP_2 ...] ...]] (neither wh_1 nor RP_2 c-commands the other)

(13) a. ... wh_1 ... wh_2 ... (both wh-elements are in situ)

   b. ... $[_{island}$ ... wh_1 ... wh_2 ...] ... (same)

   c. ... wh_1 ... $[_{island}$ ... wh_2 ...] ... (same)

   d. ... $[_{island}$ ... wh_1 ...] ... wh_2 ... (same)

   e. ... $[_{island}$ ... wh_1 ...] ... $[_{island}$ ... wh_2 ...] ... (same)

Not all of the acceptable patterns allow a pair-list interpretation, however. Indeed, the set of multiple wh-interrogatives allowing a pair-list interpretation is only a proper subset of well-formed multiple wh-interrogatives, as shown below.

Recall that the following types of sentences of the pattern in (10a) are well-formed multiple wh-questions in LA:

(14) miin šeef miin
   who saw who
   'Who saw whom?'

(15) a. miin fakkar   ?ənno saamia šeefit   miin
      who thought.3MS that   Samia saw.3FS who
      'Who thought that Samia saw whom?'

   b. miin ?ənbasaṭ   la?inno saamia ḥikyit   maʕ miin
      who pleased.3MS because Samia spoke.3FS with who
      'Who was pleased because Samia spoke with whom?'

Not all of these sentences have the same range of interpretation. A pair-list interpretation is available in (14), where the *wh*-words are quite near to each other, but not in (15), where the *wh*-words are farther apart. Multiple *wh*-questions that allow a pair-list interpretation are only a proper subset of acceptable multiple *wh*-questions. As argued by Aoun and Choueiri (1999), multiple *wh*-questions that allow a pair-list interpretation are subject to a locality condition that governs the distance between the relevant *wh*-phrases.[7] A pair-list interpretation does not arise when the *wh*-phrases are separated by two distinct Tenses in LA.[8] The *wh*-phrases in (15), but not those in (14), are separated by a clause boundary so that two distinct Tenses (one per clause) are involved. That is, in (15) the two *wh*-words are separated by Tense. (15) should be contrasted with (16), which allows a pair-list interpretation even though the two *wh*-words are also separated by a clause boundary.

(16) miin ṭalab   min saami ysallim   ʕa-miin
      who asked.3MS from Sami 3MS.greet on-who
      'Who asked Sami to greet whom?'

What distinguishes (15) from (16) is Tense: (15) contains an embedded tensed clause and (16), a tenseless (nonfinite) clause. The contrast between (15) and (16) shows that what inhibits a pair-list interpretation is Tense:

(17) a. If wh_1 and wh_2 are not separated by Tense, the pair-list
         interpretation is available.
     b. If wh_1 and wh_2 are separated by Tense, the pair-list
         interpretation is unavailable.

The Tense Condition is similar to other blocking effects on the availability of a pair-list interpretation: operators such as QPs, negation/negative polarity items, and nonovert operators also have a blocking effect (see Beck 1996; Beck and Kim 1997; Pesetsky 2000).[9]

Let us first consider the blocking effect of nonovert operators. Compare the following sentences, involving purposive clauses:

(18) ʔayya walad štara   kteeb la-taʔdm-u   la-ʔayya
      which boy   bought book for-give.2P-it to-which
      mʕallme (pair-list unavailable)
      teacher.FS
      'Which boy bought a book for you to give to which teacher?'

(19) ʔayya walad štara   kteeb la-yubsuṭ   ʔayya
     which boy   bought book for-3MS.please which
     mʕallme   (pair-list available)
     teacher.FS
     'Which boy bought a book to please which teacher?'

Even though both sentences involve a *wh*-phrase in the matrix subject
position and another *wh*-phrase in the object position of the purposive
infinitival clause, they do not have the same interpretation: (19) can have
a pair-list interpretation, but (18) cannot. The contrast can be understood
in the following way. Note that (18) contains a resumptive pronoun that
is coindexed with 'a book'. This resumptive pronoun is indirectly coindexed with 'a book' via a nonovert operator in the Spec of Comp of
the purposive clause (see Ouhalla 2001 for relevant discussion). Consequently, it is expected that, because a resumptive pronoun is involved, a
nonovert operator intervenes between the two *wh*-phrases in (18), cor-
rectly anticipating the fact that a pair-list interpretation is blocked in this
case. In contrast, the embedded infinitival clause in (19) does not have a
resumptive element coindexed with an argument in the matrix clause. A
nonovert operator thus is not present in the purposive clause in (19) and,
as expected, a pair-list interpretation obtains. The difference in interpretation between the two sentences shows that a pair-list interpretation is
blocked by an intervening operator.

Now, consider the blocking effect of QPs. A pair-list interpretation
obtains in (20b,d) but not in (20a,c). In the latter two sentences, a quantifier intervenes between the two *wh*-elements.

(20) a. miin xabbar kəll   walad ʕan   miin   (single-pair)
        who told.3MS every boy   about who
        'Who told every boy about whom?'
     b. miin xabbar saami ʕan   miin   (pair-list)
        who told.3MS Sami about who
        'Who told Sami about whom?'
     c. miin ṭalab   min kəll walad ysallim ʕa-miin (single-pair)
        who asked.3MS from each boy 3MS.greet on-who
        'Who asked each boy to greet whom?'
     d. miin ṭalab   min saami ysallim ʕa-miin (pair-list)
        who asked.3MS from Sami 3MS.greet on-who
        'Who asked Sami to greet whom?'

The cases involving negation/negative polarity items also illustrate the intervention effect of operators.[10] Consider the following contrast:

(21) a. miin ʕarraf   saami ʕa-miin   (pair-list)
        who introduced.3MS Sami to-who
        'Who introduced Sami to whom?'
     b. miin ma ʕarraf   ħadan ʕa-miin   (single-pair)
        who NEG introduced.3MS anyone to-who
        'Who didn't introduce anyone to whom?'

(22) a. miin ṭalab   min saami ysallim   ʕa-miin   (pair-list)
        who asked.3MS from Sami 3MS.greet on-who
        'Who asked Sami to greet whom?'
     b. miin ma ṭalab   min ħadan yəsallim
        who NEG asked.3MS from anyone 3MS.greet
        ʕa-miin   (single-pair)
        on-who
        'Who didn't ask anyone to greet whom?'

Even though the two *wh*-phrases are not separated by Tense, the sentences with negation/negative polarity items do not have a pair-list interpretation. We can therefore generalize the Tense Condition to the following intervention condition on the pairing of *wh*-elements:[11]

(23) *Intervention condition on* wh-*pairing*
     Two *wh*-phrases cannot be paired in case they are separated by Tense, a nonovert operator, a *wh*-operator, QP, or a negation/ negative polarity item.

This condition captures the following generalizations in LA:

(24) a. Multiple *wh*-questions that allow a pair-list interpretation are only a proper subset of well-formed multiple *wh*-questions.
     b. Two *wh*-phrases cannot have a pair-list interpretation if they are separated by Tense, a nonovert operator, a *wh*-operator, QP, or a negation/negative polarity item.[12]

3.1.3 Superiority Not As Weak Crossover
The proper subset relation between well-formed multiple *wh*-interrogatives and those allowing a pair-list interpretation as in (24) suggests that a WCO approach to Superiority, which relies on an obligatory pair-list interpretation for multiple *wh*-interrogatives, cannot be adequate. In

LA, a pair-list interpretation does not obtain when the *wh*-phrases are separated by an operator or Tense or when the *wh*-phrase in the Spec of Comp binds a singular resumptive pronoun. Specifically, (11a,c) and (13c–e) cannot have a pair-list reading; yet they are acceptable and do not violate Superiority. Moreover, the contrast between the acceptability of (11a,c) and the unacceptability of (11b,d) is significant: since (11a,c) are grammatical but do not have a pair-list (functional) interpretation, WCO does not capture the contrast between them and (11b,d). Similarly, the contrast between the unacceptability of (12a–d) and the acceptability of the corresponding (13d–e) is unaccounted for: sentences (13d–e) do not have a pair-list interpretation.

Hornstein (1995) also indicates that an island blocks a functional (pair-list) interpretation and that multiple *wh*-questions are not acceptable when a functional interpretation is unavailable. This raises the question of how the acceptable sentences that involve islands in (11a,c) and (13c–e) should be analyzed. On the other hand, Hornstein observes (pp. 231–233, n. 25) that there is an interpretive difference between *wh*-traces and unmoved *wh*-phrases in the following English cases: an unmoved *wh*-phrase, but not a *wh*-trace, can be functionally interpreted when a *wh*-island or a negative island is present:

(25) a. What$_i$ did you wonder whether everyone heard t$_i$? (functional reading unavailable)

   b. Who remembers who bought what? (functional reading available—*what* dependent on the matrix *who*)

(26) a. Who$_i$ don't you believe that everyone kissed t$_i$? (functional reading unavailable)

   b. Which man didn't sing which song? (functional reading available—*which song* dependent on *which man*)

This seems to imply that the Island Condition is not relevant in cases involving an in-situ *wh*-phrase within an island. In other words, if Hornstein's analysis were to be extended to LA, we would expect a pair-list interpretation to be available in all the patterns containing an in-situ *wh*-phrase in an island. For example, (13d–e) ought to have a pair-list interpretation. However, they do not.[13]

One possibility is to revise Hornstein's account by simply adopting the representations containing a pro without adopting the accompanying claim regarding the interpretation (the existence of a pro indicates a functional interpretation, which is a pair-list interpretation in this WCO approach). However, we would still fail to capture the (un)acceptability of the relevant data. For instance, the contrast between (11a,c) and (11b,d) and the contrast between (12a–d) and (13d–e) could not be captured. Recall that in Hornstein's account, a *wh*-phrase needs to be moved to the Spec of Comp in order to be a generator. A D-linked *wh*-phrase need not be in the Spec of Comp to be a generator: the copy in the argument position can be retained and serve as a generator. In LA, an in-situ *wh*-phrase and a *wh*-phrase related to a resumptive pronoun are both D-linked. In other words, each of the *wh*-phrases in (11a–d), (12a–d), and (13d–e) can serve as a generator directly in argument position. The copy in the Spec of Comp can be deleted. There should be no distinction among these sentences; the contrast in their acceptability is not expected. Moreover, in general, the WCO account under discussion would not capture the unacceptability of the patterns where the two *wh*-phrases are not in a c-command relation and the second *wh*-phrase is in situ, regardless of its D-linking properties.

In brief, a WCO approach to Superiority, which is built on the obligatoriness of a functional or pair-list interpretation in multiple *wh*-questions, cannot be sustained considering the LA data. We have shown that not all acceptable multiple *wh*-questions allow a pair-list interpretation. In addition, it is questionable that a pair-list interpretation is represented exactly the way a functional interpretation is represented, although this is assumed under the WCO approach to Superiority. Indeed, we show in the next section that, even more generally, a functional interpretation should be distinguished from a distributive reading for QP/*wh* interactions, which in turn differs from a pair-list interpretation for *wh*/*wh* interactions. Such distinctions contrast with the frequent claim in the literature that the three interpretations are essentially the same (see section 3.2.2).

3.2   Functional, Distributional, and Pair-List Interpretations

We have shown that certain locality conditions govern the availability of interpretations: a pair-list interpretation of multiple *wh*-interrogatives is subject to a locality condition but a single-pair interpretation is not. According to the generally accepted view, for a multiple interrogative construction, a pair-list interpretation is a functional interpretation, which is also identical to the distributive interpretation found in cases containing a QP interacting with a *wh*-phrase.

These interpretations must be distinguished, however. This can be made clear by first examining the patterns of QP/*wh* interaction that allow a distributive interpretation and those that allow a functional interpretation. We will begin by clarifying the nature of the locality condition discussed in the previous section governing the availability of a pair-list interpretation (section 3.2.1) and discussing the nature of functional and distributive interpretations in more detail (section 3.2.2).

3.2.1 The Interpretation of Multiple *Wh*-Interrogative Constructions

Recall that the pair-list interpretation available to multiple *wh*-interrogatives in LA is subject to certain intervention effects, as stated in (24). We will show that it is important to separate the locality conditions in (23) into two distinct conditions: an intervention effect by operators and a domain requirement defined by Tense.

Comparing the elements that exercise intervention effects on the possibility of a pair-list interpretation stated in (24) with the interveners discussed by Beck (1996) and Beck and Kim (1997) reveals that they are identical except for the role of Tense: Tense is relevant in LA but not in the examples discussed by Beck and Kim. Beck and Kim show that when a scope-bearing element is raised, the trace is subject to a Minimal Quantified Structure Constraint, which is defined in terms of a *quantifier-induced barrier*.

(27) *Quantifier-induced barrier (QUIB)*
     The first node that dominates a quantifier, its restriction, and its nuclear scope is a quantifier-induced barrier.

(28) *Minimal Quantified Structure Constraint (MQSC)*
     If an LF trace β is dominated by a QUIB α, then the binder of β must be dominated by α.

Stating Beck and Kim's constraint more concretely, a *wh*-phrase cannot be separated from its scope position by a quantifier, such as a negative operator or a QP.

Comparing (23)–(24) and (27)–(28), one may wonder whether Tense belongs to the same class of interveners as *wh*-operators, negation, and quantifiers—the quantification-type (Q-type) interveners. In view of insights from research on the binding theory (Chomsky 1981) concerning the distinction between the domain requirement according to which an element is bound within a domain and the antecedent requirement according to which an anaphor must be bound by an antecedent (see Aoun 1985, 1986; Aoun and Li 1993a), it is possible to speculate that Tense defines a domain and the Q-type interveners define a potential binder. In terms of minimality (Aoun and Li 1989, 1993a; Cinque 1990; Rizzi 1990), as well as the Minimalist Program (Chomsky 1995) and the notion of phase (Chomsky 2000), it is possible to assume that the Q-type interveners play a role in identifying the minimal antecedent and that Tense defines a phase. A phase defines a domain that operations can have access to, according to the Phase Impenetrability Condition (Chomsky 2000, 108). This condition states that, for a strong phase HP with head H, where the edge is the residue higher than H, either Specs or elements adjoined to HP:

(29) *Phase Impenetrability Condition*
In phase α with head H, the domain of H is not accessible to operations outside α, only H and its edge are accessible to such operations.

In other words, "... operations cannot 'look into' a phase α below its head H" (p. 108). Regarding the data we examine here, it may be postulated that Tense defines a strong phase. Given this view, only the Spec of Tense (T) is accessible to an operation outside the Tense Phrase (TP). A preverbal subject occupies the Spec of T. Therefore, a preverbal subject is available to be paired with another *wh*-phrase outside the phase as illustrated in (30), as well as another *wh*-phrase within the phase. An object, by contrast, is not at the edge of the phase and therefore is not accessible to another *wh*-phrase outside the TP. Similarly, a postverbal subject is not at the edge of the phase and should not be accessible to another *wh*-phrase outside the TP. This is true, as illustrated in (31).

(30) miin ʔaal   ʔənno miin ħa-yšuuf   l-film   (pair-list)
     who said.3MS that   who will-3MS.see the-movie
     'Who said that who would see the movie?'

(31) miin ʔaal   ʔənno ħa-yšuuf   miin l-film   (single-pair)
     who said.3MS that   will-3MS.see who the-movie
     'Who said that who would see the movie?'

In other words, (23) can be restated as (32)–(33).

(32) a. Multiple *wh*-questions that allow a pair-list interpretation are only a proper subset of well-formed multiple *wh*-questions.

    b. The relation between two *wh*-phrases that have a pair-list
       interpretation is sensitive to an intervention effect and a domain
       requirement.

(33) a. The intervention effect is defined by an intervening operator,
       such as a *wh*-operator, a QP, a negation/negative polarity item,
       or a nonovert operator.
    b. The domain requirement is defined by T: a TP is a strong phase.
       It allows only a *wh*-phrase in the Spec of T to have a pair-list
       interpretation with another *wh*-phrase outside the TP, in
       addition to another *wh*-phrase within the same TP.

The difference between the generalization discussed by Beck (1996) and
Beck and Kim (1997) and the one we have established for LA (32)–(33)
lies in the relevance of the domain requirement. The domain requirement
applies in the LA cases but not in the cases discussed by Beck and Kim.[14]
This is not surprising, as the domain requirement is not obeyed in cases
involving QP/*wh* interaction, to which we turn next.

3.2.2   The Interpretation of QP/*Wh* Constructions

Sentences involving QP/*wh* interaction are the canonical cases illustrating
the nature of functional and distributive interpretations. For instance, a
sentence like (34) can have the interpretation and answer in (35) or (36).
(35) is the individual reading and (36), the functional reading (see Groenendijk and Stokhof 1984; Engdahl 1986; Chierchia 1991, 1993; Hornstein 1995; Sharvit 1999). ((34)–(36) are from Sharvit 1999, 594, 596.)

(34) Which woman did every man invite?

(35) Of the set of contextually relevant women, which woman y is such
      that for every x, x a man, x invited y? (Possible answer: Mary)

(36) Of the set of contextually relevant woman-valued functions, which
      function f is such that for every x, x a man, x invited $f(x)$?
      (Possible answer: His mother)

In addition, (34) can be answered with a list of pairs (the pair-list interpretation, which has also been termed the distributive interpretation for
QP/*wh* interaction). A possible answer is *John invited Mary, Bill invited
Sue.* ... The question is what a pair-list or distributive interpretation is.
Some have proposed that a pair-list/distributive interpretation is just a
variant of the functional reading (Engdahl 1986): a pair-list/distributive
answer provides the extension of the actual world. Others have proposed

that the pair-list/distributive reading bears no relation to the functional reading (e.g., Groenendijk and Stokhof 1984; also see Higginbotham and May 1981; Szabolcsi 1997a,b,c). In between these two opposing positions are proposals that support a functional dependency underlying both functional and pair-list/distributive readings, where the latter is derived by an Absorption mechanism (see Higginbotham and May 1981 for Absorption) converting the two operators into one constituent (Chierchia 1993; Sharvit 1999—also see, e.g., Dayal 1996). Specifically, for both functional and pair-list readings, there is a functional, doubly indexed trace. At LF, (34) can be represented as (37) and (38) to derive the readings in (35) and (36), respectively.

(37) [which woman]$_j$ [every man]$_i$ [t_i invite t_j]

(38) [which woman]$_j$ [every man]$_i$ [t_i invite t_j^i]

(37) contains a trace that bears one index and is interpreted as an individual variable. (38) contains a functional trace that is simultaneously bound by *which woman* and by the trace of *every man*. This functional trace bears two indices: the functional index, the subscript j, bound by *which woman*; and the argument index, the superscript i, bound by the trace of *every man*. That is, the argument index can act as a bound pronoun while the functional index is bound by the *wh*-phrase in the Spec of Comp. Hornstein (1995, 113) states that "an intuitive way of thinking of this is that what we have in the a[rgument] index is a bindable pronoun analogous to the one that arises in the overt functional answer." The LF representation of a functional interpretation therefore contains a pronoun bound by the quantifier, as in (39).

(39) [(which woman) [[every man]$_i$ [t_i invite [pro$_i$ woman]]]]

According to Chierchia (1991, 1993), a functional interpretation is a necessary but not sufficient condition for supporting a pair-list reading. The function supplies a way of mapping a given domain of entities to a range of values—that is, a pair-list relating an element in the domain to an element in the range. Chierchia suggests that only some expressions can provide a domain. A universal quantifier, for instance, can provide a domain; it denotes all the supersets of a given set. A universal quantifier also allows one to retrieve a domain, which is crucial for generating a list. The quantifiers *no* and *most*, for instance, do not allow one to retrieve a domain; therefore, they do not allow a pair-list interpretation, even though they allow a functional interpretation.

(40) a. Who does no linguist admire?
        His mother.
     b. Who do most linguists admire?
        Their mothers.

With respect to the mechanism that derives a pair-list/distributive interpretation, the two quantifiers are converted into one constituent by an Absorption mechanism: ... [*wh* ... [QNP ... → ... [*wh* QNP] ... That is, the *wh*-phrase *which woman* and the subject QP *every man* in (34) are absorbed into one constituent.

In brief, the following generalization emerges, according to Chierchia, Hornstein, Sharvit, and others:

(41) Both distributive and functional readings are obtained via a
     dependency relation between the two relevant quantifiers. The two
     readings differ in the types of QPs involved. The distributive
     interpretation is derived by an Absorption mechanism that converts
     two operators into one; when this mechanism does not apply, a
     functional reading results. That is, in the case of a *wh*-operator and
     a QP, the *wh*-operator and the QP are converted into one
     constituent by Absorption to derive a distributive interpretation.

What is missing from all these discussions, however, is the fact that functional and distributive interpretations of QP/*wh* interactions can be subject to different locality conditions, which also differ from the locality conditions governing the pair-list interpretation of *wh*/*wh* interactions. In other words, with respect to locality conditions, three different interpretations need to be distinguished: pair-list for *wh*/*wh* interaction, distributive, and functional for QP/*wh* interaction.

3.2.3 Distinguishing Pair-List, Distributive, and Functional Interpretations

In the literature, the terms *pair-list interpretation* and *distributive interpretation* have been used interchangeably, because it has not been noted that the conditions for obtaining the pair-list interpretation for QP/*wh* interaction and for *wh*/*wh* interaction are different. In fact, as we will show, *wh*/*wh* interaction is subject to the domain requirement (T boundary) but QP/*wh* interaction is not. For ease of presentation, we will therefore use the term *distributive interpretation* for QP/*wh* interaction and the term *pair-list interpretation* for *wh*/*wh* interaction.

We indicated in section 3.2.1 that a pair-list reading for two *wh*-phrases is subject to a domain requirement and an intervention effect: the two *wh*-phrases cannot be separated by T or an operator. The intervention effect is also manifested in the availability of a distributive interpretation in cases of QP/*wh* interaction. For example, the distributive reading obtained in a sentence containing the universal quantifier *every* and a *wh*-phrase is subject to this effect: the QP and the *wh* cannot be separated by an operator. For instance, in the following LA examples, a distributive reading between the QP and the *wh*-phrase is not available:

(42) *QP intervening between 'every' and* wh
      kəll mʕallme badda   tʕarrif   kəll ṣabe ʕala ʔayya
      every teacher.FS want.3FS introduce.3FS every boy to which
      bənt (no distributive reading)
      girl
      'Every teacher wants to introduce every boy to which girl?'

(43) *Negation/negative polarity item intervening between 'every' and* wh
      kəll mʕallme ma badda   tʕarrif   wala ṣabe ʕala ʔayya
      every teacher.FS NEG want.3FS introduce.3FS no boy to which
      bənt (no distributive reading)
      girl
      'Every teacher doesn't want to introduce any boy to which girl?'

As before, when there is no resumptive pronoun in the purpose clause, and thus no nonovert operator, a distributive reading for the QP/*wh* interaction is available, as in (44a–b). But once a nonovert operator intervenes (its presence being indicated by the resumptive pronoun in (44c)), the distributive reading is not available.

(44) *Null operator intervening between 'every' and* wh *(purpose clauses)*
      a. kəll walad ʔəre   kteeb la-tinbiṣit   ʔayya
         every boy   read.3MS book in.order.to-3FS.happy which
         mʕallme (distributive reading)
         teacher.FS
         'Every boy read a book in order for which teacher to be
         pleased?'
      b. kəll walad ʔəre   kteeb la-yibṣut   ʔayya
         every boy   read.3MS book in.order.to-3MS.make.happy which
         mʕallme (distributive reading)
         teacher.FS
         'Every boy read a book to please which teacher?'

   c. kəll ṣabe štara   hdiyye la-yaʕṭiy-a   la-ʔayya
      every boy bought.3MS gift   in.order.to-give.3MS-it to-which
      bənt   (no distributive reading)
      girl
      'Every boy bought a gift to give it to which girl?'

Similarly, a *wh*-island containing a *wh*-operator also induces the intervention effect.

(45) Wh-*operator intervening between 'every' and* wh
    kəll mʕallme badda taʕrif   miin ħakee   maʕ ʔayya
    every teacher.FS want.3FS know.3FS who talked.3MS with which
    təlmiiz   (no distributive reading)
    student
    'Every teacher wants to know who talked with which student?'

Interestingly, however, the distributive interpretation obtained in cases of QP/*wh* interaction, in contrast to the pair-list interpretation of multiple *wh*-phrases, does not seem to be subject to the domain requirement; in other words, T does not block a distributive interpretation between a QP and a *wh*-phrase.

(46) *Tense intervening between 'every' and* wh *(adjunct, subcategorized embedding, respectively)*
    a. kəll mʕallme ʔtanaʕit   ʔənno l-mudiira   btikrah
      every teacher.FS convinced.3FS that   the-principal.FS hate.3FS
      ʔayya təlmiize (distributive reading)
      which student.FS
      'Every teacher was convinced that the principal hates which student?'
    b. kəll mʕallme fallit   ʔabl   ma   l-mudiira   ħəkyet
      every teacher.FS left.3FS before COMP the-principal.FS talked.3FS
      maʕ ʔayya təlmiiz   (distributive reading)
      with which student
      'Every teacher left before the principal talked to which student?'

In brief:

(47) *Distributive interpretation for QP/*wh *interaction*
    The availability of a distributive interpretation in cases of QP/*wh* interaction is sensitive to an intervention effect but not a domain requirement.

In addition to this distinction, another one needs to be made as well: unlike distributive and pair-list interpretations, functional interpretations do not seem to be subject to either the intervention effect or the domain requirement. Thus, even though the patterns illustrated in (42)–(45) show the relevance of an intervention effect on the availability of a distributive interpretation, the same sentences are acceptable with a functional interpretation. That is, a functional interpretation is not subject to the intervention effect. Not surprisingly, (46) is also acceptable with a functional interpretation, which indicates the irrelevance of the domain requirement to the functional interpretation.

In brief:

(48) a. Functional interpretations in QP/*wh* constructions are not sensitive to the domain requirement or the intervention effect.

b. Distributive interpretations in QP/*wh* constructions are sensitive to the intervention effect but not the domain requirement.

c. Pair-list interpretations in *wh*/*wh* constructions are sensitive to both the domain requirement and the intervention effect.

The task, of course, is to account for this distinction, a task to which we now turn.

3.3   Generating Interpretations

3.3.1   Pronoun Binding

It is not surprising, in fact, that a functional reading is insensitive to the intervention effect or the domain requirement. Adopting the insight of Chierchia (1991), Hornstein (1995), and others, we can represent a functional reading as the binding of a pronoun by the QP, as illustrated in (39). Pronoun binding, in general, is not sensitive to an intervening operator or to a domain requirement defined by T. For instance, it is quite acceptable for a pronoun to be bound by the quantifier in the following patterns, even though there is an intervening quantifier or T:

(49) a. *QP does not block pronoun binding*
  kəll təlmiize ħa-tχabbir ħadan ʔənno hiyye neeẑħa
  every student.fs will-tell.3fs someone that she passing
  'Every student$_i$ will tell someone that she$_i$ is passing.'

b. *Negation/negative polarity item does not block pronoun binding*
kəll təlmiiz waʕad l-mʕallme ma yižbur
every student.3MS promised.3MS the-teacher.FS NEG force.3MS
wala bənt tərʔuṣ maʕ-o
no girl dance.3FS with-him
'Every student_i promised the teacher not to force any girl to
dance with him_i.'

c. *Null operator does not block pronoun binding*
kəll walad ħa-yištre kteeb la-l-mʕallme tiʔraa-lo-yee
every boy will-buy.3MS book for-the-teacher read.3FS-him-it
'Every boy_i will buy a book for the teacher to read to him_i.'

d. *Wh-operator does not block pronoun binding*
kəll mʕallme btaʕrif miin ʕazam-a
every teacher.FS know.3FS who invited.3MS-her
'Every teacher_i knows who invited her_i.'

e. *T does not block pronoun binding*
kəll walad xabbar saamia ʔənno l-mʕallme
every boy told.3MS Samia that the-teacher.FS
ʔaaṣaṣit-o
punished.3FS-him
'Every boy_i told Samia that the teacher punished him_i.'

In other words, a functional interpretation, which is essentially a bound
pronoun relation, is a relation between A-elements. It is not surprising
that the relation between A-elements (pronoun binding) is insensitive to
an intervention effect by quantifiers or to a domain requirement. Accordingly, it is not surprising that a functional reading is insensitive to the intervention effect or the domain requirement.

3.3.2 Nonmovement Quantifier-Dependency Relation

How is it, then, that a distributive interpretation is sensitive to the intervention effect but not the domain requirement? It should be noted that
what is essential to a distributive interpretation is the relation between
the two quantifiers. This is the spirit of the Absorption mechanism,
which has been proposed to derive the distributive interpretation. As
noted, Absorption is used to convert two quantifiers into one constituent: [*wh* ... [QNP ... → [*wh* QNP].... Similarly, for the pair-list interpretation in cases of *wh/wh* interaction, Absorption is used to convert
two *wh*-quantifiers into one constituent. It is not possible, however, to

interpret Absorption as literally involving the merger of two quantifiers. This can be clarified by a brief digression regarding a merger approach to deriving the pair-list interpretation for multiple *wh*-interrogatives.

Aoun and Choueiri (1999) argue that a pair-list interpretation is derived by merging the two *wh*-elements: the lower *wh*-in-situ is moved to a c-commanding *wh*. The c-commanding *wh* can be in the Spec of Comp as in (50) or in situ as in (51).

(50) miin ʔarrafto   ʔa-miin
     who introduce.2P to-whom
     'Who did you introduce to whom?'

(51) saami raaħ   ʔabl-ma yʕarraf   miin ʕa-miin
     Sami left.3MS before   3MS.introduce who to-who
     'lit. Sami left before introducing whom to whom?'

The movement approach raises questions. First, the putative movement would be sensitive to the conditions on *wh*-pairing (33) yet would differ from overt *wh*-movement, which is not subject to these conditions. This difference is illustrated by the contrast between (52), where a pair-list reading is not available when the two *wh*-phrases are in separate T domains, and (53), where a *wh*-phrase easily moves out of one T domain into a higher one.

(52) miin fakkar   ʔənno saami šeef
     who thought.3MS that   Sami saw.3MS
     miin   (no pair-list interpretation)
     who
     'Who thought that Sami saw whom?'

(53) miin fakkarto   ʔənno saami šeef (overt movement possible)
     who thought.2P that   Sami saw.3MS
     'Who did you think that Sami saw?'

Second, there are cases that allow a pair-list interpretation but not overt movement. For instance, in LA, a *wh*-phrase appearing as the pre-verbal subject of an embedded clause that does not contain an operator in the Spec of Comp can be paired with another *wh*-phrase in the higher clause even when the clause has an independent T.

(54) miin ʔaal   ʔənno miin šeef   l-film (pair-list)
     who said.3MS that   who saw.3MS the-movie
     'Who said that who saw the movie?'

(55) miin ?aal   ?ənno miin ħa-yšuuf   l-film   (pair-list)
     who said.3MS that   who will-3MS.see the-movie
     'Who said that who would see the movie?'

(56) miin ?ənbasaṭ   la?inno miin wəṣil   (pair-list)
     who pleased.3MS because who arrived.3MS
     'Who was pleased because who arrived?'

However, the subject of an embedded clause does not allow overt extraction in LA.

(57) *?ayya wəleed fakkarto   ?ənno raaħo
      which boys   thought.2P that   left.3P
      'Which boys did you think that left?'

(58) *?ayya wəleed ?ənbasaṭṭo la?inno raaħo
      which boys   pleased.2P because left.3P
      'Which boys were you pleased because left?'

Third, the putative merger of the two *wh*-phrases cannot be assimilated to QR, which does not apply across clauses (see May 1977 and Hornstein 1984 regarding the clause-boundedness of QR). For instance, (59) is ambiguous: either 'every table' can be raised higher than and take wide scope over 'two tablecloths', or it can take narrow scope with respect to 'two tablecloths'. In contrast, 'every actor' in (60) cannot be raised out of the embedded clause to take scope over the object QP 'a boy'.[15] (60) is not ambiguous: the scope of 'every actor' is restricted to the embedded clause, where it cannot take scope over the object QP in the matrix clause. But a *wh*-phrase in an embedded subject position can have a pair-list interpretation with another *wh*-phrase in the matrix clause (61).

(59) keeno   ħaaṭṭiin šaršaf-een   ʕa kəll   ṭaawle   (ambiguous)
     were.3P putting.P tablecloth-DUAL on every table
     'They had put two tablecloths on every table.'

(60) xabbarit walad ?ənno kəll   mmasil sallam
     told.3FS boy   that   every actor   greeted.3MS
     ʕa-saami (unambiguous)
     on-Sami
     'She told a boy that every actor greeted Sami.'

(61) xabbarit miin   ?ənno miin sallam ʕa-saami   (pair-list)
     told.3FS whom that   who greeted on-Sami
     'Who did she tell that who greeted Sami?'

Fourth, the availability of a pair-list interpretation in (62) and (63) even though a subject intervenes between the two *wh*-phrases argues against assimilating the putative merger of the *wh*-phrases to an A-movement process because we would in that case incorrectly predict intervention effects when specifiers in an A-position intervene, given standard assumptions about A-movement.

(62) miin ṭalab   min saami ysallim   ʕa-miin   (pair-list)
     who asked.3MS from Sami 3MS.greet on-who
     'Who asked Sami to greet whom?'

(63) miin/ʔayya walad štara   kteeb la-yubsuṭ   miin/ʔayya
     who/which boy   bought book for-3MS.please who/which
     mʕallme (pair-list)
     teacher.FS
     'Who/Which boy bought a book to please whom/which teacher?'

In brief, we are led to conclude that movement is not involved in the derivation of a pair-list interpretation. An in-situ *wh*-phrase stays in situ and is not subject to covert movement, as argued in Li 1992, Aoun and Li 1993a, and Chomsky 1995, chap. 3, for instance.[16] A pair-list interpretation obtains when the conditions on pairing are satisfied.[17]

This digression shows that the intervention effect of the pair-list interpretation of multiple *wh*-interrogatives cannot be derived by any movement process because the relevant *wh*-phrases occur in contexts beyond those that can be captured by A-movement, QR, or *wh*-movement. The same considerations apply to the distributive interpretation in cases of QP/*wh* interaction. The following sentences, for instance, allow a distributive interpretation even though the *wh*-phrase is not in a position that allows movement:

(64) a. kəll mʕallme fallit   ʔabl ma   l-mudiira   ħəkyet
        every teacher.FS left.3FS before COMP the-principal.FS talked.3FS
        maʕ ʔayya təlmiiz
        with which student
        'Every teacher left before the principal talked to which student?'
     b. kəll walad ʔəre   kteeb la-yibṣut   ʔayya
        every boy read.3MS book in.order.to-3MS.make.happy which
        mʕallme
        teacher.FS
        'Every boy read a book to please which teacher?'

Not resorting to actual movement, Absorption can be interpreted as a dependency/covariation relation between two quantifiers, which may be expressed in terms of a linking relation or any other form expressing a dependency/covariation relation. Regardless of what mechanism should be adopted to express the dependency/covariation relation between two quantifiers, the intervention effect of a third quantifier on distributive interpretations can be taken as a manifestation of the notion of minimality: no relation between two quantifiers can be established if there is an intervening quantifier. By contrast, the domain requirement does not play a role. After all, the scope of a quantifier is the domain that it c-commands, regardless of whether or not T occurs within this c-command domain.

3.3.3 Agree

Finally, let us consider why a pair-list interpretation in cases of *wh*/*wh* interaction is sensitive to a domain requirement as well as an intervention effect. A pair-list interpretation of *wh*/*wh* interaction shares with a distribution interpretation of QP/*wh* interaction the property that both involve the interaction of two quantifiers. Consequently, it is expected that both readings are sensitive to the intervention of another quantifier. However, a pair-list interpretation differs from a distributive interpretation in terms of what quantifiers (*wh* or non-*wh*) are involved. Note that when a QP is a generator (the quantifier that takes the wide scope in terms of scope interaction; see section 3.1.1 and Hornstein 1995), the other quantifier can be another QP or a *wh*-phrase and a distributive reading is available in either case.

(65) a. Every doctor examined a patient.   (distributive reading available)
  b. Who did every doctor examine?   (distributive reading available)

By contrast, when the generator is a *wh*-phrase, the other quantifier must also be a *wh*-phrase if a pair-list answer is to be available. The contrast between the following two dialogues illustrates this point. In (67), a pair-list answer is not appropriate because the object is a QP, not a *wh*-phrase.

(66) a. Which doctor examined which patient?
  b. Doctor A examined patient A; doctor B examined patient B; . . .

(67) a. Which doctor examined a patient?
     b. *Doctor A examined patient A; doctor B examined patient
         B; . . .

It is possible that this requirement can be regarded as an Agree relation
between the two *wh*-phrases (Chomsky 2000). Agree is a relation between
an uninterpretable feature or an element that activates Agree by virtue of
its uninterpretable features (a probe) and a category that matches the
feature(s) (goal). A probe seeks a matching goal within an appropriate
domain. An appropriate domain (such as a TP) constitutes a strong
phase, and only the head H of a domain and its edge can be accessed by
a probe from outside the phase (the Phase Impenetrability Condition).
Agree can capture the relation between the two *wh*-phrases when a pair-
list interpretation obtains if Agree is extended to apply between elements
with interpretable features (to the extent that a [+*wh*] feature is an interpretable feature).[18]

Agree is subject to a domain requirement (i.e., Chomsky's (2000)
notion of phase). This means that the availability of a pair-list interpretation in sentences containing *wh*-phrases is sensitive to both the intervention effect and the domain requirement.[19]

3.3.4 Summary

In brief, three interpretations need to be distinguished in cases of QP/*wh*
and *wh*/*wh* interaction: functional, distributive, and pair-list. It is important to separate these three readings because they are sensitive to different
locality conditions. In cases of *wh*/*wh* interaction, the availability of a
pair-list interpretation is sensitive to both the intervention effect and
the domain requirement; in cases of *wh*/QP interaction, the availability of
a distributive interpretation is sensitive only to the intervention effect
whereas the availability of a functional interpretation is sensitive to
neither. Such distinctions follow from the types of relations that hold
between the relevant QP or *wh*-phrases. A functional interpretation is
essentially an A-relation between the relevant phrases, just like the relation between a bound pronoun and its A-antecedent. Pronoun binding is
not subject to either an intervention effect or a domain requirement. A
distributive interpretation concerns the relation between two quantifiers;
therefore, the relevance of an intervening quantifier is expected. A pair-
list interpretation includes an additional Agree requirement: the two relevant quantifiers must be *wh*-quantifiers.[20]

3.4   *Wh*-Quantifiers versus *Wh*-Variables

Before concluding the chapter, we would like to point out one more important fact concerning the interpretation of the patterns containing *wh*-phrases. We just mentioned that when a pair-list or distributive interpretation is considered, it is the quantificational part of these phrases that participates in determining the interpretation, and therefore the intervention of a quantificational expression is relevant. In this section, we present crosslinguistic evidence that further supports this point.

In discussing the conditions on the availability of a pair-list interpretation in cases of *wh/wh* interaction and the availability of a distributive interpretation in cases of QP/*wh* interaction, we concentrated on the distance between the two *wh*-phrases or between a *wh*-phrase and a QP. We have essentially considered only the overt positions of the relevant *wh*-phrases. With respect to the examples containing in-situ *wh*-phrases, one may wonder whether these *wh*-phrases undergo raising at LF, thus changing their position, in which case the domain requirement or intervention effect may be manifested differently. Even if an in-situ *wh*-phrase does not undergo movement, the question complementizer that licenses such *wh*-phrases indicates the scope of the interrogation. It is worth asking whether such a complementizer plays a role in scope interaction.

There are good empirical reasons to consider only the *wh*-phrases in their overt positions and not the question complementizer in LA. First, consider these sentences, which allow a distributive interpretation:

(68) kəll   mʕallme   ʔaaṣaṣit   ʔayya walad
     every teacher.FS punished.3FS which boy
     'Every teacher punished which boy?'

(69) ʔayya walad kəll   mʕallme   ʔaaṣaṣit
     which boy   every teacher.FS punished.3FS
     'Which boy did every teacher punish?'

It is possible to claim that (68) and (69) have the same LF representations: the *wh*-phrase is moved to the Spec of Comp to be interpreted in its scope position. At LF, the QP and the raised *wh*-phrase are not separated by an operator, and a distributive interpretation is available. However, compare the following two sentences:

(70) saami fakkar   ʔənno kariim ʕarraf   miin ʕa
     Sami thought.3MS that   Karim introduced.3MS who to
     miin   (pair-list available)
     who
     'Sami thought that Karim introduced whom to whom?'

(71) miin saami fakkar   ʔənno kariim ʕarraf   ʕa
     who Sami thought.3MS that   Karim introduced.3MS to
     miin   (pair-list unavailable)
     who
     'Who did Sami think that Karim introduced to whom?'

Recall that the contrast in the availability of a pair-list interpretation between these two sentences is due to the domain requirement: the two *wh*-phrases are within the same TP in (70), but not in (71). This indicates that the in-situ subject *wh*-phrase *miin* in (70) does not undergo raising covertly; if it did, there would be no distinction between the two sentences with respect to the domain requirement and the contrast in interpretation would not exist.[21] The contrast between these two sentences further indicates that what is considered to determine the availability of a pair-list interpretation must be the *wh*-phrases themselves. The question complementizer, which licenses the in-situ *wh*-phrases and gives them interrogative scope, does not play a role in determining a pair-list interpretation.

(72) $Qu_i \ldots [\ldots wh_i \ldots]$

Were the question complementizer the element to be considered for the pair-list interpretation, there would again be no difference in the domain requirement between (70) and (71) and the contrast in the availability of a pair-list interpretation would be unexpected.

However, this claim seems to directly contradict the claim made in Aoun and Li 1993b that the question marker licensing an in-situ *wh*-phrase in Chinese must play a role in determining the scope interaction of an in-situ *wh*-phrase and a QP in this language. This is not the only problem when we consider the relevant Chinese patterns containing multiple *wh*-phrases or a *wh*-phrase interacting with a QP. Indeed, the Chinese data show that neither the domain requirement nor the intervention effect is relevant to the availability of a pair-list interpretation. The behavior of multiple *wh*-questions in Chinese seems to be quite different from what we have discussed so far concerning LA. Recall that multiple *wh*-questions in LA allow a pair-list interpretation only when the two *wh*-phrases are not separated by T or an operator—a constraint that, for instance, excludes a pair-list reading in cases like those in (73).

(73) *No pair-list interpretation*
     a. miin fakkar   ʔənno saamia šeefit   miin
        who thought.3MS that   Samia saw.3FS who
        'Who thought that Samia saw whom?'
     b. miin ʔənbasaṭ   laʔinno saamia ħikyit   maʕ miin
        who pleased.3MS because Samia spoke.3FS with who
        'Who was pleased because Samia spoke with whom?'

Such a constraint does not seem to hold in Chinese. Thus, the Chinese counterparts to (73) do allow a pair-list interpretation.

(74) *Pair-list interpretation*
     a. shei yiwei   zhangsan kandao shei
        who thought Zhangsan see   who
        'Who thought Zhangsan saw whom?'
     b. shei yinwei wo gen shei   shuohua hen gaoxing
        who because I   with whom speak   very happy
        'Who was happy because I spoke with whom?'
     c. shei xihuan ta zai nar   xie   de shu
        who like   he at where write DE book
        'Who likes the book that he wrote where?'

That these questions allow a pair-list interpretation is shown by the fact that they can indeed be answered by a list of pairs.

(75) a. a-ming yiwei   zhangsan kandao laoshi, a-de yiwei
        A-ming thought Zhangsan saw   teacher A-de thought
        zhangsan kandao huahua, ...
        Zhangsan saw   Huahua
        'A-ming thought Zhangsan saw teacher, A-de thought Zhangsan
        saw Huahua, ...'
     b. a-ming yinwei   wo gen huahua shuohua hen gaoxing, a-de
        A-ming because I   with Huahua speak   very happy   A-de
        yinwei   wo gen minmin shuohua hen gaoxing, ...
        because I   with Minmin speak   very happy
        'A-ming was happy because I spoke with Huahua, A-de was
        happy because I spoke with Minmin, ...'

c. a-ming xihuan ta zai chengshi xie   de shu, a-de xihuan ta
   A-ming like   he at city   write DE book A-de like   he
   zai xiangcun   xie   de shu,...
   at countryside write DE book
   'A-ming likes the books that he writes in the city, A-de likes the
   books that he writes in the countryside,...'

The contrast between the Chinese sentences in (74) and the LA sentences in (73) is unexpected. It might seem to suggest that the interpretive mechanism for deriving a pair-list reading applies differently in different languages: for instance, that the interpretive mechanism is subject to an operator intervention effect in LA, but not in Chinese. Prima facie, this statement seems empirically adequate. Thus, in Chinese, an intervening QP or negation/negative polarity item does not block the availability of a pair-list interpretation, either, as illustrated by the acceptability of the answers in (77) to the questions in (76).

(76) a. shei xiwang ta yaoqiu meigeren dai   shenme lai
        who hope   he ask   everyone bring what   come
        'Who hopes that he will ask everyone to bring what?'
     b. shei mei yao renheren dai   shenme lai
        who not ask anyone   bring what   come
        'Who did not ask anyone to bring what?'

(77) a. a-ming xiwang ta yaoqiu meigeren dai   shu   lai,   a-de
        A-ming hope   he ask   everyone bring book come A-de
        xiwang ta yaoqiu meigeren dai   qian   lai,...
        hope   he ask   everyone bring money come
        'A-ming hopes that he will ask everyone to bring books, A-de
        hopes that he will ask everyone to bring money,...'
     b. a-ming mei yao renheren dai   shu   lai,   a-de mei yao
        A-ming not ask anyone   bring book come A-de not ask
        renheren dai   qian   lai,...
        anyone   bring money come
        'A-ming did not ask anyone to bring books, A-de did not ask
        anyone to bring money,...'

Although at first glance this empirical generalization appears to be correct, it is quite unexpected that the interpretive mechanisms for deriving a pair-list reading would differ in different languages (see Higginbotham 1985 and Aoun and Li 1993a regarding interpretive invariance). More importantly, relaxing the intervention and domain conditions on the interpretive mechanism turns out not to be empirically adequate when we examine a wider range of data. Consider cases involving the interaction of QPs and *wh*-phrases. Even though a simple sentence like (78a), with a QP and *wh*-phrase in a single clause, has a distributive interpretation (illustrated by the availability of a distributive answer in (78b)), embedding the QP and *wh*-phrase in an island, as in (79a), seems to prevent a distributive interpretation (illustrated by the unavailability of a distributive answer in (79b)).

(78) a. meigeren dou maile   shenme ne
     everyone all   bought what   QU
     'What did everyone buy?'

    b. a-ming maile   shu, a-de maile bi,...
      A-ming bought book A-de bought pen
      'A-ming bought books, A-de bought pens,...'

(79) a. ni   maile   [[meigeren dou zai nar   kandao de] shu] ne
     you bought   everyone all at where saw   DE book QU
     'You bought books that everyone saw where?'

    b. *Impossible answer*
      wo maile   a-ming zai xuexiao kandao de shu, a-de zai
      I   bought A-ming at school   saw   DE book A-de at
      shudian   kandao de shu,...
      bookstore saw   DE book
      'I bought books that A-ming saw at school, A-de saw at the bookstore,...'

    c. *Possible answer*
      wo maile   meigeren dou zai xuexiao kandao de shu
      I   bought everyone all at school saw   DE book
      'I bought books that everyone saw at school.'

Further complicating the picture, a distributive interpretation does become available when the QP occurs in the matrix clause.

(80) a. meigeren dou maile [[ta zai nar   kandao de] shu] ne
     everyone all   bought he at where saw   DE book QU
     'Everyone bought books that he saw where?'

    b. a-ming maile   ta zai xuexiao kandao de shu, a-de maile   ta
      a-ming bought he at school   saw   DE book A-de bought he
      zai shudian   kandao de shu,...
      at bookstore saw   DE book
      'A-ming bought books that he saw at school, A-de bought books that he saw at the bookstore,...'

Indeed, we have suggested elsewhere (Aoun and Li 1993b) that what enters into scope relations in such instances is actually the QP and the question operator or particle (Qu) binding the *wh*-phrase. We adopted the proposal that a *wh*-phrase in Chinese is an indefinite expression licensed by Qu (see Cheng 1991, 1995; Li 1992; Tsai 1994; also see Kuroda 1965 and Nishigauchi 1990 for Japanese and Kim 1991 for Korean). A *wh*-phrase in Chinese is not a quantificational expression. It is only licensed and interpreted according to the contexts it occurs in. For instance, *shei* in the following examples may be interpreted as a universal quantifier due to licensing by *dou* 'all', as an existential quantifier due to licensing by the *if* clause, and as an interrogative due to licensing by the *wh*-question marker *ne*:

(81) a. shei dou xihuan shu
         who all like   book
         'Everyone likes books.'
     b. ruguo ni   xihuan shei, jiu   qing ta   lai
         if   you like   who then ask him come
         'If you like someone, then invite him over.'
     c. shei xihuan ni   ne
         who like   you QU
         'Who likes you?'

In other words, a *wh*-word in Chinese does not have its own independent interpretation and is analyzed instead as an indeterminate nonquantificational expression. Because it is not a quantificational expression, it does not enter into scope relations with other quantificational expressions. In cases like (81a–b), it is the universal and existential quantifiers licensing and interpreting the relevant *wh*-word that play a role in scope interpretation. In (81c), it is the Qu licensing and interpreting the *wh*-word that is the scope marker for this *wh*-word and enters into scope relations with other quantificational expressions. In Aoun and Li 1993b, we claimed that a Qu can be generated in a Question projection (or a Σ projection along the lines of Laka 1990—also see Baker 1970; Pesetsky 1987). It need not be generated in the clause where its interrogative scope is appropriately represented. It can be generated in a lower clause. If it is generated in a lower clause and interpreted as having scope in a higher clause, it must then undergo movement to its scope position. This movement obeys locality conditions. Regardless of whether the Qu undergoes raising, it must be generated in a position c-commanding the related *wh*-word in order to license it. This pattern can be represented by the diagram in (82), where the scope position indicates the scope of interpretation of the *wh*-phrase and where the movement process need not occur (when Qu is base-generated in the appropriate scope position).

(82) ... scope position ... Qu ... *wh*

movement   licensing

This proposal amounts to saying that, in cases involving islands, it must be that a Qu is generated outside the island, binding the *wh*-phrase inside the island.

(83) ... scope position ... Qu ... [$_{island}$ ... *wh* ...]

movement   licensing

Recall that it is the Qu, not the *wh*-word, that plays a role in scope interaction. It therefore follows that, in (83), it is the position of the Qu outside the island, not the *wh*-word inside the island, that must be considered for scope interpretation. This captures the following facts:

(84) a. In (78) and (80), the scope of the question is the matrix clause, which indicates that the Qu should be in the matrix clause. The QP is also in the matrix clause. The Qu and the QP in the matrix clause can interact with each other and have the reading according to which the QP has a wide scope interpretation (i.e., the distributive interpretation).

b. (79), however, contains a QP in a relative clause, even though the Qu is in the matrix clause. This structure does not give rise to a wide scope reading for the QP. That is, the distributive interpretation is unavailable.

Clarifying the roles played by *wh*-words and Qu in scope interaction adequately captures the Chinese facts in (84). However, this account presents a further problem. It reveals a direct conflict when we bring together our discussions of LA and Chinese: the LA data require the *wh*-phrase, not the question complementizer, to enter into scope relations, whereas the Chinese data require Qu, not the *wh*-phrase, to enter into scope relations. Moreover, we still have not explained why the Chinese sentences in (74) and (76) can have a pair-list interpretation, although the intervention and domain requirements are not met.

We show below that this conflict can be resolved by considering the morphological composition of question words more carefully. Our solution in turn provides a more adequate account for the behavior of QP/*wh* and *wh*/*wh* interactions in both Chinese and LA.

As mentioned in section 2.4.2, we follow Chomsky (1964), Katz and Postal (1964), Klima (1964), Kuroda (1965), Fiengo et al. (1988), Nishigauchi (1990), and Kim (1991) in analyzing a question word as a composition of three parts: Question, Quantification, and Restriction (also see analyses of *wh*-questions in the semantics literature such as Hamblin 1973 and Karttunen 1977). The Question can be base-generated in a Question projection and raised to the appropriate scope position to express the scope of interrogation. The Restriction is where the *wh*-phrase is base-generated, generally in the argument position. The issue is where the Quantification is located. If the Quantification plays a role in scope interactions, its position is revealed by the behavior of scope interactions. As mentioned, Chinese *wh*-phrases are not quantificational: they do not have any quantificational force on their own and are interpreted according to their contexts. This amounts to saying that, in Chinese, the Quantification part of a question word is not situated where the *wh*-phrase is. Indeed, the facts discussed in (78)–(80) indicate that the position of the Question, not the position of the *wh*-phrase, is relevant in scope interactions, which also suggests that the Quantification is not situated where the *wh*-phrase is. Rather, it is situated close to where the Question is, perhaps, for instance, being incorporated with the Question or occurring in the Question projection (and possibly being left behind after the Question is raised to the appropriate interrogative scope position).[22]

In contrast, *wh*-phrases in LA are generally not considered to be indeterminate nonquantificational expressions interpreted according to their context. Certainly, they do not have the same range of interpretive possibilities as *wh*-phrases in Chinese, such as being interpreted as a universal or existential quantifier according to the context. Thus, even though a *wh*-phrase can stay in situ in LA just as in Chinese, it is not a nonquantificational expression as it is in Chinese. The difference between Chinese and LA *wh*-phrases lies in a difference in quantification: a *wh*-phrase is quantificational in LA but not in Chinese. In other words, the Quantification is generated with the *wh*-phrase in LA but with the Question in Chinese.[23] Such a distinction between Chinese and LA can be schematically represented as in (85).[24]

(85) a. *Chinese*

Question + Quantification ... Restriction

|

wh-words

b. *LA*

Question ... Quantification + Restriction

|

wh-words

This distinction may now provide an account for why a pair-list interpretation is possible in the Chinese sentences in (74) but not in the corresponding LA sentences in (73). It is appropriate to assume that when two quantificational expressions enter into scope relations, the relevant part must be the Quantification part of such expressions. In Chinese, when the Quantification is situated where the Question is, it is not surprising that an interrogative sentence containing two *wh*-phrases separated by an island (74) can have a pair-list interpretation. The Quantification parts related to the two *wh*-phrases are in the matrix clause because the Question parts are in the matrix clause. The availability of a pair-list interpretation is simply the same as it is with single-clause cases like 'Who saw what?' It is also not surprising that a QP or negation/negative polarity item does not block a pair-list interpretation when the two *wh*-phrases are separated by it, as illustrated in (76) and (77), because the *wh*-phrases are not relevant for scope interactions at all. The overt positions of the *wh*-phrases are not indicators of the relative quantificational scope; instead, the Question is. In LA, on the other hand, the position of the Quantification is indicated by the position of the *wh*-phrase. When the *wh*-phrase is separated from a QP or another *wh*-phrase by an operator, the Quantification related to this *wh*-phrase cannot interact with such a QP or *wh*-phrase. This captures the generalization regarding the contexts that allow a pair-list interpretation in LA.

In brief, the contrast between LA and Chinese in the availability of a pair-list or distributive interpretation is not due to any difference in interpretive mechanisms. These languages differ only in the morphological structure of their *wh*-phrases. A *wh*-interrogative consists of three parts: Question, Quantification, and Restriction. Different languages vary with respect to where these three components are generated. In LA, the Quantification is generated with the Restriction (the *wh*-phrase); in Chinese, the Quantification is generated with the Question. Accordingly, even though both Chinese and LA allow *wh*-phrases in situ, they differ with respect to where the Quantification is situated. The clue to where the Quantification is situated resides in the behavior of *wh*-phrases. *Wh*-phrases in Chinese are nonquantificational. They are interpreted according to their contexts. In contrast, *wh*-phrases in LA are quantificational. They do not have the range of interpretations found with Chinese *wh*-phrases. This provides an account for the difference in the availability of a pair-list interpretation between LA and Chinese: in LA, what matters is the position of the *wh*-phrase; in Chinese, the position of the *wh*-phrase is not directly relevant to scope interactions. The domain requirement and the intervention effect can apply equally in the relevant constructions in the two languages.

3.5 Summary

After demonstrating in chapter 1 that Superiority cannot be accommodated by a movement approach and in chapter 2 that an approach incorporating the Minimal Match Condition is desirable, we began this chapter by clarifying that such an MMC approach to Superiority, crucially, cannot be assimilated to the interpretation of multiple *wh*-interrogatives, despite attempts to do so, best represented by Hornstein's (1995) WCO approach. We established that such a WCO approach to Superiority cannot accommodate the relevant facts in LA because it is built on an obligatory functional interpretation of multiple *wh*-interrogatives (a functional interpretation being identical to a pair-list interpretation), whereas, importantly, well-formed multiple *wh*-interrogatives do not require a functional interpretation. Multiple *wh*-interrogatives allowing a functional (pair-list) interpretation are only a subset of the *wh*-interrogatives that do not violate Superiority. Moreover, it is not enough to distinguish a functional interpretation from a pair-list interpretation. Instead, three types of nonindividual/single-pair interpretations must be distinguished: (1) a pair-list interpretation obtained in cases of *wh*/*wh* interaction, (2) a distributive interpretation obtained in cases of QP/*wh* interaction, and (3) a functional interpretation obtained in cases of QP/*wh* interaction. This distinction is necessary because these three readings are subject to different locality conditions, as summarized in (48), repeated here.

(48) a. Functional interpretations in QP/*wh* constructions are not
          sensitive to the domain requirement or the intervention effect.

    b. Distributive interpretations in QP/*wh* constructions are sensitive to the intervention effect but not the domain requirement.

    c. Pair-list interpretations in *wh*/*wh* constructions are sensitive to both the domain requirement and the intervention effect.

This distinction is understood in the following way: a functional interpretation is a dependency relation between A-elements (pronoun binding), in contrast to a distributive or pair-list interpretation, which is a dependency relation between quantifiers. This explains why an intervention effect by an intervening quantifier is relevant to pair-list and distributive interpretations, but not to functional interpretations. Furthermore, pair-list and distributive interpretations are distinguished by the fact that the former, but not the latter, require an Agree relation between multiple *wh*-phrases. This explains why a domain requirement is relevant to pair-list interpretations, but not to distributive interpretations.

We further showed from a crosslinguistic perspective that a pair-list or distributive interpretation indeed is concerned with the quantificational part of *wh*-questions. Recognizing the role of quantification and different morphological compositions of *wh*-phrases in different languages enabled us to capture different distributional facts regarding the availability of pair-list and distributive interpretations without needing to stipulate different interpretive mechanisms in the languages discussed, Chinese and LA.[25]

PART II

Relativization: Derivation and Structure

Chapter 4

Head-Initial Relative Constructions

Relative constructions[1] have received a great deal of attention in recent years largely owing to Kayne's (1994) revival of the *promotion analysis* of relative constructions, in contrast to the prevailing *wh-movement analysis* widely adopted since Chomsky 1977b. The promotion analysis was originally proposed by Schachter (1973), who also cited Brame (1968), and by Vergnaud (1974). An early form of the *wh*-movement analysis was labeled the *matching analysis* by Schachter (1973), referring to an analysis whereby the derivation of a relative clause involves the deletion of a nominal expression in the relative clause under identity with the base-generated Head. (See Lees 1960, 1961; Chomsky 1965; Kuroda 1968. See also Montague 1974; Partee 1975; and, for an extensive review and list of references, Vergnaud 1974.) In addition to differing proposals for deriving the Head by movement or base-generation, different structures have been entertained: the relative construction involves an adjunction structure as in Chomsky 1977b or a complementation structure as in Kayne 1994.

Although both the promotion analysis and the matching analysis have been pursued, it has widely been assumed that one analysis suffices (see, e.g., Carlson 1977; Grosu and Landman 1998). However, a detailed investigation of restrictive relative constructions reveals the need to distinguish different types of relative constructions within as well as across languages. This state of affairs can be accommodated only if both analyses are adopted.

Different types of relative constructions require different empirical generalizations. More precisely, relative constructions differ with regard to whether the Head of a relative construction can be reconstructed. For instance, LA distinguishes between definite and indefinite relative constructions, which differ in the availability of reconstruction: the Head can be reconstructed in a definite relative but not in an indefinite relative. To a certain extent, the same contrast is found between English relative constructions with a *wh* relative pronoun and those without: the former do not allow reconstruction but the latter do. This contrast suggests that (1) in cases where reconstruction of the Head is allowed, the Head of a relative construction can be derived by movement and (2) in cases where reconstruction is not allowed, the Head cannot be derived by movement (i.e., the Head must be base-generated). Nonetheless, we show that even in relative constructions that do not allow reconstruction of the Head (Head not derived by movement), empirical generalizations exist that support an analysis according to which operator movement applies to derive these constructions, in addition to the option of base-generation. Accordingly, a *wh*-operator movement analysis (the matching analysis referred to above) should also be available. This indicates that two movement strategies are available to derive relative constructions: (1) a promotion strategy that moves the Head of the relative construction, and (2) an operator movement strategy (matching analysis). In addition, (3) a direct base-generation strategy is needed in contexts where movement is not available.

The availability of different strategies to derive relative constructions does not necessarily mean that both adjunction and complementation structures need to be adopted in a particular language. In a language that positions the Head of a relative construction before the relative clause (Head-initial relative construction) such as English or LA, the complementation structure alone is sufficient to generate different types of relative constructions. We will also show in chapter 5 that adjunction structures alone are sufficient to generate Head-final relative constructions in Chinese.

We first sketch the main arguments for the existence of the two movement strategies, promotion and operator movement (section 4.1). We then show that various empirical generalizations, especially with regard to reconstruction possibilities of the Head in English, support the claim that the promotion analysis and the *wh*-movement (matching) analysis are both available (section 4.2). Finally, we show that similar empirical generalizations concerning the availability of reconstruction are found in LA relative constructions (section 4.3). In this language, two types of relative construction are distinguished: definite and indefinite. The former exhibits reconstruction effects, but the latter does not. It follows that definite relatives are derived by a promotion analysis. In contrast, the lack of reconstruction effects in indefinite relatives suggests that they cannot be derived by raising the Head; instead, the Head must be base-generated. LA, again, shows that more than one means should be available to derive relative constructions.

4.1 Promotion versus Matching (Operator Movement)

Relative constructions, especially those of English, have been studied quite extensively. Essentially, two lines of research have been pursued.

4.1.1 The Promotion Analysis

In the early 1970s, the significant observation was made that the Head of a relative clause can be interpreted as if it is in the gap position inside the relative clause (reconstruction effects). This led to the proposal that the Head is moved from within the relative clause—the so-called promotion analysis (Schachter 1973; Vergnaud 1974). This analysis has received much renewed attention since the advent of Kayne's (1994) Antisymmetry approach to word order and phrase structures, which in principle rules out any right-adjunction structures in the grammar of natural languages. In essence, according to Kayne (1994) and Bianchi (1999, 2000a,b), the promotion analysis involves the following complementation structure and the Head movement process:

(1) *The promotion analysis*
   $[_{DP} \text{ D } [_{CP} \text{ NP/DP}_i \text{ } [_{C} \text{ } [_{IP} \dots t_i \dots]]]]$[2]

Important empirical generalizations support the raising of the Head to its surface position (Head raising) in deriving the relative construction. Consider English relative constructions, for instance. There are arguments for Head raising based on the distribution of idiom chunks, binding, and scope properties, that is, reconstruction effects.

First, regarding idioms, it has been shown that part of an idiom can occur as the Head of a relative clause that contains the other part of the idiom. Consider the [V + O] idioms in (2), for instance. The O part can be the Head of the relative clause and the V part is the verb of the relative clause. Given that the parts of an idiom need to be generated as a unit, such examples argue that movement is involved (see Schachter 1973, 31–32).

(2) a. The careful track that she's keeping of her expenses pleases me.
    b. The headway that Mel made was impressive.
    c. I was offended by the lip service that was paid to civil liberties at
      the trial.

Second, reconstruction effects are illustrated by the binding possibilities
in the following examples from Schachter 1973, 32–33; compare (3) with
(4) and (5) with (6).[3]

(3) a. John$_i$ painted a flattering portrait of himself$_i$.
    b. *Himself$_i$ painted a flattering portrait of John$_i$.

(4) a. The portrait of himself$_i$ that John$_i$ painted is extremely
      flattering.
    b. *The portrait of John$_i$ that himself$_i$/he$_i$ painted is extremely
      flattering.

(5) a. [John and Mary]$_i$ showed a fleeting interest in each other$_i$.
    b. *Each other$_i$ showed a fleeting interest in [John and Mary]$_i$.

(6) a. The interest in each other$_i$ that [John and Mary]$_i$ showed was
      fleeting.
    b. *The interest in [John and Mary]$_i$ that each other$_i$ showed was
      fleeting.

Third, certain examples illustrating scope interaction argue for the
availability of reconstruction: the Head nominal can be interpreted as
having narrow scope with respect to another quantifier within the relative
clause. The following examples are the English counterparts of Italian
examples provided by Bianchi (1999, 45–46, 122–123):

(7) a. Every doctor will examine two patients.
    b. Every doctor will examine the two patients.
    c. I phoned the two patients that every doctor will examine
      tomorrow.

(7a) contains the object QP *two patients*, which can be interpreted as
having narrow scope with respect to the subject QP *every doctor*; that is,
there can be twice as many patients as doctors. (7b), whose object contains a definite article, has only the reading according to which a total of
two patients are examined by the doctors. Interestingly, in (7c) the relativized nominal *(the) two patients* can be interpreted as in (7a), that is, as
having narrow scope with respect to the subject QP in the relative clause.

This fact indicates that the Head can be interpreted in the direct object position, and hence that it must have been raised from that position (see section 4.1.3.3 regarding the determiner's role in heading a complex nominal).

Fourth, the distribution of bound pronouns also exhibits reconstruction effects.

(8) a. The picture of his$_i$ mother that every student$_i$ liked best was an old black and white.

b. We admired the picture of his$_i$ mother that every student$_i$ painted in art class.

In brief, there is ample evidence that reconstruction takes place in relative constructions in English; that is, the promotion analysis adequately accounts for the relative construction in English.

4.1.2   *Wh*-Movement: The Matching Analysis

In contrast, citing similarities among the many constructions that share the properties listed in (9), Chomsky (1977b) suggests that, like *wh*-interrogatives, relative clauses are derived via *wh*-movement (as are clefts, comparatives, topicalizations, *easy-to-please* constructions, etc.).

(9) a. The construction contains a gap.

b. Long-distance relations are available.

c. Island constraints are relevant.

(10) and (11) illustrate these properties. (10) illustrates the existence of a gap, which, moreover, can be related to the relative pronoun *who* across clause boundaries (a long-distance relation). In such a structure, the relative pronoun is interpreted with the Head *boy* via a predication rule or agreement relation (Chomsky 1977b; Safir 1986; Browning 1987), which is also a matching relation between the Head and the relativized *wh*-phrase.[4] The examples in (11) illustrate the relevance of island conditions. This analysis is conveniently labeled the *matching analysis*.[5]

(10) the boy$_i$ [who$_i$ Mary thinks [t$_i$ is the smartest]]

(11) a. *the boy$_i$ [who$_i$ I like the teacher [who has taught t$_i$]]

b. *the boy$_i$ [who$_i$ I will be happy [if you like t$_i$]]

c. *the boy$_i$ [who$_i$ I wonder why [John has taught t$_i$]]

Schematically, then, the matching analysis can be represented as follows, according to, for instance, Chomsky (1977b):

(12) *The matching analysis*
$[_{\text{NP/DP}}[_{\text{Head}} \text{NP/DP}_i \ldots] [_{\text{Relative CP}} wh_i [_{\text{IP}} \ldots t_i \ldots]]]$

4.1.3 The Promotion Analysis and the Matching Analysis: A Comparison

The promotion analysis and the matching analysis differ in two major respects. One difference concerns reconstruction effects. Under the promotion analysis, the Head is derived by direct movement and reconstruction is possible. Under the matching analysis, the Head is base-generated. A *wh*-operator is moved to a position close to the Head (i.e., the peripheral position of the relative CP) and bears a predication or agreement relation to the Head. Since the Head does not undergo direct movement according to this analysis, reconstruction of the Head does not occur.

The other difference concerns structures. The matching analysis has an adjunction structure: the relative CP is adjoined to the Head. The Head-initial word order in English means the relative clause is right-adjoined to the Head, under this analysis. However, such a right-adjunction structure is not allowed if phrase structures are to be understood in terms of Antisymmetry as Kayne (1994) proposes. Consequently, Kayne suggests that the structure does not involve adjunction. Instead, he claims that it involves a complementation structure: the D of the complex nominal takes a CP as its complement, as illustrated in (1), repeated here.

(1) $[_{\text{DP}} \text{D} [_{\text{CP}} \text{NP/DP}_i [_C [_{\text{IP}} \ldots t_i \ldots]]]]$

The differences between the two analyses can be summarized as follows:

(13)	Structure	Derivation
Promotion analysis	complementation	Head derived by movement
Matching analysis	adjunction	Movement of an operator in predication/agreement relation with a base-generated Head

However, the promotion analysis has not always adopted a complementation structure. Earlier versions of the promotion analysis, such as Schachter's (1973) or Vergnaud's (1974), assume an adjunction structure: the relativized nominal is moved from within the relative clause to the Head position outside the relative clause, where it is adjoined. It is only in the version of the promotion analysis proposed by Kayne (1994) that the Head occupies the Spec of the relative CP and the CP is a complement to D—the complementation structure. There is important evidence to support the complementation structure, as shown below.

According to the complementation structure, the following properties hold:

(14) a. Because the relative CP is the complement of D, the presence of a relative CP entails the presence of D.

   b. A selection relation exists between D and CP.

   c. D does not form a constituent with the Head NP, which is in the Spec of CP.

As we will show, these characterizations are supported empirically.

4.1.3.1 The Obligatoriness of a DP Structure   (14a) indicates that the presence of a relative clause entails a DP projection. This requirement can be supported by some interesting constraints on the distribution of relative clauses. Specifically, the following coordination facts show the relevance of a DP projection in relative constructions. Generally, English allows *and* to conjoin DPs, NPs, and NPs modified by adjectives.

(15) a. He saw [[an actor] and [a producer]].   (DP coordination)

   b. He is an [[actor] and [producer]].   (NP coordination)

   c. He is a [[great actor] and [brilliant producer]].   (Adj + NP coordination)

Interestingly, however, when relative clauses occur in coordinate relative constructions, a determiner must occur in each conjunct, suggesting that what is conjoined must be DPs; compare (16a) and (16b). The relative clause in (16c) must modify both of the conjuncts, not just one of them. Nonetheless, a relative clause can, in principle, modify only one conjunct: specifically, in case that conjunct has a determiner (16d). These facts support the necessity of a DP projection when a relative clause occurs.[6]

(16) a. *He is an [[actor that wants to do everything] and [producer that wants to please everyone]].

   b. He is [[an actor that wants to do everything] and [*a* producer that wants to please everyone]].

   c. He is an [[actor] and [producer]] that wants to please everyone.

d. He is [[an actor] and [[a producer] that does not know how to produce]].[7]

4.1.3.2 Selection Relation between D and CP   There is a very close dependency relation between the relative clause and the determiner (Bianchi 1999; Alexiadou et al. 2000). The D and the CP must co-occur in the following expressions:

(17) a. the Paris *(that I knew)   (Vergnaud 1974, 265)
     b. the three books of John's *(that I read)   (cf. Kayne 1994, 86)
     c. the four of the boys *(that came to dinner)

Other examples illustrating the same close D/CP dependency can be found in Schmitt 2000, 311–312. They include type expressions (18), measure expressions (19), resultatives (20), and *with* expressions (21). The co-occurrence of a definite article in such expressions is made acceptable by the use of a relative clause.[8]

(18) a. I bought one type of bread.
     b. *I bought the type of bread.
     c. I bought the type of bread you like.

(19) a. Maria weighs forty-five kilos.
     b. *Maria weighs the forty-five kilos.
     c. Maria weighs the forty-five kilos Susana would love to weigh.

(20) a. John painted the house a nice color.
     b. *John painted the house the nice color.
     c. John painted the house the nice color his girlfriend liked.

(21) a. Mary bought a house with windows.
     b. *Mary bought a house with the windows.
     c. Mary bought a house with the windows that she liked.

In brief, such examples illustrate a close relation between D and the relative CP.[9]

4.1.3.3 External Determiner   In addition, it has been argued that structurally, the definite determiner *the* lies outside the relative CP (the external determiner hypothesis). Such arguments are mainly based on facts demonstrating that *the* cannot have occurred inside the relative clause, as discussed by Bianchi (1999, 43–48). First, the trace of the relativized nominal is not interpreted as definite. (22a–b), for instance, which involve the existential *there* construction, show that the relativized trace is indefinite because it occurs in a context that typically disallows a definite expression. This indicates that the determiner *the* cannot be part of the relativized nominal itself.

(22) a. *There were *the* men in the garden.
      b. *The* men that there were t in the garden were all diplomats.

A second argument is based on the fact that *the* occurs in a relativization structure even when the relativized nominal generally cannot co-occur with *the*. The contrast between the pairs of expressions in (23), for instance, shows that *the* cannot occur with certain idioms but is allowed when a relative clause co-occurs.

(23) a. *They made the fun of me.   (Fabb 1990, 71)
      b. the fun that they made of me
      c. *We made the headway on that problem.   (Browning 1987, 130)
      d. the headway that we made on that problem

A third argument concerns scope assignment under reconstruction, as illustrated by the interpretation of sentences involving QPs such as those in (7), repeated here.[10]

(7) a. Every doctor will examine two patients.
     b. Every doctor will examine the two patients.
     c. I phoned the two patients [that every doctor will examine t tomorrow].

As mentioned earlier, the object QP *two patients* in (7a) can have a narrow scope interpretation. (7b), whose object contains a definite article, has only the reading according to which a total of two patients are examined by the doctors. Importantly, (7c), where the relativized nominal is preceded by a definite article, has the same interpretation as (7a), not (7b). (7c)'s similarity to (7a), not (7b), indicates that the relativized trace behaves like a nominal phrase without a definite article. In other words, the definite article is not part of the relative CP.[11]

4.1.3.4 DP An additional property of such a complementation structure needs to be clarified: the relation between the external D and what is moved to the Spec of CP. According to Kayne (1994), what is moved can be an NP. However, according to Borsley (1997), what is moved cannot be an NP. Moving an NP means the trace is an NP. However, this NP trace occurs in a position where one would expect a DP. Note that an NP cannot occupy an argument position.

(24) *Bill liked picture.

In addition, the trace behaves like a DP because it can bind a pronoun, obey the binding principles, control a PRO, license a parasitic gap, and occur in a Case-marked position.

(25) a.   the man that t_i thought he$_i$ saw a UFO
     b.   the man that t_i tried PRO$_i$ to fool everybody
     c.   the book that Bill criticized t_i without reading pg$_i$
     d.   *the man that it seems t to know the answer

With respect to locality conditions, the movement of a DP and of an NP should obey weak island conditions differently, according to Borsley. A DP is referential; therefore, extracting it across a weak island should be quite acceptable. An NP, however, is nonreferential; therefore, extracting it across weak islands should be more difficult, paralleling extraction of a nonreferential *wh*-phrase, as illustrated in (26). Relativization across weak islands such as factive complements and infinitival *wh*-complements is acceptable, as in (27), in stark contrast to the unacceptability of *wh*-extraction of nonreferential expressions across factive islands and infinitival *wh*-complements, as in (26). Relativization patterns with DP movement, not NP movement.

(26) a.   *How do you wonder what to say?
     b.   *Why did you regret that John read the book?

(27) a.   the book that we wondered how to afford
     b.   the book that we regretted that John read

Accordingly, Bianchi (1999, 2000b) proposes that what is moved is not an NP, but a DP with an empty D. The empty D needs to be licensed; its licenser is the external D of the relative construction, *the* in (28).

(28) [$_{DP}$[$_D$ the] [$_{CP}$[$_{DP}$ Ø man] [$_{C'}$ that [$_{IP}$ came here]]]]

Moreover, the Head DP (D being empty) in the CP-peripheral position provides an NP that is necessary for the interpretation of the external D. That is, the relation between the external D and the Head DP in the Spec of the relative clause is double-edged: the external D licenses the internal empty D of the DP in the Spec of the relative CP, and the external D has an NP to be interpreted with.

How is the internal empty D licensed by the external D, and how is the external D interpreted with the NP that is selected by the internal D? According to Bianchi (1999, 2000b), the licensing of the internal D by the external D is achieved by incorporating the former to the latter. The incorporation is possible when the two Ds are adjacent to each other. This incorporation process in turn makes it possible for the external D to be interpreted with the NP selected by the internal D. After incorporation, the external D and the internal D in a sense have become one unified entity. Accordingly, the relation between the internal D and the NP it selects *is* the relation between the external D and this NP.[12]

The relation between the Head DP and the external D can be summarized as follows:

(29) a. In the relative construction [$_{DP}$ D [$_{CP}$ DP$_i$ [C [$_{IP}$ ... e$_i$ ...]]]], the DP in the Spec of CP (the Head) contains an empty D (the internal D).
   b. The empty internal D needs to be licensed.
   c. The external D needs to be interpreted with an NP.
   d. The empty internal D is licensed by the external D.
   e. The external D is interpreted with the NP selected by the internal D.
   f. (d) and (e) are achieved by incorporating the internal D to the external D.
   g. Incorporation takes place when the two Ds are adjacent to each other, as in the configuration in (a).

4.1.3.5 Structure and Derivation We have shown that relative constructions exhibit reconstruction effects and that a close relation exists between the external D and the relative clause. The reconstruction effects argue for the promotion analysis, where the Head is moved to its surface position, not base-generated there as in the matching analysis. The close relation between the external D and the relative clause supports the complementation structure, which is the structure adopted by the promotion analysis as in (1), not by the matching analysis as in (12). Given the evidence we have shown for a complementation structure, should the promotion analysis be adopted and the matching analysis dispensed with? On the other hand, if there is any indication that operator movement exists (recall the basic tenet of a *wh*-operator analysis of relativization: the similarities among numerous constructions that all share the properties of *wh*-movement), must the adjunction structure be adopted? In other words, does the existence of reconstruction effects argue for the complementation structure and the operator analysis for the adjunction structure (and vice versa)? More fundamentally, are the arguments for reconstruction and complementation structures that we have presented so far applicable to all relative constructions?

In this chapter and those to follow, we will argue that both the promotion analysis and the matching analysis can capture important generalizations regarding different types of relative constructions in various languages. However, a more appropriate description of the generalizations regarding various types of relative constructions requires that we not adopt the two analyses as they stand. Instead, the promotion analysis (1) and the matching analysis (12) should be deconstructed into the subparts in (30) and (31).

(30) a. Complementation structure: the relative clause is a complement to D
     b. Adjunction structure: the relative clause is adjoined to the Head

(31) In cases where a relative clause contains a trace, two analyses are available.
     a. Head raising/Promotion: The nominal to be relativized moves to the Head position; that is, the trace in the relative clause is derived by movement of the Head.
     b. Head base-generation/operator movement: The Head is base-generated in its surface position and interpreted with the relative clause via a *wh*-operator moved to the Spec of the relative CP; that is, the trace in the relative clause is derived by operator movement.[13]

An important consequence of (31a–b) concerns the availability of reconstruction.

(32) a. The Head-raising analysis allows the Head to be reconstructed.
     b. The Head base-generation/operator movement analysis does not allow the Head to be reconstructed.

The separation of (30)–(31) indicates the logical possibility that derivations should be independent of the structures adopted in these analyses. The existence of operator movement does not entail an adjunction structure, and Head raising does not entail a complementation structure. Operator movement can apply in a complementation structure, and Head raising can apply in an adjunction structure. We will further argue that languages do not exclusively apply either Head raising (31a) or operator movement (31b) to derive their relative constructions. Both derivations are available. The choice of either option is based on morphosyntactic properties of the relative construction and other general conditions of the grammar. Drawing on data from Head-initial relative constructions in English and LA, we will demonstrate in this chapter that both strategies in (31), Head raising and Head base-generation/operator movement, are available to derive relative constructions, and that both derivations can simply have a complementation structure. (In the following chapters, we turn to Head-final relative constructions in Chinese and Japanese.)

4.2 Relative Constructions in English

4.2.1 Head Raising or Not?

As shown in section 4.1.1, deriving English relative constructions by Head raising is supported by important facts about the distribution of idioms and about reconstruction effects in relative constructions containing anaphors, bound pronouns, and QPs. Nonetheless, arguments have also been made against this analysis. It has been noted that all relative constructions do not show reconstruction effects and that the Head is not necessarily raised from within the relative clause. McCawley (1981), for instance, observes that the Head can be an idiom chunk related to the matrix verb in some instances, rather than being related to the verb of the relative clause (cf. (2)).

(33) John *pulled the strings* that got Bill the job.

Carlson (1977) argues that finer distinctions should be made among different types of relative clauses: that is, in addition to distinguishing appositive relatives, a distinction between amount relatives and restrictive relatives should be made (also see Heim 1987; Grosu and Landman 1998). He suggests that amount relatives are derived by Head raising but restrictive relatives are not necessarily so derived. Although amount relatives show reconstruction effects, this is not the case with restrictive relatives, as briefly described below.

According to Carlson, important properties distinguish amount relatives (ARs) from restrictive relatives (RRs). ARs do not allow a *wh*-relative pronoun, and they allow only those determiners that can be followed by a number expression. Carlson demonstrates the differences with the examples in (34), which illustrate the unacceptability of a *wh*-pronoun in an AR (the relevant sentences have only an amount interpretation), and the sentences in (35), which illustrate the fact that when *some* is the determiner, only a restrictive interpretation is possible. The table in (36), from Carlson 1977, 525, illustrates the two types of determiners that are acceptable or unacceptable (i.e., cannot occur with a number expression) in ARs.

(34) a.   Marv put everything that he could in his pocket.
     b.   *Marv put everything which he could in his pocket.

(35) a.   Marv put something which was bigger than his fist in his pocket.
     b.   Marv put something that was bigger than his fist in his pocket.

(36)
Type I	Type II
the forty men	**ten* many people
these few insects	**few* several incidents
every ten minutes	**lots of* many boys
any five cigars	**many* twelve pounds
all fifty Vikings	**a* several clods
what few remarks	**some* eight mammals
-er many bottles	**a few* ten oboes
these two answers	**several* many ladies
these five criminals	**most* nine squids
my many dreams	**each* fifty minutes

Carlson suggests that the ARs should be accounted for by a raising (promotion) analysis: the Head is derived by raising the relevant nominal. Noting that ARs exhibit reconstruction effects with respect to the distribution of idiom chunks but that RRs do not, as illustrated in (37), he suggests that the promotion (Head-raising) analysis applies to ARs and that recognizing ARs as distinct from RRs "undercuts some reasons that have been given for a Raising analysis of RR's (though by no means all; and even with the facts from idioms, a Raising analysis of RR's is not ruled out entirely)" (p. 541).

(37) a.   {The/All/That/What} headway (that) Mel made was astounding.
     b.   *{Some/Much/Most/Little/This/Ø} headway that Mel made was satisfactory.

Even though Carlson does not claim that restrictive relatives absolutely cannot be derived by a raising analysis and does not clarify when a restrictive relative can or cannot be derived by a raising analysis, he does question the validity of the reconstruction tests for restrictive relatives used in the literature. He notes that the arguments given for a raising analysis of restrictive relatives run the risk of conflating ARs and RRs: "But a glance through Schachter [1973] reveals that the determiner of the head N is invariably *the*, no *wh*-forms are used; ... Vergnaud [1994] consistently uses the French definite article *le*. ... The definite article may, of course, head an AR; so, in the examples used, we run the risk of conflating AR's and RR's" (p. 535).

It is quite plausible that the choice of determiners and the choice of *wh* or *that* (or Ø) can affect the availability of Head raising in English relatives. It is less clear, however, whether the distinction lies in the semantics: amount relatives versus restrictive relatives. Note that it is not easy to understand how relative clauses like the one in (4a) (repeated here), for instance, express amount (reconstruction possible), in contrast to the counterparts in (38a–c), which cannot express amount, because of the use of *wh* and nonamount determiners (type II in (36)).

(4) a. The portrait of himself$_i$ that John$_i$ painted is extremely flattering.

(38) a. The portrait of Mary which John painted is extremely flattering.
　　 b. Some portraits of Mary that John painted are extremely flattering.
　　 c. Some portraits of Mary which John painted are extremely flattering.

The questions, then, are when and why Head raising can apply to derive the different types of relative constructions. Moreover, how is the relative construction derived when Head raising does not apply? We show below that Head raising is available in principle, but it may not be realized for independent reasons. In those cases where Head raising is not available, movement properties are still manifested, suggesting that the operator movement analysis (with a base-generated Head, (31b)) must also be available. Carlson's insight can be recast in the syntactic terms of Head raising failing to apply instead of the semantic distinction between amount and restrictive relatives. The use of *wh* instead of *that* and the use of type II determiners instead of type I determiners are morphosyntactic indications of the absence of Head raising.

4.2.2   Operator Movement

Extending Carlson's observation, note that the use of *wh*-pronouns and type II determiners not only prevents idiom chunks from serving as the relative Head but also prohibits reconstruction in cases containing pronouns or quantifiers.[14]

(39) *No reconstructed bound pronoun interpretation*
   *some boys of his$_i$ class [who$_j$ I know everyone$_i$ would bring t$_j$ to the party]

(40) *No reconstructed narrow scope interpretation for* some
   some boys [who$_j$ I know everyone$_i$ would bring t$_j$ to the party]

Despite the lack of reconstruction, such constructions still show movement properties: they contain a gap and the gap cannot occur inside an island.

(41) a. *[some boys [who$_i$ John met [the student [that saw t$_i$ yesterday]]]]
   b. *[some boys [who$_i$ [[if John saw t$_i$] Mary would be happy]]]
   c. *[some boys [who$_i$ [that John saw t$_i$] was important]]

These facts suggest that relative constructions can be derived by operator movement, rather than by Head raising alone. Indeed, for some speakers, the use of a *wh*-pronoun indicates derivation by operator movement, a *wh*-pronoun being the clue to the existence of a *wh*-operator.[15] Accordingly, there is a systematic contrast with respect to the availability of reconstruction between a relative construction that uses a *wh*-relative pronoun (referred to as a *wh*-relative) and one that does not (referred to as a non-*wh*-relative). For instance, compared with the relative constructions in (2), repeated here, relative constructions whose Heads involve idioms are worse when *that* is replaced by *which*.

(2) a. The careful track that she's keeping of her expenses pleases me.
   b. The headway that Mel made was impressive.
   c. I was offended by the lip service that was paid to civil liberties at the trial.

(42) a. ??The careful track which she's keeping of her expenses pleases me.
   b. ??The headway which Mel made was impressive.
   c. ??I was offended by the lip service which was paid to the civil liberties at the trial.

By contrast, when the idiom chunk is not inside the relative clause, the use of *which* is quite acceptable:

(43) John pulled the strings which got Bill the job.

(44) and (45) differ minimally from (4a) and (6a) in using a *wh*-pronoun in place of *that*, and they differ accordingly in acceptability, being worse than (4a) and (6a) with respect to the reconstructed interpretation.

(44) ??The portrait of himself$_i$ which John$_i$ painted is extremely
       flattering.

(45) ??The interest in each other$_i$ which John and Mary$_i$ showed was
       fleeting.

(46) and (47) show the same contrast in a variety of contexts with different types of verbs.

(46) a. The picture of himself$_i$ (that) John$_i$ painted in art class is
          impressive.
      b. The picture of himself$_i$ (that) John$_i$ likes best is impressive.
      c. *?The picture of himself$_i$ which John$_i$ painted in art class is
          impressive.
      d. *?The picture of himself$_i$ which John$_i$ likes best is impressive.

(47) a. We admired the picture of himself$_i$ (that) John$_i$ painted in art
          class.
      b. We admired the picture of himself$_i$ (that) John$_i$ likes best.
      c. *We admired the picture of himself$_i$ which John$_i$ painted in art
          class.
      d. *We admired the picture of himself$_i$ which John$_i$ likes best.

The corresponding *wh*-interrogatives easily allow reconstruction.

(48) a. Which picture of himself$_i$ did John$_i$ paint in art class?
      b. Which picture of himself$_i$ does John$_i$ like best?
      c. We wondered which picture of himself$_i$ John$_i$ painted in art
          class.
      d. We wondered which picture of himself$_i$ John$_i$ likes best.

The following examples illustrate the same contrast in embedded contexts:

(49) a. The picture of himself$_i$ that/??which John$_i$ thinks Mary painted
          in art class is impressive.

b. The picture of himself$_i$ that/??which John$_i$ thinks Mary likes the best is really ugly.

c. We admired the picture of himself$_i$ that/?*which John$_i$ thinks Mary painted in art class.

d. We admired the picture of himself$_i$ that/?*which John$_i$ thinks Mary likes the best.

e. The picture of himself$_i$ that/*which Mary thinks John$_i$ painted in art class is impressive.

f. We admired the picture of himself$_i$?that/*which Mary believes John$_i$ painted in art class.

g. The picture of himself$_i$?that/*which every student$_i$ bought was a rip-off.

h. The picture of himself$_i$?that/*which Mary said every student$_i$ painted in art class is impressive.

Again, *wh*-interrogatives allow reconstruction easily.

(50) a. Which picture of himself$_i$ did John$_i$ think Mary painted in art class/liked the best?

b. We wondered which picture of himself$_i$ John$_i$ thinks Mary painted in art class/liked the best.

c. Which picture of himself$_i$ does Mary believe John$_i$ painted in art class?

d. We wondered which picture of himself$_i$ Mary believes John$_i$ painted in art class.

e. Which picture of himself$_i$ did every student$_i$ say that Mary painted in art class/liked the best?

f. I wonder which picture of himself$_i$ Mary said every student$_i$ painted in art class.

g. I wonder which picture of himself$_i$ every student$_i$ thinks Mary liked the best.

The examples above show a consistent contrast with respect to the interpretation of anaphors between *wh*-relatives and non-*wh*-relatives in the availability of reconstruction. *Wh*-relatives further contrast with *wh*-interrogatives in reconstruction availability.

Bound pronouns exhibit the same contrast between *wh*-relatives and non-*wh*-relatives and between *wh*-relatives and *wh*-interrogatives.

(51) a. I would like to collect the best pictures of his$_i$ best friend that everyone$_i$ will bring tomorrow.

    b. ??I would like to collect the best pictures of his$_i$ best friend which I think everyone$_i$ will bring tomorrow.

(52) a. The picture of his$_i$ mother that/?*which every student$_i$ painted in art class is impressive.

    b. The picture of his$_i$ mother that/?*which every student$_i$ liked best was an old black and white.

    c. We admired the picture of his$_i$ mother that/?*which every student$_i$ painted in art class.

    d. We admired the picture of his$_i$ mother that/?*which every student$_i$ liked best.

    e. The picture of his$_i$ mother that/?*which every student$_i$ thought (that) Mary had painted in art class is impressive.

    f. The picture of his$_i$ mother that/?*which every student$_i$ thought (that) Mary liked best is impressive.

    g. We admired the picture of his$_i$ mother that/*?which every student$_i$ thought (that) Mary had painted in art class.

    h. We admired the picture of his$_i$ mother that/?*which every student$_i$ thought (that) Mary liked best.

    i. The picture of his$_i$ mother ?that/*which Mary thought that every student$_i$ painted in art class is impressive.

    j. The picture of his$_i$ mother that/*which Mary thought that every student$_i$ liked best is impressive.

    k. We admired the picture of his$_i$ mother ?that/*which Mary said every student$_i$ painted in art class.

    l. We admired the picture of his$_i$ mother that/*which Mary said that every student$_i$ liked best.

(53) a. Which picture of his$_i$ mother does every student$_i$ think Mary painted in art class?

    b. Which picture of his$_i$ mother did Mary say that every student$_i$ painted in art class?

With respect to scope interpretation, it is interesting to note that there is also a contrast between *wh*- and non-*wh*-relatives.

(54) a. I phoned the two patients (that) every doctor will examine tomorrow.

    b. I phoned the two patients who every doctor will examine tomorrow.

The relative with *that* allows a reading according to which each of the doctors examines two different ad hoc patients (a distributive interpretation), a reading not available for the relative with *who* (Barry Schein, personal communication). Moreover, the following two sentences contrast in the availability of a wide scope interpretation for the quantifier *most* in the relative clause, a wide scope interpretation of *most* being available for the non-*wh*-relative only:

(55) a. I will interview the two students (that) most professors would recommend.
   b. I will interview the two students who most professors would recommend.

The following generalizations emerge:

(56) a. Non-*wh*-relatives exhibit reconstruction effects; that is, the Head can be derived by movement from the position where it is interpreted to its surface position.
   b. *Wh*-relatives do not exhibit reconstruction effects; that is, the Head is not derived by movement from the position where it is interpreted to its surface position. It is base-generated in its surface position.

Moreover, as mentioned, when a gap occurs in a *wh*-relative (as well as a *that* relative), the relation between the gap and the *wh*-relative obeys the island conditions.

(57) a. *the girl [who$_i$ I have seen [the boy$_j$ [who e$_j$ loves e$_i$]]]
   b. *the girl [who$_i$ I am happy [because the boy$_j$ loves e$_i$]]

In brief, the two types of relatives[16] can be derived by a Head-raising process and an operator movement process, respectively.[17]

(58) a. Non-*wh*-relatives are derived by Head raising.
   b. *Wh*-relatives are derived by operator movement.[18]

Before concluding this section, we would like to emphasize that the contrast between (58a) and (58b) cannot be reduced to the difference between amount relatives and restrictive relatives. It is doubtful that the empirical contrast observed so far with respect to reconstruction concerns the semantic notion of amount. Just as the contrast between (4a) and (38a–c) can hardly be understood as a contrast between amount and restrictive relatives, so it is difficult to understand that the *that* relatives in the examples we have presented so far are amount relatives. Consider for instance (59a–b), where replacement of *that* by a *wh*-pronoun, as in (60a–b), would putatively turn them into restrictive relatives.

(59) a. We admired the picture of himself$_i$ that John$_i$ painted in art class.
      b. We admired the picture of himself$_i$ that John$_i$ likes best.

(60) a. *We admired the picture of himself$_i$ which John$_i$ painted in art class.
      b. *We admired the picture of himself$_i$ which John$_i$ likes best.

Note further that the *that* relatives that exhibit reconstruction effects also allow stacking; see (61a–b) (and cf. (61c)).

(61) a. We admired the picture of himself$_i$ that he$_i$ painted in art class that he$_i$ likes best.
      b. We admired the picture of himself$_j$ for her$_i$ mother that Picasso$_j$ had painted that every girl$_i$ had requested.
      c. Every girl$_i$ requested the picture of himself$_j$ for her$_i$ mother that Picasso$_j$ had painted.

Stacking is a property of restrictive relatives, not amount relatives, according to Carlson (1977, 540).[19]

(62) a. I dreamed of several books which I saw yesterday which I had hoped to buy.
      b. *Jake noticed the headway we made that Fred said we couldn't make.

In brief, the generalizations in (58a–b) cannot be reduced to the purely semantic distinction between amount relatives and restrictive relatives. What these generalizations claim is that, even among restrictive relatives, the use of a *wh*-pronoun makes a distinction: when a *wh*-pronoun is used, reconstruction is not available; when a *wh*-pronoun is not used (as in a *that* relative), reconstruction is available. Since amount relatives do not use *wh*-pronouns, the fact that they allow reconstruction is a subset of a more general observation that non-*wh*-relatives allow reconstruction and can be derived by Head raising.

4.2.3 Determiners

As we have just shown, the use of a *wh*-pronoun indicates that the structure is derived by movement of a *wh*-operator that is in a predication/

agreement relation with the base-generated Head (the matching analysis). This is one part of Carlson's observation regarding the use of *wh* versus *that/Ø*. The other part concerns the use of determiners: relatives with type II determiners in (36) should not be derived by Head raising—that is, they should not exhibit reconstruction effects. This is quite true with the cases illustrating scope interaction. For instance, a type II determiner cannot be interpreted as having narrow scope with respect to another quantifier in the relative clause.

(63) a. [some patients [that Mary said every doctor would examine
         tomorrow]][20]

     b. [two patients [that I think every doctor will examine tomorrow]]

Idiom chunks with type II determiners are also worse than cases with type I determiners, as Carlson notes.

(64) *Some/Much headway that Mel made was satisfactory.

Cases involving anaphors and bound pronouns, however, are less clear. Nonetheless, if a contrast exists, it seems to be in the right direction, as the following examples illustrate (compare (65) with (66) and (67) with (68)):

(65) a. ??I saw some pictures of his$_i$ mother that Mary said everyone$_i$
         liked the best.[21]

     b. ??I saw some pictures of himself$_i$ that Mary said everyone$_i$ liked
         the best.

     c. ??I brought two pictures of [each other]$_i$ that [John and Bill]$_i$
         took.

(66) a. I saw the pictures of his$_i$ mother that Mary said everyone$_i$ liked
         the best.

     b. I saw the pictures of himself$_i$ that Mary said everyone$_i$ liked the
         best.

     c. I brought the two pictures of [each other]$_i$ that [John and Bill]$_i$
         took.

(67) a. *I know a story about himself$_i$ that no student$_i$ would tell to
         the class.[22]

    a'. No student$_i$ would tell a story about himself$_i$ to the class.

     b. *I know a story about his$_i$ friend that no student$_i$ would tell to
         the class.

    b'. No student$_i$ would tell a story about his$_i$ friend to the class.

(68) a. I know the story about himself$_i$ that no student$_i$ would tell to the class.

   b. I know the story about his$_i$ friend that no student$_i$ would tell to the class.

In brief, both parts of Carlson's observation are manifested in relatives that can hardly be interpreted as denoting amount (i.e., nonamount, restrictive relatives): the choice between *wh*-pronouns and *that*/Ø, and the choice of different determiners. The effect of different determiners mirrors the same distinction found in LA relatives: definite determiners in LA license an empty D, but indefinite determiners do not, as we will illustrate in section 4.5. Because of this difference in licensing ability, a relative construction with a definite determiner allows DP raising (Head-raising analysis), but a relative construction with an indefinite determiner does not.[23] Taken together, the similar distinctions found in English and LA suggest that, if Carlson is correct in distinguishing the two types of determiners, type I determiners can license an empty D, but type II determiners cannot. The issue, of course, is why this should be so. We may speculate that, given that type II determiners must not occur with a number expression, they probably represent the conflation of D and Number nodes, which fails to license an entity that is simply D (licensing requires identity of nodes, for instance). We will leave this issue for further research.

Nonetheless, the following claim can still be made: in those relative constructions containing a gap and not exhibiting reconstruction, operator movement (the matching analysis) must have applied. Relative clauses in English always obey island conditions, as long as there is a gap. It does not matter what determiners are used or whether a *wh*-pronoun occurs. In other words, we arrive at the following conclusion: both the Head-raising analysis (31a) and the operator movement analysis (the matching analysis, (31b)) are needed to derive relative constructions. Further evidence supporting a *wh*-operator movement analysis for relatives with type II determiners lies in the contrast between the following (a) and (b) sentences:

(69) a.   Who introduced the man that talked about what?

   b. ??Who introduced a/some man that talked about what?

(70) a.   Who saw the man (that) who introduced?

   b. ??Who saw a/some man (that) who introduced?

The (b) sentences in (69)–(70) become acceptable when the *wh*-phrase inside the relative is replaced by a non-*wh*-phrase.

(71) a. Who introduced the man that talked about sports?
     b. Who introduced a/some man that talked about sports?

These contrasts show that when a relative is headed by the determiner *the*, which allows Head raising and does not involve a *wh*-operator, a *wh*-phrase can occur inside the relative clause. In contrast, when the determiner is *a/some*, the relative is derived by *wh*-operator movement and contains a *wh*-operator. A *wh*-island is present in the latter but not in the former, which accounts for the differing acceptability of another *wh*-phrase in the relative.

4.2.4 Structures

The discussion so far provides important empirical evidence for distinguishing different types of relative constructions—for example, distinguishing *wh*-relatives from non-*wh*-relatives within the class of restrictive relatives. It argues that both a Head-raising analysis and an operator analysis are needed (31a–b).

Does the existence of both Head raising and operator movement with a base-generated Head suggest that both the complementation structure and the adjunction structure should be adopted? The discussion in section 4.1.3 indicates that the complementation structure is well supported. Indeed, the conjunction facts show that a relative construction, either a *wh*-relative or a non-*wh*-relative, must be projected as a DP. Just as (16) argues that a non-*wh*-relative construction is projected as a DP, so (72) argues that a *wh*-relative must be projected as a DP.

(72) a. *He is an [[actor who wants to do everything] and [producer who wants to please everyone]].
     b. He is [[an actor who wants to do everything] and [*a* producer who wants to please everyone]].

If the complementation structure is sufficient and desirable for both types of relative constructions (those derived by Head raising and those derived by operator movement), the adjunction structure can be dispensed with, making right-adjunction structures unnecessary (see section 4.1.1 regarding Kayne's (1994) Antisymmetry approach to phrase structures).

We show below that a complementation structure such as the one Bianchi (1999) develops, refining Kayne's (1994) proposal, is sufficient for both Head raising and operator movement. Indeed, allowing both options in this complementation structure has a further advantage: it dispenses with the stipulations necessary for Kayne's and Bianchi's analysis. We will illustrate these claims with both *wh*-relatives and non-*wh*-relatives in English.

Recall that under a Head-raising analysis, the Head DP, with empty D, is raised to the peripheral position of the CP. That is, a non-*wh*-relative has the following structure and derivation:

(73) [DP D [CP DP_i [C [IP ... t_i ...]]]]

(74) [DP the [CP[DP Ø picture]_i [C' that [IP Bill liked t_i]]]]

According to Kayne, relative constructions containing *wh*-phrases are derived in a similar manner. Kayne (chap. 8) suggests that a *wh*-relative is derived by first raising a *wh*-phrase to the Spec of CP and then raising the NP to the Spec of the *wh*-phrase—that is, by means of a two-step movement process.

(75) [DP[D the] [CP[DP boy_i [who t_i]] [C'[IP I like]]]]

Bianchi refines this analysis, claiming that the NP is not moved to the Spec of the *wh*-phrase. Instead, adopting a split-CP analysis (Rizzi 1997), she proposes that it is moved to the Spec of a higher projection, as in (76).

(76)

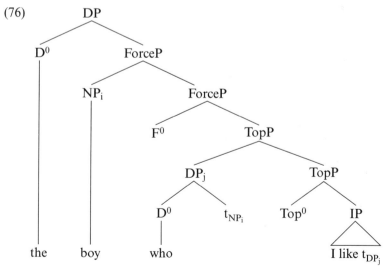

In brief, according to Kayne and Bianchi, a relative clause with a *who* phrase is derived by base-generating [*who* NP] in the argument position.

The phrase [*who* NP] is moved from within the relative IP to the Spec of a Topic projection that is complement to a Force projection. The NP of the phrase [*who* NP] undergoes further movement: it moves from inside the DP occupying the Spec of TopP to the Spec of ForceP.

This analysis needs to assume that the structure in (76) base-generates phrases such as [*who* NP], [*why* NP], [*where* NP], and [*when* NP], which are generally not found in other contexts (such as the interrogative patterns). The NP, which is selected by the *wh* in the D position, needs to undergo movement to be interpreted with the external D (so that the external D itself can be interpreted; see (29e)). In such a structure, the internal D is a lexical *wh*. Unlike DPs where an empty D is incorporated with the external D so that the two Ds can become one, these cases with *wh*-phrases need to have an NP interpreted with two lexical Ds. It would be an improvement if these assumptions could be dispensed with.

Moreover, in the same way that (77) has the structure in (78), where the NP *book* has moved from the Spec of DP occupying the Spec of TopP to the Spec of ForceP, we should be able to derive (79) from (80). However, (79) is not acceptable. *Which* in fact cannot occur when the Head is animate even though [*which* + animate NP] is perfect. That is, we need to generate the otherwise unacceptable [*who boy*], as in (76), in order to derive a well-formed relative construction. If we generate the acceptable [*which boy*], we cannot derive a well-formed relative construction.[24]

(77) the book which I like

(78)

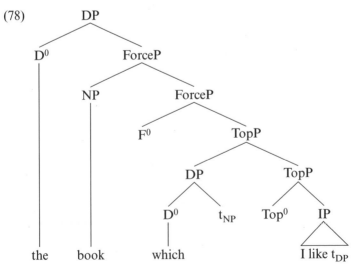

(79) *the boy which I like

(80)

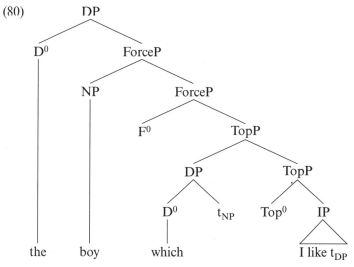

In cases with *why*, as in (81), for instance, it is not clear how the relevant *wh*-word fits into structure (76). It is not clear how the adverb *why* can be represented as a DP structure that has an NP as complement of D, in order for the noun to be raised to the Spec of ForceP.

(81) the reason why he did not come

As noted, it would be desirable to eliminate the assumptions and questions outlined above. A good place to start is to reconsider what occupies the Spec of TopP in (76), (78), and (80). Note that independently, a *wh*-word such as *who* is itself a DP. *Who* has substantive features such as [+human], which generally are situated in N, D being the location for grammatical features such as definiteness. Other *wh*-words such as *why* and *when* are XP categories as well, as they can occur in XP positions. These *wh*-words do not take a lexical NP as their complement: *who person/why reason/when time*. Accordingly, we propose that what occupies the Spec of TopP is simply the *wh*-word—*who, why, where, when, which,* and so on. This proposal is in line with Chomsky's (1977b) original suggestion that relativization is derived by the movement of a *wh*-operator to (the Spec of) Comp. The *wh*-word is an operator predicated of the Head NP in the Spec of ForceP position. In other words, in contrast to the structure in (76), where the NP in the Spec of ForceP is moved from within the DP in the Spec of TopP, we suggest that the NP is *not* moved from within the *wh*-phrase. If it is not moved to the Spec of ForceP, it must be base-generated there. Accordingly, it is base-generated in the Spec of ForceP and a *wh*-operator occupies the Spec of TopP. The NP is the Head of the relative construction and enters into either a predication relation with the *wh*-operator or an agreement relation (see Chomsky 1977b; Safir 1986; Browning 1987). That is, English has two relative structures: (82) and (83).[25]

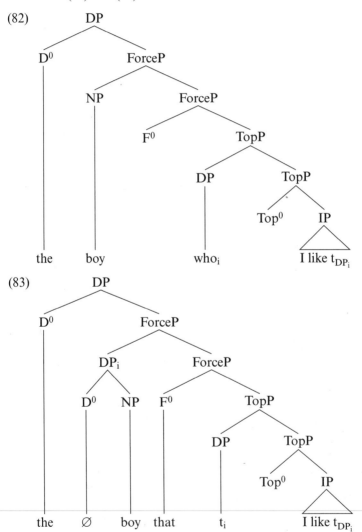

(82)

(83)

(82) differs from the structure (76) adopted by Bianchi in the following two respects. First, the NP in the Spec of ForceP is base-generated in this position, rather than being moved there. Second, what occupies the Spec of TopP is a *wh*-operator, which can be an XP itself, without a lexical NP as complement of the *wh*-operator.

Modifying (76) as in (82) allows us to dispense with the stipulations mentioned earlier. We do not need to assume that [*who* NP], [*why* NP], [*where* NP], [*when* NP], and so on, must be generated for the sole purpose of deriving *wh*-relatives. We do not need to stipulate that [*which boy*] cannot be generated for the purpose of relativization. We do not need to assume that the derivations and structures in (78) and (80) are possible only when the NP in [*which* NP] is [−human]. More importantly, unlike (76), the structure in (82) captures the interesting empirical generalization noted earlier concerning the distinction between *that* relatives and *wh*-relatives.

As noted, (82) contains a base-generated Head, standing in a predication/agreement relation with a *wh*-operator. The Head is not related to the gap in the relative IP via movement. Accordingly, we would expect English *wh*-relatives, in contrast to non-*wh*-relatives, to not exhibit reconstruction effects involving the Head. This would contrast with the prediction of the promotion analysis (76), where a two-step process derives the *wh*-relative. Under the copy-and-merge theory of movement, the Head NP should exhibit reconstruction effects: the full representation of the relative construction in (76), for instance, should be as shown in (84), where a copy of the NP appears in the argument position inside the IP.

(84) [$_{DP}$ the [$_{ForceP}$[$_{NP}$ boy]$_j$ [$_{ForceP}$ F [$_{TopP}$[who [boy]$_j$]$_i$ [$_{IP}$ I like [who boy]$_i$]]]]]

As shown in the previous section, the reconstruction facts argue for the structure in (82), rather than (76).

In brief, we have shown that English relative clauses containing a gap should be classified into two types: those derived by Head raising and those derived by operator movement. The latter are realized as *wh*-relatives and the former as non-*wh*-relatives. Both types can be accommodated by a complementation structure.[26] An adjunction structure is therefore unnecessary.[27]

Further extending the discussion on the distinction between a Head-raising analysis and an operator analysis, we now show that Head raising is not always available in English, either.

4.2.5   Adjunct Relativization

There are certain relativization cases that require operator movement. Recall that our analysis indicates two derivations for relative constructions: movement of a DP with an empty D to the Head position as in (82) or movement of an operator to stand in a predication/agreement relation with the base-generated Head as in (83). In the former case, the empty D of the DP will be adjacent to the external D and be licensed by it. The two Ds behave like one, and therefore the relation between the NP and the internal D can be taken to be the relation between the NP and the external D. Accordingly, the external D is properly interpreted. This predicts that, if what is moved does not contain an empty D close enough to the external D so that the external D can be associated with the NP via the empty D it licenses [external D [empty internal D + NP] ...], the derivation will crash because the external D will not have an NP to be interpreted with. The Head-raising analysis, then, cannot be adopted for such constructions, and reconstruction of the Head should not be possible. This should be so regardless of whether a *wh*-pronoun occurs overtly. Even if a *wh*-pronoun does not occur overtly, the relative construction is still derived by movement of an operator, not by direct movement of the Head. This is indeed the case with typical adjunct relativization.[28] Such relative constructions do not allow reconstruction.

(85) a. *We accepted [[the reason of his$_i$ own choosing] [that every student$_i$ was late e]].

   b. *We imitated [[the method advocated by his$_i$ father-in-law] [(whereby) every mechanic$_i$ fixed the car e]].[29]

This analysis of relative constructions makes a further prediction: even when a relative clause does not contain a *wh*-pronoun in adjunct relativization, it should still behave like a *wh*-island (see (69)–(70)). Again, this prediction is borne out. In the following sentences, argument relativization can be derived by Head raising, which does not involve a *wh*-operator. In contrast, adjunct relativization is derived by *wh*-operator movement and constitutes a *wh*-island.[30]

(86) a. Who introduced the man that talked about what?
   b. ??Who introduced the man who talked about what?
   c. ??Who did it with the method whereby John did what?
   d. ??Who wrote to John for the same reason that Bill wrote to whom?
   e. ??Who wrote to John for the same reason why Bill wrote to whom?

(87) a. Who believes John bought what?
    b. ?Who wonders whether John bought what?
    c. ?Who wonders how John did what?
    d. ?Who wonders why John did what?

4.2.6 Summary

Starting with the two competing analyses for relative constructions, we showed that both the promotion (Head-raising) analysis and the matching (*wh*-operator movement) analysis are necessary to derive different subpatterns of relative constructions in English. The need for both analyses arises from facts about reconstruction possibilities.[31]

(88) a. Head reconstruction available—Head raising
        non-*wh*-relatives with type I determiners
    b. Head reconstruction unavailable—operator movement
        wh-relatives, non-*wh*-relatives with type II determiners

The choice of derivation for relative constructions depends on what is generated as the phrase to be relativized: either a DP with an empty D or a *wh*-DP.

(89) a. If the phrase to be relativized is a DP with an empty D, then DP undergoes movement so the empty D can be licensed. Licensing is successful in non-*wh*-relatives with type I determiners but not type II determiners.
    b. If the phrase to be relativized is a *wh*-phrase, then it undergoes operator movement, coindexed with a base-generated Head.

Although the Head-raising option is available only to the relative constructions exhibiting Head reconstruction (88a), the *wh*-movement option, in principle, should be available to the relative constructions that do not exhibit Head reconstruction (88b) as well as those that do (88a). However, the effect of an alternative derivation for (88a) is not visible because of the availability of the Head-raising option.

Fundamentally, then, what determines the derivation of a relative construction lies in the choice of the phrase to be relativized, as summarized in (89a–b). The morphosyntactic behavior of such phrases determines what is moved and what is reconstructed.

In the next section, we demonstrate that our approach is adequate to account for the properties of relative constructions in another language with Head-initial relative constructions: LA.

4.3   Relative Constructions in Lebanese Arabic

The properties and analysis of various relative constructions in LA are the theme of Aoun and Choueiri 1997 and especially Choueiri 2002. We will not repeat the authors' detailed arguments and examples here, instead simply summarizing the main properties of these constructions and illustrating with a few examples. The main point demonstrated by LA relative constructions is, again, that relative constructions do not have uniform derivations. Specifically, definite relatives need to be distinguished from indefinite relatives in LA. The former can be derived by Head raising but the latter cannot.

4.3.1   Reconstruction and Head Raising

The important facts regarding LA relative constructions and the account of these facts proposed in the works just cited can be summarized as follows:

(90) a. A relative construction in LA can be definite or indefinite.
   b. A definite relative Head is introduced by a strong determiner and the relative clause has a definite complementizer, *yalli*.
   c. An indefinite relative Head is introduced by a null (indefinite) determiner or a numeral.
   d. In both definite and indefinite relative constructions, a resumptive pronoun must occur in any nonsubject argument position.
   e. A definite relative construction exhibits reconstruction only when the resumptive pronoun is not separated from the Head by an island.
   f. An indefinite relative construction never exhibits reconstruction.
   g. The reconstruction facts indicate that a definite relative construction is derived by movement in nonisland contexts and is base-generated in island contexts, and that an indefinite relative construction is always base-generated.

The following examples illustrate the definite and indefinite relative constructions in LA.

Definite relatives always occur with the complementizer *yalli*.

(91) a. l-kteeb   *(yalli) štarayt-o   mbeeriħ   ḍaaʕ
       the-book   that bought.1s-it yesterday is.lost.3MS
       'The book that I bought yesterday is lost.'

    b. tʔaaṣaṣ   l-walad *(yalli) (huwwe) xazzaʔ l-kteeb
       punished.3MS the-boy   that   he   tore.3MS the-book
       'The boy that tore up the book was punished.'

Indefinite relatives do not have such a complementizer.

(92) a. ʕam fattiš   ʕa kteeb (*yalli) ḍayyaʕt-o l-yom
       ASP look.1s for book   that lost.1s-it   today
       'I am looking for a book that I lost today.'
    b. ʕam fattiš   ʕa walad (*yalli) ḍarab kariim
       ASP look.1s for boy   that hit.3MS Karim
       'I am looking for a boy that hit Karim.'

Definite relatives exhibit a reconstruction effect, which can be illustrated by the following examples of scope reconstruction:

(93) a. badda   l-mudiira   tətʕarraf ʕala l-mara   yalli kəll
       want.3FS the-principal.FS meet.3FS on   the-woman that every
       mwazzaf   žeeb-a   maʕ-o   ʕa-l-ḥafle
       employee.3MS brought.3MS-her with-him to-the-party
       'The principal wants to meet the woman that every employee
       brought with him to the party.'
    b. maʕʔuule yḥaʔʔiʔo   maʕ l-kam ḥaaris yalli ṭalab
       possible   question.3P with the-few guard that asked.3MS
       r-raʔis   ʔənno ywaʔfuw-un ʔədeem kəll   bineeye
       the-president that   stand.3P-them in.front every building
       'It is possible that they question the few guards that the
       president asked that they make them stand in front of every
       building.'

As indicated in Choueiri 2002, chap. 2, these sentences allow a reading according to which the Head is reconstructed.

Similarly, the following sentences from Choueiri 2002, 138, illustrate reconstruction in cases involving bound pronouns:

(94) a. ʕaleemit faḥṣ-[o]ᵢ yalli ʔarrarit   l-mʕallme   ʔənno
       grade   exam-his that decided.3FS the-teacher.FS that
       tfeeži?   [kəll   təlmiiz]ᵢ fiy-a raḥ tətlaʕ   bukra
       surprise.3FS every student in-it will come.out.3FS tomorrow
       'The grade of hisᵢ exam that the teacher decided to surprise
       every studentᵢ with will be ready tomorrow.'

b. šažareet žnaynt-[o]ᵢ yalli nada btaʕrif   ʔənno [wala žnayneete]ᵢ
   trees   garden-his that Nada know.3FS that   no   gardener
   byəhməl-un   ballašo   yzahhro
   neglect.3MS-them started.3P bloom.3P
   'The trees of hisᵢ garden that Nada knows that no gardenerᵢ
   neglects started to bloom.'

In both (94a) and (94b), a pronoun contained within the Head can be
bound by a quantificational phrase within the relative clause. This means
that both sentences are acceptable under a distributive reading of the
quantifier inside the relative clause. Notice that in both cases, the quantifier inside the relative clause occurs in an embedded clause (which rules
out the possibility of generating the distributive reading by QR, which is
generally clause-bound, as opposed to generating it by reconstruction).

Without further elaboration or quotations from the works cited, it is
sufficient to point out that there is ample evidence for the existence of
reconstruction effects in definite relative constructions in LA. Therefore,
clearly, definite relatives are derived by Head raising in this language.

In contrast, an indefinite relative construction in LA does not display
any reconstruction effects. For instance, as illustrated in (95), a pronoun
contained within an indefinite relativized DP can never be bound by a QP
in the indefinite relative clause.

(95) a. *šəft   [ṣuura la-ʔəbn-aᵢ]ⱼ [kəll   mwazzafe]ᵢ badda
        saw.1s picture of-son-her   every employee.FS want.3FS
        tʕalləʔ-a   bi-maktab-a
        hang.3FS-it in-office-her
        'I saw a picture of her son every employee wants to hang in her
        office.'
     b. *šəft   [ṣuura la-ʔəbn-aᵢ]ⱼ [kəll   mwazzafe]ᵢ ʔaalit   ʔənno
        saw.1s picture of-son-her   every employee.FS said.3FS that
        badda   tʕalləʔ-a   bi-maktab-a
        want.3FS hang.3FS-it in-office-her
        'I saw a picture of her son every employee said she wants to
        hang in her office.'

Using reconstruction as a diagnostic for the availability of movement,
Aoun and Choueiri (1997) and Choueiri (2002, sec. 4.3) interpret the
absence of reconstruction effects in indefinite relatives as indicating the
absence of movement in that construction.

4.3.2 What Moves?

Why is a definite relative derived by Head raising in LA whereas an indefinite relative is not? Choueiri (2002, chap. 4) argues that Head raising is in principle available to derive relative constructions. However, using this process to derive an indefinite relative results in an ill-formed representation. The derivation crashes.

Recall that under a Head-raising analysis, what moves is a DP with an empty internal D. This empty D needs to be licensed. Such licensing is not always available, however. As noted, different types of determiners are allowed in the external D of a relative construction in LA: for a definite relative, D is occupied by a definite determiner; for an indefinite relative, D is occupied by a number expression or takes a null form. For convenience, we refer to the determiner of a definite relative as a *definite determiner* and the null determiner of an indefinite relative as an *indefinite determiner*. Choueiri (2002, secs. 4.2.4–4.2.6) argues that the main distinction between the two types of relatives in LA is that a definite determiner, but not an indefinite determiner, can co-occur with (license) a DP that contains a null determiner.

Returning to the derivation of relative constructions, the raised nominal is a DP (with a null determiner). This raised element, thus, cannot co-occur with an indefinite determiner. This is why Head raising is not available in indefinite relatives. Indefinite relatives in LA, as Aoun and Choueiri (1997) and Choueiri (2002) argue, are base-generated.

In brief, the analysis of LA relatives argues against relying exclusively on a Head-raising approach to relativization, since Head raising turns out to be unavailable for indefinite relatives in this language. Thus, the following conclusions can be drawn:[32]

(96) a. Relativization can be derived either by Head raising or by base-generation.
   b. Reconstruction is available in Head-raising structures (definite relatives) and is not available in base-generation structures (indefinite relatives).

4.4 Summary

Beginning with the two competing analyses for relative constructions, we have shown that both the promotion (Head-raising) analysis and the matching (*wh*-operator movement) analysis are necessary to derive different subpatterns of relative constructions that contain a gap in the relativized position. The need for both analyses is clear from various facts regarding reconstruction possibilities:

(97) a. Head reconstruction is available in LA definite relatives and English non-*wh*-relatives with type I determiners.

   b. Head reconstruction is unavailable in LA indefinite relatives, English *wh*-relatives, and English non-*wh*-relatives with type II determiners.

The different reconstruction possibilities indicate that Head raising is available to derive the constructions listed in (97a) but not those listed in (97b). This is because a DP with an empty D is licensed in the former cases but not the latter. When the Head is not derived by movement, it is base-generated. In such a case, operator movement applies if the relative clause contains a gap in the relativized position.

Chapter 5

Head-Final Relative
Constructions

In the previous chapter, we argued that the properties of Head-initial relative constructions in English and LA follow straightforwardly from a complementation structure in which the Head either can be base-generated in the position where it overtly occurs or can come to occupy the initial position via movement. The availability of movement, manifested in various reconstruction effects, depends on the possibility of licensing the empty internal D by the external D. In other words, Head-initial relative constructions invariably have a complementation structure, and differences in behavior with respect to reconstruction of the Head follow from differences in the availability of an external D to license the internal D.

All else being equal, a complementation structure results in a Head-initial relative construction, according to Kayne's (1994) Antisymmetry approach to word order and phrase structure. Nonetheless, as is well known, there are languages where relative constructions are Head-final. In this chapter, we focus on how such relative constructions are derived, taking Chinese as an example and arguing that relative constructions do not necessarily require complementation structures and that what is moved is not necessarily a DP. Instead, the evidence shows that relative constructions in Chinese involve adjunction structures and NP, not DP, movement. The support for NP movement, in contrast to DP movement, comes from reconstruction: Chinese exhibits reconstruction effects different from those in English or LA. Whereas English and LA exhibit effects of DP reconstruction, Chinese exhibits NP reconstruction effects. Moreover, the NP Head can itself be a relative construction. That is, the projection of a relative clause and its Head can be an NP, as indicated by reconstruction facts, further supporting an adjunction structure analysis for relative constructions.

The chapter is organized as follows. Because we have used reconstruction as the diagnostic to determine the derivation of relative constructions in LA and English, we also begin this chapter with reconstruction effects in Chinese relative constructions (section 5.1). An interesting contrast emerges: unlike English and LA, which exhibit reconstruction effects with respect to both binding and scope, Chinese allows reconstruction with respect to binding but not scope properties. Because of the morphosyntactic structure of QPs in Chinese, the contrast follows straightforwardly if what is reconstructed is an NP, not a DP. An NP reconstruction analysis is further supported by some novel and interesting coordination facts demonstrating that when a relative clause is adjoined to an NP Head, the resulting complex nominal can still be an NP (section 5.2). Our analysis not only argues for NP reconstruction but also supports an adjunction structure for relative constructions in Chinese, which have the same structural properties as true adjectives in this language (section 5.3). This also argues against adopting a complementation structure in Chinese, an analysis further supported by the lack of determiner and selection properties corresponding to those in English discussed in section 4.1.3. The difference between Head-initial and Head-final relatives thus can be reduced to a difference in their phrase structures, complementation versus adjunction—a result that accords with Kayne's (1994) Antisymmetry theory of the linearization of phrase structure.

5.1 Reconstruction in Chinese Relativization

In Chinese, the evidence for movement initially seems to be conflicting. In support of a movement analysis, it seems possible for reconstruction to take place when reflexives are involved: a reflexive contained in the relativized Head can be bound by an antecedent within the relative clause.

(1) a. wo jiao zhangsan quan   mei-ge-ren$_i$ kai ziji$_i$ de chezi
       I   ask Zhangsan persuade every-CL-person drive self DE car
       lai
       come
       'I asked Zhangsan to persuade everyone to drive self's car over.'
    b. [[wo jiao zhangsan quan   mei-ge-ren$_i$ kai   t lai   de] ziji$_i$
        I   ask Zhangsan persuade every-CL-person drive   come DE self
       de chezi]
       DE car
       'self's car that I asked Zhangsan to persuade everyone to drive over'

A reconstruction effect is also exhibited in the following cases, which involve bound pronouns contained in a relativized Head:

(2) a. wo xiang mei-ge   xuesheng$_i$ dou neng ba wo gei ta$_i$de shu
       I hope every-CL student   all can BA I give his book
       dai lai
       bring come
       'I hope every student$_i$ can bring the book that I gave to him$_i$.'

    b. ni hui kandao [[wo xiang mei-ge   xuesheng$_i$ dou neng dai   t
       you will see   I   hope every-CL student   all can bring
       lai   de] wo gei ta$_i$de shu]
       come DE I give his book
       'You will see the book that I gave to him$_i$ that I hope every
       student$_i$ will bring.'

    c. mei-ge-ren$_i$ dou yiwei wo yijing mai-dao wo yao song gei
       every-CL-person all think I   already bought I   will give to
       ta$_i$ de liwu
       him DE present
       'Everyone thought I already bought the present that I was going
       to give to him.'

    d. [[mei-ge-ren$_i$ dou yiwei wo yijing mai-dao t de] wo yao
        every-CL-person all think I   already bought DE I   will
       song gei ta$_i$ de liwu]
       give to him DE present
       'present that I was going to give to him that everyone thought I
       already bought'

With respect to scope interaction, however, there are cases where reconstruction is unavailable.

(3) a. wo hui zhengli [[mei-ge-ren   dou hui kan t de] san-ben
       I will arrange every-CL-person all will read DE three-CL
       shu] (same 3 books)
       book
       'I will put the three books that everyone will read in order.'

    b. [[mei-ge-ren   dou hui kan t de] san-ben shu], wo hui
        every-CL-person will all read DE three-CL book I   will
       zhengli (same 3 books)
       arrange
       'The three books that everyone will read, I will put in order.'

However, these expressions involve *dou* 'all'. When 'all', which occurs with the QP in the relative clause, disappears, the reconstruction effect seems to reappear.

(4) wo hui zhengli [[mei-ge-ren   hui kan t de] san-ben
    I   will arrange   every-CL-person will read   DE three-CL
    shu]   (different 3 books)
    book
    'I will put the three books that everyone will read in order.'

This raises the question of why reconstruction seems to be available only in some cases.

Note that the contrast in the availability of reconstruction cannot be due to the (in)definiteness of the complex nominals (recall the contrast between definite and indefinite relatives in LA and English in chapter 4). That is, one cannot suggest that the lack of scope reconstruction in (3) might be due to the fact that no overt determiner occurs in such expressions, hence that they must correspond to the English expressions without *the*. This is not possible because a Chinese nominal expression without an overt determiner can be translated as definite or indefinite. Indeed, (3b) requires the relevant nominal in the preposed topic position to be definite, corresponding to expressions with *the* in English.

Furthermore, note that the observed contrast in the availability of reconstruction corresponding to the absence or presence of 'all' does not appear in nonrelative constructions that allow reconstruction. For instance, a contrastive topic construction allows reconstruction regardless of whether or not 'all' is present. The following examples illustrate that a fronted QP in a contrastive topic construction can be reconstructed and interpreted as if it were in the base-generated argument position regardless of the presence or absence of 'all':

(5) mei-ge-ren   (dou) hui kan san-ben shu   (different 3 books)
    every-CL-person all   will read three-CL book
    'Everyone will read three books.'

(6) san-ben shu, wo xiang mei-ge-ren   (dou) hui kan, bu zhi
    three-CL book I   think every-CL-person all   will read not only
    liang-ben shu   (different 3 books)
    two-CL   book
    'Three books, I think everyone will read, not just two books.'

These facts indicate that relative constructions and contrastive topic constructions do not behave alike with respect to reconstruction. Reconstruction is sensitive to the presence or absence of 'all' in the former, but not in the latter. It would be quite odd if we were forced to stipulate that reconstruction behaves differently in different constructions. Fortunately, there is a more logical option: we may question whether reconstruction is indeed available in relative constructions. In fact, we show below that reconstruction of QPs that take the form $[Q + Cl + N]$ is not available in relative constructions. The apparent reconstruction effects regarding scope interaction should more appropriately be analyzed as the result of direct scope interaction between the Head QP and the QP inside the relative clause.

Elsewhere (Aoun and Li 1993a, chap. 5), we discuss a contrast between the following pair of sentences (see Lee 1986 for extensive discussion of the relation between a QP and 'all'):

(7) a. [[mei-ge-ren   xie   t de] wenzhang] dou hen you yisi
        every-CL-person write DE article   all very have interest
        'The articles that everyone wrote are all interesting.'
    b. [[t xie   mei-ge-ren   de] wenzhang] dou hen you yisi
         write every-CL-person DE article   all very have interest
        'The articles that described everyone are all interesting.'
    c. wo kanle [[mei-ge-ren   dou xie] de wenzhang]
        I   read   every-CL-person all write DE article
        'I read the article that everyone wrote.'

(7b), in contrast to (7a), must have a group reading. This is because the QP *meigeren* 'everyone' related to 'all' must be within the "government" domain of 'all'.[1] The subject QP 'everyone' in (7a), but not the object QP 'everyone' in (7b), can be raised out of the relative clause to be in the government domain of 'all', resulting in an interpretation according to which 'everyone' takes scope over *wenzhang* 'article' (everyone wrote a different article). The locality condition on QP raising allows the subject QP to raise out of the relative clause (owing to the absence of Agreement in Chinese) but prohibits the object from raising within the relative clause. Similarly, the QP in (7c) cannot be raised out of the relative clause to take scope over 'article' because of the domain (government) requirement between 'all' and the related QP.

In Aoun and Li 1993a, we further note that the contrast between (8a) and (8b) follows from an account of QR and the domain requirement of 'all'.

(8) a. wo kanle [[mei-ge-ren   dou xie   t] de liang-pian wenzhang]
      I   read   every-CL-person all write DE two-CL   article
      'I read the two articles that everyone wrote.'
   b. wo kanle [[mei-ge-ren   xie   t] de liang-pian wenzhang]
      I   read   every-CL-person write DE two-CL   article
      'I read the two articles that everyone wrote.'

Because of the domain requirement on the relation between 'all' and the phrase related to it, a QP such as 'everyone' in (8a) cannot be raised to a position outside the relative clause. The QP's failure to be raised outside the relative clause of course makes it impossible for it to be raised to a position c-commanding the QP in the Head of the complex nominal expression. Consequently, (8a) does not have the interpretation according to which 'everyone' has wide scope. In contrast, (8b) does not have 'all', so the issue of domain requirements is irrelevant. The subject QP can be raised out of the relative clause and c-command the Head QP. This derives the reading according to which the subject QP has wide scope.

Note that this account is adequate only if the Head QP is not reconstructed within the relative clause. If it *is* reconstructed, all of the above sentences, including those with 'all', should allow the narrow scope interpretation of the Head QP. This can best be illustrated by the contrast between (8a) and (8b). If the Head QP were interpreted in the position inside the relative clause from which it is relativized, the interpretation of (8a) should not differ from that of (9).

(9) mei-ge-ren   dou xie   liang-pian wenzhang
    every-CL-person all write two-CL   article
    'Everyone wrote two articles.'

However, (9) clearly has the interpretation according to which 'everyone' has scope over 'two articles', an interpretation unavailable in (8a). This contrast argues against reconstruction for scope interpretation in relativization structures. Therefore, the availability of the wide scope interpretation for the subject QP is not due to reconstruction; instead, it is due to raising of the subject QP 'everyone' out of the relative clause. This account is further supported by the fact that, when QR fails to raise 'everyone' outside the relative clause, it no longer has scope over the relativized QP, even though it c-commands the position where the relativized QP originated. This is illustrated by (10a–c), where the QP in the embedded clause cannot be raised outside the relative clause and the sentence is not ambiguous: the Head has unambiguous wide scope over the QP in the most deeply embedded clause.

(10) a. wo hui zhengli [[ta xiwang mei-ge-ren   hui kan t de]
         I   will arrange he hope   every-CL-person will read DE
         san-ben shu] (same 3 books)
         three-CL book
         'I will put the three books that he hopes that everyone will read
         in order.'

     b. [[ta xiwang mei-ge-ren   hui kan t de] san-ben shu], wo hui
            he hope   every-CL-person will read DE three-CL book I   will
         zhengli (same 3 books)
         arrange
         'The three books that he hopes that everyone will read I will put
         in order.'

     c. ta xiang kan [[ni yiwei mei-ge-ren   yao nian t] de
         he want read you think every-CL-person will read DE
         liang-pian wenzhang] (same 2 articles)
         two-CL   article
         'He wants to read the two articles that you thought everyone
         would read.'

In brief, in Chinese a QP as Head of a relative clause does not reconstruct to interact with another QP inside the relative clause.

Furthermore, note that it is not true that reconstruction never takes place with respect to scope. It is only when the Head itself is a QP that scope reconstruction is not available. If a QP is contained in a modifier adjoined to a nominal, together constituting the Head of a relative clause, this complex Head can be reconstructed and a reconstructed scope interpretation is available. For instance, in (11), *san-ge zuojia* 'three authors' is not the Head itself. It is just a modifier adjoined to a nominal, *shu* 'book', and the two together 'books by three authors' is the complex Head of the relative clause '(that) everyone likes'. This Head, which contains the adjoined QP 'three authors', can undergo reconstruction in the relative construction. The sentence has the interpretation according to which 'three authors' takes narrow scope with respect to 'everyone'. This contrasts with (12), whose Head is itself a QP and does not reconstruct; 'everyone' in the relative clause does not take scope over the Head.

(11) *Reconstruction (wide scope for 'everyone') available*
[[mei-ge-ren   dou xihuan t$_i$ de] [$_{NP}$[san-ge   zuojia (xie) de]
  every-CL-person all like   DE   three-CL author write DE
shu]$_i$]
book
'the books (written) by three authors that everyone likes'

(12) *Reconstruction (wide scope for 'everyone') unavailable*
[$_{NP}$[mei-ge-ren   dou xihuan t$_i$ de] san-ben shu$_i$]
    every-CL-person all like   DE three-CL book
'three books that everyone likes'

The following two sentences show the same contrast:

(13) a. *Wide scope for 'everyone' unavailable*
       [$_{NP}$[mei-ge   xuesheng dou nian-wan   t$_i$ de] san-ben shu$_i$]
         every-CL student   all   read-finish   DE three-CL book
       'three books that every student has read'
   b. *Wide scope for 'everyone' available*
       [$_{NP}$[mei-ge   xuesheng dou nian-wan   t$_i$ de] san-ge   zuojia
         every-CL student   all   read-finish   DE three-CL author
       xie   de shu]
       write DE book
       'books by three authors that every student has read'
       (Uttered in a context where each student is given sets of different
       books. The set of different books each student gets contains
       2-author books, 3-author books, 4-author books, and so on.)

With respect to idioms, both reconstruction (movement from within relative clauses) and base-generation are possible. There are instances where parts of an idiom, occurring as a relativized Head, are related to the relative clause (14) and other instances where they are related to the matrix clause (15).[2]

(14) a. [[ta *chi* e$_i$ de] *cu*$_i$]   bi   shei dou da[3]
         he *eat* DE *vinegar* compare who all   big
       'Lit. The vinegar he eats is greater than anyone else's.'
       'His jealousy is greater than anyone else's.'
   b. wo ting-bu-dong   [[ta *you* e$_i$ de] *mo*$_i$][4]
       I   listen-not-understand   he *hu-* DE *-mor*
       'Lit. I do not understand the -mor that he hu-ed.'
       'I do not understand his humor.'

(15) a. ta laoshi ai *chi* [[rang ren   shou-bu-liao   de] *cu*]
        he always like *eat* let   people receive-not-complete DE *vinegar*
        'Lit. He always likes to eat vinegar that cannot be put up with.'
        'He always likes to be jealous to such a degree that is beyond
        what can be put up with.'
    b. ta zhi hui *you* [[meiren ting-de-dong   de] *mo*]
        he only can *hu-* nobody listen-DE-understand DE *-mor*
        'Lit. He can only hu- the -mor that nobody understands.'
        'He can only say humorous things that nobody can understand.'

The discussion in this section, summarized in (16), shows that the conclusions we reached concerning the availability of reconstruction in Chinese relative constructions are not quite consistent.

(16) a. Reconstruction is possible for binding relations involving
      anaphors, bound pronouns, and so on, in the Head.
    b. Reconstruction is not possible for structures involving a Head
      QP interacting with another QP inside a relative clause for scope
      interpretations.
    c. Idiom chunks involving a relativized Head can be related to the
      relative clause. Therefore, reconstruction is possible when idiom
      chunks are involved. However, the idiomatic Head is not always
      necessarily related to the relative clause. It can be related to the
      matrix clause.

By contrast, the relevant English and LA relative constructions exhibit reconstruction effects systematically. Why is it that QPs in Chinese behave differently from those in English and LA, and how can we make sense out of such seemingly incoherent reconstruction effects?

The reconstruction facts regarding binding certainly argue for an analysis that derives the relative Head by movement. On the other hand, the QP scope interaction facts do not support direct movement to the Head. How can the two seemingly conflicting sets of facts be reconciled? The answer lies in the morphosyntactic properties of QPs. Note that the relevant scope interaction facts involve QPs containing number + classifier expressions. The occurrence of number + classifier expressions necessarily projects a QP expression beyond an NP to a larger structure that includes the number and classifier projections, given that Chinese nominals have the structure shown in (17) (Tang 1990; Li 1998, 1999a,b).

(17)

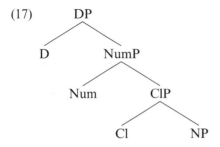

On the other hand, a modifier (including a relative clause) together with the NP it modifies can be projected as an NP. The object of a [V + O] idiom can also be an NP, as such object idiom chunks are generally non-referential. The NP/non-NP distinction provides an answer to the apparently conflicting reconstruction effects: what is reconstructed in Chinese is an NP. An NP can be an idiom chunk or can have a modifier that contains an anaphor or a pronoun. In contrast, an NP cannot be a QP because of the lack of number and classifier projections (and consequent lack of the Q or D projection). In other words, if what is reconstructed can only be an NP, instead of a DP, the seemingly inconsistent reconstruction facts follow straightforwardly: QPs, which necessarily contain a number + classifier expression, must be projections larger than NP; the non-QP cases, which do not contain a number + classifier expression, need not be larger than an NP. The distinction between NP reconstruction and DP reconstruction not only captures the seemingly inconsistent reconstruction facts in Chinese but also accounts for crosslinguistic differences—namely, the unavailability of the full range of reconstruction effects in Chinese versus their availability in the relevant English and LA relative constructions.

Even though the distinction between NP reconstruction and DP reconstruction captures the interesting variations in reconstruction effects within Chinese relative constructions and between Chinese on the one hand and English and LA on the other,[5] numerous questions arise. Why is it that an NP is reconstructed in Chinese, rather than a DP as in English and LA? Moreover, among the examples used to illustrate reconstruction effects in Chinese, some even contain a relative clause in the reconstructed Head. In (2b), for instance, what is reconstructed is *wo gei ta de shu* 'the book that I gave to him' and in (2d), *wo yao song gei ta de liwu* 'the present that I was going to give to him'. This amounts to saying that the projection containing a Head and a relative clause can itself be an NP. If the Head is an NP and the addition of a relative clause produces something that is still an NP, a relative clause construction can be an adjunction structure, not a complementation structure. Is this correct? Is it true that Chinese relativization indeed involves an adjunction structure, in contrast to the complementation structure found in English or LA? What are the properties of such an adjunction structure? These questions are resolved in the following sections and the next chapter, which investigate in detail the structure and derivation of relative constructions in Chinese.

5.2 NP Projection

We start by showing that the projection containing a relative clause and its Head can indeed be an NP. The evidence comes from the behavior of different connectives in various types of conjunction structures.

First of all, note that conjunction of two NPs is possible, as in the English example (18).

(18) He is a [secretary and typist].

The expression *secretary and typist* describes the dual roles of one individual. Chinese also allows such NP conjunction.

(19) ta shi [mishu   jian daziyuan]
      he is   secretary and typist
      'He is a secretary and typist.'

The number + classifier expression *yi-ge* 'one-CL', more or less like an indefinite determiner in English, can also occur before the conjunction.

(20) ta shi yi-ge   [mishu   jian daziyuan]
      he is   one-CL secretary and typist
      'He is a secretary and typist.'

(21a–b) are further examples of a conjunction describing one individual.

(21) a. wo xiang zhao yi-ge   [mishu   jian
          I   want   find one-CL secretary and
          daziyuan] (one person being sought)
          typist
          'I want to find a secretary and typist.'

b. wo yao zuo yi-ge   [yisheng jian
   I   want do one-CL doctor and
   hushi]   (doctor and nurse simultaneously)
   nurse
   'I want to be a doctor and nurse.'

Relevant to our discussion is the use of the connective *jian* in such examples. Unlike English, which uses *and* to conjoin like phrases of basically any category, Chinese has a rich set of connectives used to connect different types of like categories. For instance, *he* or *gen* connects two individual-denoting expressions, whereas *jian* connects two properties pertaining to one individual. (21a–b) should be contrasted with (22a–b), where the conjunction of two individuals requires *he/gen* and is indicated by the addition of a number + classifier expression to the second conjunct as well as the first.

(22) a. wo xiang zhao [[yi-ge   mishu]   he/gen [yi-ge   daziyuan]]
        I   want find   one-CL secretary and   one-CL typist
        'I want to find a secretary and a typist.'
     b. wo yao kan [[yi-ge   yisheng] he/gen [yi-ge   hushi]]
        I   want see   one-CL doctor   and   one-CL nurse
        'I want to see a doctor and a nurse.'

In addition to number + classifier + noun expressions denoting individuals, other individual-denoting expressions such as proper names, pronouns, and expressions with demonstratives can be connected by *he/gen*.

(23) a. wo hen xihuan [[zhe-ge xuesheng] he/gen [na-ge xuesheng]]
        I   very like   this-CL student   and   that-CL student
        'I like this student and that student.'
     b. wo hen xihuan [[ta] he/gen [zhangsan]]
        I   very like   him and   Zhangsan
        'I like him and Zhangsan.'

Such conjunction of individual-denoting expressions is not possible with *jian*. Thus, replacing *he/gen* in (22) and (23) with *jian* is unacceptable.

(24) a. *wo xiang zhao [[yi-ge   mishu] jian [yi-ge   daziyuan]]
         I   want find   one-CL secretary and one-CL typist
         'I want to find a secretary and a typist.'
     b. *wo yao kan [[yi-ge   yisheng] jian [yi-ge   hushi]]
         I   want see   one-CL doctor   and one-CL nurse
         'I want to see a doctor and a nurse.'

(25) a. *wo hen xihuan [[zhe-ge xuesheng] jian [na-ge   xuesheng]]
         I   very like   this-CL student   and that-CL student
         'I like this student and that student.'
    b. *wo hen xihuan [[ta] jian [zhangsan]]
         I   very like   him and Zhangsan
         'I like him and Zhangsan.'

In addition to connecting two properties describing one individual, *jian* can connect two activities performed by one individual; that is, it can connect two VPs.[6]

(26) a. zhangsan [[nian-shu] jian [zuo-shi]], hen mang
         Zhangsan study   and work   very busy
         'Zhangsan studies and works; (he is) busy.'
    b. wo [[sheji] jian [huatu]], ta [[shigong] jian [jiangong]], women
         I   design and draft   he construct and supervise   we
         hezuo-de   hen hao
         cooperate-DE very well
         'I design and draft; he constructs and supervises; we cooperate very well.'

When two clauses are connected, none of these connectives (*he*/*gen*/*jian*) are used. Instead, *erqie* is used.[7]

(27) a. [[wo xihuan ta] erqie [zhangsan ye   xihuan ta]]
          I   like   him and Zhangsan also like   him
          'I like him and Zhangsan also likes him.'
    b. [[wo xihuan ta] erqie [zhangsan hui zhaogu ta]]
          I   like   him and Zhangsan will care   him
          'I like him and Zhangsan will take care of him.'

In sum, the function of Chinese connectives can be described as follows:

(28) a. *Jian* connects two properties of a single individual or two
         activities performed by one individual. In terms of categories,
         jian can connect NPs or VPs.[8]
    b. *He*/*gen* connects two individual-denoting expressions (i.e., two
         DPs), which can be proper names, pronouns, expressions
         containing demonstratives, or expressions containing
         number + classifier expressions.
    c. *Erqie* connects two nonnominal categories, including clauses,
         adjective phrases, and VPs not expressing dual properties/
         activities of one individual.[9]
    d. These connectives are not interchangeable.

The unique distribution of these connectives provides an important test for the categorial status of complex nominals. Suppose that [$_{DP}$ D CP] were an appropriate structure for Chinese relative constructions; then we would expect conjunction of relative clauses with Heads (excluding D) to be possible with the CP connective *erqie*. This expectation is not met.

(29) a. *wo xiang zhao yi-ge   [[fuze   yingwen de mishu]
         I   want find one-CL charge English DE secretary
         erqie [jiao   xiaohai de jiajiao]][10]
         and   teach kid   DE tutor
         'I want to find a secretary that takes care of English (matters)
         and tutor that teaches kids.'

     b. *wo yao dang yi-ge   [[neng yin shi   de shiren] *erqie* [neng
         I   want be   one-CL can sing poem DE poet   and   can
         hua huar   de huajia]]
         draw picture DE artist
         'I want to be a poet that can sing poems and artist that can
         draw pictures.'

Indeed, such sentences can only be made acceptable by replacing *erqie* with *jian*, the connector of a single individual's properties. Neither *he* nor *gen* is possible.

(30) a. wo xiang zhao yi-ge   [[fuze   yingwen de mishu]   *jian* [jiao
         I   want find one-CL charge English DE secretary and teach
         xiaohai de jiajiao]]
         kid   DE tutor
         'I want to find a secretary that takes care of English (matters)
         and tutor that teaches kids.'

     b. wo yao dang yi-ge   [[neng yin shi   de shiren] *jian* [neng
         I   want be   one-CL can sing poem DE poet   and   can
         hua huar   de huajia]]
         draw picture DE artist
         'I want to be a poet that can sing poems and artist that can
         draw pictures.'

(31) a. *wo xiang zhao yi-ge   [[fuze   yingwen de mishu]
         I   want find one-CL charge English DE secretary
         he/gen [jiao   xiaohai de jiajiao]]
         and   teach kid   DE tutor
         'I want to find a secretary that takes care of English (matters)
         and tutor that teaches kids.'

b. *wo yao dang yi-ge   [[neng yin shi   de shiren] *he/gen* [neng
   I   want be   one-CL can sing poem DE poet   and   can
   hua   huar   de huajia]]
   draw picture DE artist
   'I want to be a poet that can sing poems and artist that can
   draw pictures.'

Not surprisingly, (31a–b) can be rescued by adding a number + classifier
expression in the second conjunct, which turns them into conjunctions of
two individual-denoting expressions (cf. (22)).

(32) a. wo xiang zhao [[yi-ge   fuze   yingwen de mishu]
         I   want find   one-CL charge English DE secretary
         he/gen [yi-ge   jiao   xiaohai de jiajiao]]
         and   one-CL teach kid   DE tutor
         'I want to find a secretary that takes care of English (matters)
         and a tutor that teaches kids.'
     b. wo yao   dang [[yi-ge   neng yin shi   de shiren] *he/gen* [yi-ge
         I   want be   one-CL can sing poem DE poet   and   one-CL
         neng hua   huar   de huajia]]
         can   draw picture DE artist
         'I want to be a poet that can sing poems and an artist that can
         draw pictures.'

The acceptability of (32) is not surprising; after all, a complex nominal
can be an individual-denoting expression (DP). It is the use of *jian* in (30)
that is significant. Recall that a complex nominal in English or LA is
always a DP and the category inside D is a CP. However, the appearance
of *jian*, the NP connective, not the CP connective *erqie* or the DP connective *he/gen*, suggests that the connected categories are NPs, not CPs
or DPs. Indeed, if a complex nominal were always a DP, we would not
expect the conjuncts of NP conjunction to contain any relative clause.
Recall that in English, for instance, the occurrence of a relative clause forces
the projection of a DP. Two of the relevant examples are repeated here.

(33) a. *He is an [[actor that wants to do everything] and [producer that
         wants to please everyone]].
     b. He is [[an actor that wants to do everything] and [*a* producer
         that wants to please everyone]].

In brief, the contrast between the Chinese examples in (30) and the
English examples in (33) clearly argues for the different categorial status

of complex nominals in these two languages: a complex nominal can be an NP in Chinese but it must be a DP in English. It is therefore not surprising that instances like (2) show the reconstruction of a phrase containing a relative construction: the Head itself is a complex nominal, which is an NP. An NP Head can be reconstructed.

The above discussion gives rise, then, to the following important generalizations concerning Chinese relative constructions:

(34) a. Chinese relative constructions allow NP reconstruction, but not DP reconstruction.
  b. The Head of a relative construction can itself be a relative construction and undergoes reconstruction: it is an NP.
  c. The projection of a relative clause and its Head can itself be an NP.

The fact that the addition of a relative clause to an NP Head results in a structure that is still an NP suggests an adjunction structure for relative constructions. In the next section, we show that relative clauses behave like adjuncts within nominal expressions.

5.3 Adjunction

We begin with an observation regarding word order. In Chinese nominal expressions, in addition to the fact that the Head noun must always be final (in traditional terminology, the language is head-final within nominal expressions), the only other elements that display fixed ordering are demonstratives, numbers, and classifiers: they must occur in the order [Demonstrative + Number + Classifier + Noun]. To account for this fixed ordering, it has been proposed that each of these elements is the syntactic head of its respective projection (see, e.g., Tang 1990; Li 1998, 1999a,b). The fixed ordering is therefore accounted for by the hierarchical projections.

In contrast, traditional "modifiers" such as adjectives and relative clauses can occur in any position: before a demonstrative, between a demonstrative and a number, and between a classifier and a noun.[11] The marker *de* immediately follows the modifier.[12]

(35)   Demonstrative + Number + Classifier + Noun[13]
      ↑   ↑   (↑)   ↑

(36) a. hong de na   shi-ben shu
        red   DE that ten-CL book
        'those ten red books'
   b. na   hong de shi-ben shu
      that red   DE ten-CL book
      'those ten red books'
   c. na   shi-ben hong de shu
      that ten-CL red   DE book
      'those ten red books'

(37) a. meiren yao de na   shi-ben shu
        nobody like DE that ten-CL book
        'those ten books that nobody likes'
   b. na   meiren yao de shi-ben shu
      that nobody like DE ten-CL book
      'those ten books that nobody likes'
   c. na   shi-ben meiren yao de shu
      that ten-CL nobody like DE book
      'those ten books that nobody likes'

One may account for the distribution of adjectives by suggesting that they are simply a subcase of relative clauses. Indeed, adjectives can often function as predicates. When they do function as predicates, the intensifier *hen* 'very' generally co-occurs, its meaning having been bleached (i.e., its intensive meaning having been lost), a test that is usually accepted as distinguishing verbs from adjectives.[14] An adjectival predicate can also be negated by the verbal negator *bu* 'not'. When an adjective occurs prenominally and can function as a predicate, it is possible to analyze it as a reduced relative clause. (38a–c) illustrate prenominal adjectives and (39a–b) illustrate the predicative use of such adjectives.

(38) a. zhongyao de shiqing
        important DE matter
        'important matters'
   b. hen zhongyao de shiqing
      very important DE matter
      'very important matters'
   c. bu zhongyao de shiqing
      not important DE matter
      'unimportant matters'

(39) a. zhe-jian shiqing hen zhongyao
          this-CL matter very important
          'This matter is important.'
     b. zhe-jian shiqing bu zhongyao
          this-CL matter not important
          'This matter is not important.'

However, some adjectives cannot be regarded as reduced relative clauses because they cannot be used predicatively.[15]

(40) a. zhuyao de daolu
          main   DE road
          'the main road'
     b. *daolu (hen/bu) zhuyao[16]
          road   very/not main
     c. *hen/bu zhuyao de daolu
          very/not main   DE road

(41) a. weiyi de daolu
          only DE road
          'the only roadway'
     b. *daolu (hen/bu) weiyi
          road   very/not only
     c. *(hen/bu) weiyi de daolu
          very/not only DE road

(42) a. gongtong de shiye
          shared   DE business
          'shared business'
     b. *zhexie dongxi (hen/bu) gongtong
          these things   very/not shared
     c. *hen/bu gongtong de shiye
          very/not shared   DE business

We thus need to recognize the existence of prenominal adjectives that cannot be reduced relative clauses. Logically, an adjective can occupy two possible positions: inside an independent projection with a head that is not the noun it modifies (e.g., in the Spec of some higher functional projections—see Cinque 1994, 1999; Rizzi 1997), or as sister of the modified element (an adjunction analysis—see, e.g., Jackendoff 1977; Valois 1991; Bernstein 1993).[17]

The main argument for independent projection analyses and against adjunction analyses is fixed ordering among adjectives. It has been observed that in English, adjectives generally need to occur in a fixed order. For instance, a size expression generally occurs before a color expression, as in the following examples:

(43) a.   a small red car
     b.   *a red small car

In Chinese, the situation is different. Consider these examples:[18]

(44) a.   hong (se)   de xiao chezi
          red   color DE small car
          'red small car'
     b.   xiao de hong chezi
          small DE red   car
          'small red car'
     c.   xiao de hong (se)   de chezi[19]
          small DE red   color DE car
          'small red car'
     d.   hong (se)   de xiao de chezi
          red   color DE small DE car
          'red small car'
     e.   xiao hong che
          small red   car
     f.   ??hong xiao che
            red   small car

When *de* does not occur (as in (44e–f)), the adjective forms a compound with the head noun. When compounding takes place, the ordering of adjectives is strict. It is basically the same as the ordering found in many other languages, such as English. In contrast, when *de* occurs (as in (44a–d)), the adjective is not compounded with the head noun, and in this case the ordering is quite free. This is surprising if each adjective heads a functional projection: the hierarchy of these projections would have to be quite free, hence there could be no ordering relation among them. The motivation for postulating various functional projections to account for word order possibilities would be lost. On the other hand, the relatively free ordering is expected if adjectives with *de* are adjoined structures. They are adjoined to the head they modify, which can precede a demonstrative, a number, or a noun.

(45) a. zhuyao de na   san-tiao daolu
         main   DE that three-CL road
         'those three main roads'
     b. na   zhuyao de san-tiao daolu
         that main   DE three-CL road
         'those three main roads'
     c. na   san-tiao zhuyao de daolu
         that three-CL main   DE road
         'those three main roads'

Similarly, in addition to the fact that a relative clause can freely occur in various positions, the ordering of relative clauses among themselves and with adjectives is also fairly free—a behavior expected of adjunction structures. The following examples show that the ordering of relative clauses among themselves is free:

(46) a. wo kan-guo de fang-zai ta jia   de shu
         I   see-ASP DE place-at he home DE book
         'books that are at his home that I have seen'
     b. fang-zai ta jia   de wo kan-guo de shu
         place-at he home DE I   see-ASP DE book
         'books that I have seen that are at his home'

The following examples show that the ordering between a relative clause and an adjective (not derived from a relative clause) is also quite free:

(47) a. wo kan-guo de zhuyao de xiangmu
         I   read-ASP DE main   DE items
         'the main items that I have read'
     b. zhuyao de wo kan-guo de xiangmu
         main   DE I   read-ASP DE items
         'the main items that I have read'

A relative clause can also be conjoined with a prenominal modifier, which cannot be a predicate. In this case, the connective *erqie*, which conjoins nonnominal categories, is used.[20]

(48) a. zhuyao de erqie women yijing   taolun-guo de shiqing
         main   DE and we   already discuss-ASP DE matter
         'the main matters that we have discussed'
     b. gongtong de erqie meiren keyi dai hui-qu   de dongxi
         common DE and nobody can take back-go DE thing
         'things that are shared and nobody can take back'

Thus, it is straightforward to claim that relative clauses, just like pre-nominal adjectives, are adjoined structures. They can be adjoined to almost all projections within a nominal expression, as illustrated earlier. The conjunction examples further indicate that a relative clause is very much like an adjective.[21]

5.4 Complementation Structure

So far, we have shown that Chinese relative constructions involve an adjunction structure, instead of a complementation structure, as in English and LA (the relative being a complement of D: $[_{DP}$ D CP]). Adopting a $[_{DP}$ D CP] complementation structure in Chinese would not account for the fact that the projection containing a relative clause and its Head can still be an NP. Nor would it account for the contrast between English and LA relative constructions, which are obligatorily projected to DP, and Chinese relatives, which can be projected to NP.

These arguments supporting an adjunction structure argue against a complementation structure for Chinese relative constructions. Furthermore, the general arguments that have been proposed in favor of adopting a complementation structure do not hold in Chinese. In order to consider them, we will first examine Kayne's (1994, chap. 8) proposal that, like Head-initial relative constructions, Head-final relative constructions display a $[_{DP}$ D CP] complementation structure. The reverse word order of a Head-final construction is derived by movement of the entire IP to the Spec of DP.

(49) $[_{DP}[_{IP} \ldots t_i \ldots]_j [_{D'}$ D $[_{CP}$ DP$_i$ [C t_j]]]]

That is, (50a) should have the structure in (50b) (English gloss only), which does not derive the Head-final word order of Chinese relativization directly. To derive this word order, the IP needs to be raised to the Spec of DP, as in (50c).

(50) a. [ta kan de] shu
       he read DE book
       'the book he read'
    b. $[_D[_{CP}$ book $[_{IP}$ he read]]]
    c. $[_{DP}[_{IP}$ he read] $[_D[_{CP}$ book $[_{IP}$ e]]]]

This makes the IP higher than D. According to Kayne, a relative clause is nonrestrictive if it is outside the c-command domain of D. A structure like (50c) is Kayne's representation for a nonrestrictive relative clause (1994, 110–115).[22] Under this analysis, because of the word order, a Chinese relative clause is always higher than D, that is, outside the c-command domain of D. A Chinese relative therefore should always be interpreted as nonrestrictive. This is not the case, however. The relative clause in (51), for instance, is interpreted as restrictive (see Chao 1968 and Huang 1982 regarding the restrictive status of such relative clauses).[23] Indeed, it has only a restrictive interpretation, which is like the one given in the English translation: the reference of the book is restricted by the relative clause.

(51) [ta kan-guo de] (na/yi-ben) shu
     he read-ASP DE that/one-CL book
     '(the/a) book that he has read'

In addition to the problem of word order and interpretation, there is no evidence that D can select a CP in Chinese (see section 4.1.3). Chinese does not have a definite or indefinite article, corresponding to *the* or *a* in English. The most likely candidates for D are the demonstratives *zhe/na* 'this/that' and quantifiers such as *mei* 'every'. Take idiomatic expressions, for example. The object part of some [V + O] idioms can occur as the relative head with a demonstrative; others do not allow a demonstrative. What is important, however, is that in such cases, a demonstrative is equally acceptable (or unacceptable) with or without a relative clause.

(52) a. [ta kai de] [na-ge   dao] hen
         he open DE that-CL knife very
         chenggong   (*kai-dao* 'open-knife = operate')
         successful
         'That operation he performed was successful.'
     b. deng ta [kai-wan]   [na-ge   dao] zai zou
         wait he open-finish that-CL knife then leave
         'Don't leave till he finishes the operation.'
     c. *[ta chi de] [na-xie doufu] tai duo
         he eat DE those tofu   too much
         le[24]   (*chi-doufu* 'eat tofu = flirt')
         LE
         'He flirted too much.'
     d. *deng ta [chi-wan] [na-xie doufu] zai   zou
         wait he eat-finish those tofu   then go
         'Don't leave till he finishes flirting.'

The unavailability of scope reconstruction in Chinese, in contrast to its availability in the relevant Head-initial relative constructions in English and LA, also argues against the structure in (49c). The interpretation of (53c) is like (53b), rather than (53a).

(53) a. mei-ge-ren   dou wenle liang-ge wenti
        every-CL-person all   asked two-CL   question
        'Everyone asked two questions.'
     b. mei-ge-ren   dou wenle na   liang-ge wenti
        every-CL-person all   asked that two-CL   question
        'Everyone asked those two questions.'
     c. mei-ge-ren   dou wen de na   liang-ge wenti
        every-CL-person all   ask DE that two-CL   question
        'the two questions that everyone asked'

In the literature on Chinese relative constructions, attempts have been made to apply the promotion analysis proposed by Kayne (1994) to Chinese (see, e.g., Chiu 1998; Simpson 2001, 2002; Wu 2001). Closer examination, however, reveals no support for such an approach. Chiu (1998) argues for a promotion analysis because children learning Chinese place a copy of the head noun in the relative clause.

(54) luotuo chi *caomei*   de caomei
     camel eat strawberry DE strawberry
     'the strawberry which the camel ate (strawberry)'

However, the presence of a copy in the relative clause can hardly argue for a promotion analysis. Repetition of noun (phrases) often occurs in Chinese even in structures that are generally not analyzed as being derived by movement.

(55) a. laoshi   dai   laoshi   de pengyou lai   le
        teacher bring teacher DE friend   come LE
        'The teacher brought the teacher's friend (his/her friend) here.'
     b. luotuo pao, luotuo tiao
        camel run camel jump
        'Camels run; camels jump.'

The conclusion that relative clauses in Chinese involve a promotion analysis would be more convincing if, during this stage of language acquisition, children use a copy not only in relative clauses but also in other NP/DP movement structures. Furthermore, even if the facts illustrated in (54) could be interpreted as arguing for a movement analysis, they would only argue for the existence of movement. They have no bearing on the existence of a complementation structure in relative clauses.

Wu (2001, chap. 3) relies on examples involving tone changes in Taiwanese relative constructions to argue for a promotion analysis. However, as she herself notes, the facts regarding tone changes do not specifically entail a promotion analysis; they simply argue that a relative clause is adjoined to the Head or in the Spec of the Head in Taiwanese.

Clearly, no positive evidence supports accounting for Chinese relative constructions via a complementation structure and a promotion analysis in Kayne's (1994) sense. Can we, then, step back and claim that, for the sake of uniformity, a complementation structure/promotion analysis should be adopted for Chinese because it is adopted for English and some other languages? No, because taking such a step obscures the interesting contrasts between English and Chinese, particularly the facts concerning coordination and scope reconstruction.

In brief, the type of evidence supporting the dependency relation between D and CP in English and LA simply does not exist in Chinese,[25] and there is no evidence in favor of a complementation structure in Chinese.[26] Adopting a complementation structure for Chinese misses important differences between English/LA and Chinese relative constructions.

5.5 Summary

We began this chapter by observing the seemingly chaotic array of reconstruction effects exhibited in Chinese relative constructions. We demonstrated that these apparently inconsistent reconstruction effects in fact follow straightforwardly from the assumption that what is raised to the Head position is an NP, rather than a DP. Accordingly, the reconstruction of the Head is NP reconstruction, not DP reconstruction. This analysis captures the impossibility of reconstructing a Head that is itself a QP (necessarily a projection larger than NP), in contrast to the possibility of reconstructing a Head that is an NP and can contain an adjoined phrase. The phrase adjoined to the NP Head (adjunction resulting in an NP projection) may be a relative clause, an adjective, or even a QP. The last possibility gives rise to the QP reconstruction cases in (11).

The characteristics of Chinese relativization can be summarized as follows:

(56) a. What is relativized can be an NP. That is, the Head of a relative construction can be an NP, which can undergo reconstruction.

b. A relative clause and its head can be projected as an NP.

c. The distribution of a relative clause is very much like that of a prenominal adjective modifying the head N.

d. Like an adjective, a relative clause enjoys freedom of ordering, in contrast to other elements within nominal expressions that require fixed ordering, such as demonstratives, number and classifier expressions, and deverbal nominal structures.

These characteristics argue for the following adjunction structure for relativization in Chinese:

(57)

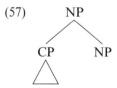

This contrasts with the complementation structure defended for English and LA relativization constructions in chapter 4. We have established that such a contrast should exist. The evidence favoring the [$_{DP}$ D CP] structure in English and LA does not exist in Chinese; moreover, there is evidence against adopting such a structure. Chinese does not exhibit the close dependency between a determiner and a relative clause that exists in languages such as English and LA. In addition to the lack of positive evidence, we have demonstrated that there is direct evidence against such a structure in Chinese. Importantly, there is a contrast between the Chinese (30) and the English (33), repeated here.

(30) a. wo xiang zhao yi-ge   fuze   yingwen de mishu   *jian* jiao
      I   want find one-CL charge English DE secretary and teach
      xiaohai de jiajiao
      kid   DE tutor
      'I want to find a secretary that takes care of English (matters) and tutor that teaches kids.'

b. wo yao   dang yi-ge   neng yin shi   de shiren *jian* neng hua
   I   want be   one-CL can sing poem DE poet   and can   draw
   huar   de huajia
   picture DE artist
   'I want to be a poet that can sing poems and artist that can draw pictures.'

(33) a. *He is an actor that wants to do everything and producer that
         wants to please everyone.
     b. He is an actor that wants to do everything and *a* producer that
         wants to please everyone.

The unacceptability of the English sentence (33a) follows from the fact
that a relative construction must be a DP in English. The acceptability of
the Chinese (30a–b) argues for the NP status of relative constructions in
that language, a status that is allowed when a relative construction is
derived by adjunction.

The adjunction structure is further supported by the free ordering of
relative clauses and the distributional similarity between relative clauses
and adjectives, which are adjoined structures.

Indeed, an adjunction structure for Chinese relativization is not unexpected given Kayne's (1994) Antisymmetry approach to phrase structure,
which allows left-adjunction. A relative clause in Chinese precedes its
head, an ordering that can be straightforwardly derived by left-adjoining
the relative clause to its head.

The adjunction structure in (57) and the NP reconstruction effects,
although supported empirically by the facts discussed in this chapter,
raise two questions Why is it NP, not DP, that is relativized in Chinese?
and How can movement derive an adjunction structure like (57)? We turn
next to these questions.

Chapter 6

Adjunction Structure and Derivation

Our study of Chinese relative constructions has revealed numerous previously unnoted empirical generalizations, which have led us to adopt an NP-raising relativization process operating on an adjunction structure. Though empirically supported, this approach raises three important theoretical questions.

First, if Kayne's (1994) Antisymmetry approach to word order and phrase structure is correct, we have seemingly proposed a structure that requires an illicit operation. Specifically, we have proposed an adjunction structure where the Head is raised from the relative clause, as shown in (1).

(1)

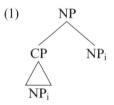

According to Kayne, the CP must antisymmetrically c-command the NP in (1) in order for it to appear on the left side. In other words, the NP cannot c-command the CP. If the NP does not c-command the CP, it cannot c-command the trace within the CP derived by Head raising. This raises the question of whether such a movement is licit.

A second question concerns what is generated and raised in the Head-raising process. The Head-raising process we proposed for Chinese relative constructions is NP raising. Head raising moves an element from within the relative clause to the Head position. In the case of argument relativization, the nominal expression in an argument position is raised to the Head position. The existence of NP Head raising means, then, that an NP can be generated in an argument position in a relative clause in this language, a point contested by Borsley (1997), as discussed in chapter 4 concerning DP raising in English. Why is it that Chinese allows NP raising but English does not?

A third question concerns the strategies available for deriving relative constructions in Chinese. As just indicated, relativization in Chinese involves raising an NP Head. In chapter 4, we argued that in a Head-initial language such as English, relative constructions are derived not only by raising the Head (the promotion analysis) but also by base-generating the Head in its surface position, where it enters into an agreement/predication relation with an operator in a relative clause (operator movement/matching analysis). Is an operator movement/matching analysis also available for Chinese relative constructions?

We answer these questions in the following sections. We show that the proposed movement of an NP out of a seemingly adjoined CP in Chinese is licit if the structural condition on movement is cast in terms of an extension condition applied in the process of derivation, rather than in terms of a c-command relation applied to representations. Moreover, we establish that what makes NP raising possible in Chinese relativization is the internal structure of nominal expressions in Chinese, which is manifested in the composition of *wh*-words and the distribution of the plural/collective morpheme *-men* in this language. Finally, we demonstrate that an operator movement process is available to derive Chinese relative constructions. Support comes from facts regarding reconstruction, adjunct relativization, island effects, the "resumptive" use of some *wh*-expressions, and so on. The discussion reveals additional interesting empirical generalizations, many of which have rarely, if ever, been discussed and which would in any case be mysterious according to previous analyses. These facts lend further support to our analysis.

6.1   Derivation

Let us consider how movement can apply to a structure like (1). Such a derivation is not unexpected if we hold the view that trees are built up step by step and that conditions on movement are checked derivationally, in line with the Minimal Link Condition discussed in Chomsky 1995 (esp. p. 264; also see section 2.4.1 above).

First, consider how a relative construction in Chinese can be derived. The reconstruction facts noted in chapter 5, repeated here, argue for the existence of an NP Head-raising process.

(2) a. Reconstruction is possible for binding relations involving anaphors, bound pronouns, and so on, in the Head.

    b. Reconstruction is not possible for structures involving a Head QP interacting with another QP inside the relative clause for scope interpretations.

    c. The Head can be an idiom chunk related to the other part of the idiom within the relative clause.

Note further that Chinese must not allow DP movement; if it did, the fact that reconstruction is not available in cases concerning scope interaction with a QP Head of a relative construction would be unexpected.

The derivation therefore proceeds as follows, given the earlier claim that a relative clause is adjoined to its Head:

(3) a. A CP is generated.

    b. The CP is merged with an NP. The NP can be a copy of an NP inside the CP:

    c. NP projects.

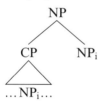

This shows the derivation of NP raising and captures all the facts in (2). Importantly, however, in order for this derivation to be licit, we must establish that (1) the structural condition on movement (e.g., that the head must c-command the tail in a movement chain) is not violated, (2) an NP can occur in an argument position to be relativized, and (3) DP movement does not take place even though a DP can be generated in an argument position. We discuss these issues in the following subsections.

6.1.1 Licit Movement

Movement generally is considered to obey a c-command requirement. However, if we adopt a definition of c-command incorporating the notion of segments (May 1985; Chomsky 1986a), the CP is in fact not c-commanded by the two-segment NP in (3): the adjunction creates a two-segment category NP. The CP is not dominated by the NP category because it is not excluded by the NP (one segment of the NP dominates the CP). In fact, the CP c-commands the NP. When the CP c-commands the NP, the Head (the lower NP segment) cannot c-command the trace inside the CP.[1] In other words, the moved phrase fails to c-command the trace generated by movement. Without a c-command relation, is the movement licit?

We suggest below that such a movement can be licit if we recast the c-command requirement on movement in terms of a derivational notion of *extension*. A derivational notion of extension not only allows the movement in question but also unifies substitution and adjunction processes under the same umbrella of extension, in contrast to Chomsky's (1995, 190–191) account, which makes adjunction an exception to the extension requirement.

In his discussion of the role of extension, the strict cycle, and cases of licit and illicit movement, Chomsky (1995, 190–191) claims that operations (Generalized Transformation (GT) or Move α) require a substitution site to be *external* to the targeted phrase marker K (movement and GT are taken to be substitution operations). For adjunctions like those in (4a–b), Chomsky states that "adjunction need not extend its target. For concreteness, let us assume that the extension requirement holds only for substitution in overt syntax, the only case required by the trivial argument for the cycle" (p. 191).

(4) a. [$_X$ Y X]
     b. [$_{XP}$ YP XP]

However, adjunction need not be an exception, if we determine the extension requirement derivationally. Suppose the following derivational steps are taken:

(5) a. Establish a structure (a set of phrase markers) that is a CP.
     b. Targeting CP, insert Ø external to CP, forming a phrase marker α.

     c. Substitute YP for Ø, which can be a copy identical to a phrase inside CP (Move) or a new copy.

d. Determine the projection of α: does CP or YP project? If CP projects, YP is an adjunct; if YP projects, CP is an adjunct.

The procedure in (5) creates an adjunction structure. This derivational procedure can be identical to the one for true substitution (vs. adjunction) cases if CP is replaced with, for instance, C′ (or C).

(6) a. Establish a structure (a set of phrase markers) that is a C′ (or C).
    b. Target the C′ (or C), insert Ø external to C′ (or C), forming a phrase marker α.

c. Substitute YP for Ø, which can be a copy identical to a phrase inside C′ (or C) (Move) or a new copy.

d. Determine the projection of α: does C′ (or C) or YP project? If C′/C projects, YP is a specifier/complement; if YP projects, C′/C becomes a maximal projection, which will then be, as in (5), an adjunction structure.

Note that for both derivations, each step is licit. The extension requirement is satisfied because the position Ø is created before α is labeled, that is, before it is determined which element is projected. Because of the derivational approach, the extension requirement is blind to the distinction between adjunction and substitution. Both processes can be viewed as substitution, if the position indicated by Ø in (5)–(6) is created first in order for the YP to replace it. Alternatively, both processes can be viewed simply as Merge (including a resulting adjunction structure), if the position indicated by Ø in (5)–(6) is not created first in order for the YP to replace it.[2] Indeed, at the stage where the two phrase markers YP and CP/C′ are combined, it is not relevant to distinguish adjunction from substitution. It is at the stage where α is labeled that this distinction matters. Since the extension condition applies at the stage when the two phrase markers are merged, the distinction is irrelevant.

After the phrase markers are derived and all the nodes are labeled, linearization can take place. At this point, α has been labeled and, if α is YP, CP is not c-commanded by YP. This allows the Antisymmetry approach to linearization to remain intact but, at the same time, movement is licit. It also enables us to accommodate both substitution and adjunction under the same extension condition, rather than making adjunction an exception (see Nunes's (1995, 2001) proposal concerning sideward movement).[3]

Having established the legitimacy of a movement process, we next show that what is moved can indeed be an NP, a claim supported by the morphosyntactic properties of *wh*-words in Chinese and other related phenomena concerning the placement of quantifiers and restrictions.

6.1.2 NP Movement

As mentioned in chapter 4, questions regarding NP movement in relative constructions were first raised by Borsley (1997), arguing against Kayne's (1994) NP-raising approach to relativization. Recall that Kayne suggests that a relative clause without *wh*-words in English is derived by moving an NP directly to the Spec of CP.

(7) [$_{DP}$ the [$_{CP}$ picture$_i$ [$_{C'}$ that [$_{IP}$ Bill liked t$_i$]]]]

Borsley argues that what moves cannot be an NP because if it were, an NP trace would have to occur in a position where one would expect a DP and because such NP movement behaves like DP movement (see section 4.1.3.4). Accordingly, Bianchi (1999, 2000b) proposes that what moves is *not* an NP, but a DP with an empty D. The empty D needs to be licensed. It is licensed by being incorporated into the external D of the relative construction. This licensing requirement on the internal D proves to be instrumental in capturing the derivation of different types of relative constructions in LA and English.

The problem, however, is that Chinese does allow NP movement. The trace derived by NP movement can still enter into binding or control relations with a DP in the relative clause. For instance, (8) and (9) contain the NP connective *jian*, which indicates that the conjoined complex nominals are NPs (and the Head is an NP). The binding of an anaphor or PRO by the relativized nominal is acceptable. The acceptability of (9) also shows that the Head containing the reflexive must be reconstructed in order to be bound by the subject *ta* 'he'. In other words, the Head must be moved from within the relative clause *ta neng xinlai* 'he can trust *x*'. Yet this complex nominal can still be conjoined with another one by *jian*, signaling NP conjunction.

(8) wo xiang zhao yi-ge   [[e_i neng zhaogu $ziji_i$ jiating] de $zhufu_i$]
    I   want find one-CL   can care   self family DE housewife
    jian [e_j neng zhudong shefa PRO_i chuang shiye   de] nu
    and   can initiate attempt   create business DE female
    qiang ren_i]
    strong person
    'I want to find a housewife that can take care of self's family and strong woman that can take initiatives to try to create business (an individual that is a capable housewife and creative strong woman).'

(9) wo xiang gei ta   zhao yi-ge   [[ta_i neng xinlai e de] [$ziji_i$ fumu
    I   want for him find one-CL   [[he can trust   DE self parent
    ye   hui xihuan de nu pengyou]] *jian* [[e neng bangmang PRO
    also will like DE girl friend   and   can help
    zhaogu fumu de] taitai][4]
    care   parent DE wife
    'I want to find a girl friend for him that he can trust and that self's (his) parents also like and wife that can help care for parents (a girl that is trustworthy and likable and has filial piety).'

These examples show that, even though relativization in Chinese is clearly a process of NP movement, the trace generated by NP movement can still bind a reflexive or a PRO. How is this to be reconciled with Borsley's and Bianchi's claim that relativization must be DP movement? A clue to the solution can be found in the special properties of the nominal to be relativized.

Note that, even though Bianchi's revision concerning what moves solves the problems raised by Borsley, her analysis crucially relies on the claim that the D of the nominal to be relativized (referred to as the internal D) is empty. But why must it be empty?[5] Further, recall that the D of a complex nominal phrase must be external to the Head and the relative clause—the external determiner hypothesis.[6] Under this view, it is possible to think that the Head DP with an empty D is very much like an NP in terms of its relation with the external D.[7]

(10) a. D [Head [Relative Clause]]
     b. D [NP]

The relation shown in (10) and the peculiar properties of the internal D make it plausible to entertain the option that the Head is an NP and the relativization process moves an NP, if it is possible to allow an NP to be generated in an argument position and behave like an argument. Since an argument position requires a DP, an empty D is postulated as the internal D in order to make the representation well formed. Further note that even when the Head is a DP with a lexical D, the NP associated with the internal lexical D still needs to be preposed to be interpreted with the external D, according to Kayne and Bianchi. This refers to the cases of [*wh*-NP], which have a lexical *wh* in D. When the D is [+*wh*], the NP associated with this D still needs to be moved to the Spec of D in order to be associated with the external D. In other words, regardless of whether the internal D is empty or lexical (*wh*), the NP in the Head position needs to be interpreted via the external D. From the perspective of NP licensing, the internal D alone is inadequate to license the nominal to be relativized. The NP needs to wait for licensing until it is raised and enters a licensing relation with the external D. For interpretation, the relativized nominal cannot just rely on the internal D. The external D plays a crucial role. This leads to the following conclusion: it is possible to claim that the DP-like properties of the raised Head (as in (11)) are obtained *after* the relativized nominal is interpreted with the external D.

(11) a.   the man that t_i thought he$_i$ saw a UFO
     b.   the man that t_i tried PRO$_i$ to fool everybody
     c.   the book that Bill criticized t_i without reading pg$_i$
     d.   *the man that it seems t to know the answer

The external D is responsible for the DP properties of the relativized nominal. There is no reason not to allow relativization to be derived by NP movement, if we can show that an NP can be generated in an argument position.

Indeed, it is possible to show that an NP can be generated in an argument position in Chinese. Moreover, this conclusion has already been argued for independently. Evidence comes from the behavior of *wh*-phrases and of the plural/collective marker *-men* in this language.

Recall our discussion of the composition of *wh*-expressions in chapter 3. We argued that, in contrast to English, whose *wh*-words which consist of (Question) Quantification and Restriction, Chinese allows the three components to be generated in different positions. Most importantly, Chinese allows *wh*-phrases to consist simply of a Restriction.[8] For instance, the following *wh*-words are interpreted as existential or universal when bound by the existential quantifier in a conditional clause or by the universal quantifier *dou*, respectively:

(12) a. ruguo ni   xihuan shei, wo jiu   ba ta   jieshao   gei ni
         if   you like   who I   then BA him introduce to you
         'If you like someone, I will introduce him to you.'
     b. shei dou lai   le
         who all   come LE
         'Everyone came.'

Note that such "Restriction only" *wh*-words can occupy argument positions. Moreover, these *wh*-words still behave like a quantificational DP with respect to binding and control in relation to another DP.

(13) a. shei$_i$ dou bu gan ba ziji$_i$/ta$_i$ de yisi   shuo chulai
         who all   not dare BA self/he DE intent speak out
         'Nobody dares to speak out self's/his intent.'
     b. shei$_i$ dou xiang [PRO$_i$ qu]
         who all   want   go
         'Everyone wants to go.'

In other words, the behavior of *wh*-words in this language indicates that NPs (Restriction) can occupy an argument position and be interpreted with a quantifier in a separate position.

That an NP can be generated in an argument position in Chinese is further supported by facts concerning the plural/collective morpheme -*men* in this language. To account for the distribution of -*men* and its interaction with the ordering options among the constituents of nominal expressions, Li (1998) suggests that the plural/collective marker -*men* is the realization of a number feature occupying the head position of a Number projection. This marker is realized only on an element that has undergone movement through an empty Classifier (Cl) to D. This is because of the interaction of the Chinese nominal structure and the Head Movement Constraint. Recall that a full nominal in Chinese has the following structure:

(14) [$_{DP}$ D [$_{NumP}$ Num [$_{ClP}$ Cl [$_{NP}$ N]]]]

A noun is generated in N, a classifier in Cl, the plural marker in Num, and a demonstrative or proper name or pronoun in D. If Cl is not lexically filled (a classifier is not present), an N can be raised to Num (suffixing -*men*) and then further raised to D to check the definite feature in D.[9]

(15) laoshi   dui *xuesheng-men* hen hao
      teacher to student-MEN   very good
      'The teacher is nice to the students.'

If Cl is lexically filled (a classifier is present), an N cannot be raised and combine with the plural marker in Num (the Head Movement Constraint). This accounts for the unacceptability of the expressions:

(16) *laoshi dui (*zhe/na*)   san-ge   xuesheng-men tebie   hao
       teacher to these/those three-CL student-MEN especially good
       'The teacher is especially nice to (these/those) three students.'

An N can also move up to Num only when D is occupied (e.g., by a demonstrative) and Cl is not lexically filled. This captures the contrast in grammaticality between the following sentences containing -*men* phrases:

(17) a.   laoshi dui *zhe/na-xie xuesheng-men* tebie   hao
          teacher to these/those student-MEN especially good
          'The teacher is especially nice to these/those students.'
     b. *laoshi dui *zhe/na*   ji-ge   xuesheng-men tebie
          teacher to these/those several-CL student-MEN especially
          hao
          good
          'The teacher is especially nice to these/those couple of
          students.'
     c. *laoshi *dui zhexie/naxie-ge xuesheng-men* tebie   hao
          teacher to these/those-CL student-MEN especially good
          'The teacher is especially nice to these students.'

In (17a), D is occupied by the demonstrative but Cl is empty. The noun can move up to Num and realize the plural feature -*men*. In (17b–c), Cl is occupied, so N-to-Num movement is blocked by the intervening Cl (the Head Movement Constraint) and the -*men* form is not possible. Importantly, however, bare nouns with -*men* must be interpreted as definite. Citing Rygaloff (1973) and Yorifuji (1976), Iljic (1994, 94) writes that "N-*men* always refers to the definite. As a rule, one can neither posit nor negate the existence of N-*men*."

(18) a. *you   ren-men   cf. you   ren
        have person-MEN   have person
        'there is/are some person(s)'
   b. *mei you   ren-men   cf. mei you   ren
        not have person-MEN   not have person
        'there is nobody'

(19) ta hui dai   xuesheng-men hui   jia
    he will bring student-MEN   back home
    'He will bring the students back home.'
    *'He will bring (some) students back home.'

As mentioned, a definite N-*men* is derived by moving N first through an empty Cl and then through Num to D, which has a [+definite] feature.[10] The definiteness requirement on N-*men*, however, does not follow straightforwardly from the movement account: if N-*men* is possible as long as no classifier is present and if an indefinite noun has a full nominal projection [D + Num + Cl + N] with the D hosting an existential quantifier (Longobardi 1994), N in this case can still be raised to Num to combine with -*men* and obtain an indefinite interpretation (see (17a)). The only difference between (17a) and an indefinite N-*men* would simply be the different contents of D. But this would be wrong, as N-*men* must always have a definite interpretation.

A solution to the problem of N-*men*'s definiteness requirement is as follows. We suggest that D should simply be a projection for [+definite], not hosting a default existential operator when [+definite] is not present as suggested by Longobardi (1994) for English and Romance languages.[11] An indefinite noun can simply be projected as an NP, not a DP.[12] It is licensed by an existential quantifier (via the existential closure discussed in Diesing 1992) or other available quantifier in the context, conforming to the general tendency in Chinese that the Restriction can be generated separate from the Quantification, as illustrated by the behavior of *wh*-words in this language. It should be noted again that indefinite NPs can still function like DPs with respect to binding and control.

(20) wo zhao xuesheng$_i$ [PRO$_i$ ba ziji$_i$ de jiaren   qing lai]
    I   find student   BA self DE family ask   come
    'I will find students to ask self's family to come.'

In brief, the morphological composition of *wh*-words and the distribution of -*men* in Chinese indicate that an NP can be generated in an argument position, as long as the NP is not a definite expression (recall that definite expressions require the generation of a [+definite] D). Regarding relativization, we note that the relativized nominal inside a relative clause is not a definite expression. Even when it is a proper name or a pronoun, it does not refer to the unique individual normally referred to by the proper name or the pronoun. Instead, it functions like a common noun (see Del Gobbo 2001 for the claim that relative clauses in Chinese cannot be appositives).

(21) ta xinshang de bali/ni   yijing bu fu   cunzai le
      he appreciate DE Paris/you already not again exist   LE
      'The Paris/you that he appreciates no longer exists.'

When an argument position allows an NP, relativization in Chinese can be a process of NP movement. That is, the nominal to be relativized is an NP. The licensing/interpretation of the NP can be delayed until it is combined with any external structures (external quantifier, Cl higher than the NP, etc.).[13] NP movement is a process allowed in a language like Chinese, which tends to generate the Quantification and the Restriction in separate positions and allows an indefinite nominal to be projected as an NP.

Having shown that NP movement is indeed licit, we turn next to the strategies available for deriving relative constructions. We have shown that NP Head raising is one option. In the following section, we consider base-generation and movement, or resumption and gaps, which will provide further evidence for the operation of both Head raising and operator movement in relativization.

6.2 Base-Generation

Recall from section 5.1 that, just like English, Chinese allows the Head to be an idiom chunk related to the matrix and not the relative clause. Compare, for instance, *He pulled the strings that got him the job* and (22a–b) (where the idioms are italicized).

(22) a. ta laoshi ai *chi* [[meiren shou-de-liao   de] *cu*]
         he always like *eat* nobody receive-able-complete DE *vinegar*
         'Lit. He always likes to eat vinegar that nobody can put up with.'
         'He always likes to be jealous to such a degree that is beyond what can be put up with.'

b. ta zhi hui *you* [[meiren ting-de-dong   de] *mo*]
   he only can *hu-* nobody listen-able-understand DE *-mor*
   'Lit. He can only hu- the -mor that nobody understands.'
   'He can only say humorous things that nobody can understand.'

This possibility for idioms suggests that direct NP movement is not the only option for deriving relative clauses, unless the assumption that an idiom is generated as a unit is abandoned. Therefore, it must be the case that the Head is not moved from within the relative clause. It can be base-generated. It is not surprising that base-generation of the Head is available to derive relative constructions. The second step of the derivation outlined in (3) can do without the statement "The NP can be a copy of an NP inside the CP." That is, the NP need not be a copy of an NP inside the relative CP. It can be a different lexical item in the numeration; therefore, base-generation is available.

Other evidence independently suggests that the Head of a relative clause is not always derived by movement. In the following examples, an overt pronoun occurs where the Head is interpreted in the relative clause; that is, the overt pronoun is a resumptive pronoun in the relative clause:

(23) a. *wo xiang kan [[ni   shuo meigeren$_j$ hui dai   ta$_i$ huilai de]
         I   want see   you say   everyone will bring him back DE
         [ziji$_j$ de pengyou]$_i$]
         self DE friend
         'I want to see self's friend that you said that everyone would bring back.'

     b. *wo xiang kan [[ni   shuo meigeren$_j$ hui dai   ta$_i$ huilai de]
         I   want see   you say   everyone will bring him back DE
         [wo yijing jieshao   gei ta$_j$ de pengyou]$_i$]
         I   already introduce to him DE friend
         'I want to see the friend that I have introduced to him that you said everyone would bring back.'

Reconstructing the Head back to the relative clause is not possible, as indicated by the unacceptability of the binding of the anaphor or the bound pronoun by the QP within the relative clause. This contrasts with the following cases where an empty category replaces the overt pronoun and reconstruction becomes possible:

(24) a. wo xiang kan [[ni   shuo meigeren$_j$ hui dai   Ø$_i$ huilai de]
         I   want see   you say everyone   will bring   back DE
         [ziji$_j$ de pengyou]$_i$]
          self DE friend
         'I want to see self's friend that you said that everyone would
         bring back.'

    b. wo xiang kan [[ni   shuo meigeren$_j$ hui dai   Ø$_i$ huilai de]
         I   want see   you say everyone   will bring   back DE
         [wo yijing   jieshao   gei ta$_j$ de pengyou]$_i$]
          I   already introduce to   him DE friend
         'I want to see the friend that I have introduced that you said
         everyone would bring back.'

(23), involving resumptive pronouns, can be made acceptable by not
forcing the reconstructed interpretation—in other words, if reconstruction does not apply. Thus, if the index of the resumptive pronoun is
changed (say, to k), the sentences are acceptable; so is the following sentence, which does not contain an anaphor or a bound pronoun:

(25) wo xiang kan [[ni   shuo zhang hui dai   ta$_i$ huilai de] [xiaohai]$_i$]
     I   want see   you say Zhang will bring him back   DE   child
     'I want to see the child that you said that Zhang would bring back.'

Moreover, the Head can be related to a resumptive pronoun in a position
inaccessible to movement—for example, inside an island.

(26) a. wo xiang kan [na-ge [ni [yinwei ta$_i$ bu hui lai]   hen
         I   want see   that-CL you because he not will come very
         shengqi de] [xuesheng]$_i$]
         angry   DE student
         'I want to see the student that you are angry because he would
         not come.'

    b. wo xiang kan [na-ge [ni yaoqing [dai ta$_i$ lai   de ren]
         I   want see   that-CL you invite   bring him come DE person
         lai   zher de] [xuesheng]$_i$]
         come here DE   student
         'I want to see the student that you invited the person over that
         brought him over.'

The acceptability of sentences like (26a–b) requires a base-generation
strategy to derive the relative construction. The following representa-

tion, where the pronoun is base-generated, is available to relative constructions:

(27) $[[_{CP} \ldots \text{pronoun}_i \ldots] [\text{Head}_i]]$

More precisely, it can be shown that the relative CP in (27) contains a relative operator. Chinese relatives with resumptive pronouns not only disallow reconstruction but also cannot contain a *wh*-interrogative. (28a) and (29a) show that a *wh*-interrogative phrase can occur inside a relative clause and be interpreted as having matrix scope when relativization leaves a gap (Head raising). The occurrence of a resumptive pronoun eliminates this possibility, as (28b) and (29b) show. Replacing the *wh*-interrogative with a name, as in (28c) and (29c), makes the sentences acceptable. These contrasts follow straightforwardly if the occurrence of a resumptive pronoun precludes the possibility of deriving the relative construction by Head raising and instead involves a *wh*-operator, creating a *wh*-island.[14]

(28) a. shei xihuan [[shei dasuan qing $\emptyset_i$ lai   yanjiang de] zuojia$_i$]
          who like   who plan   ask   come talk   DE author
          'Who likes the author that who planned to ask $\emptyset$ to come to talk?'

     b. *shei xihuan [[shei dasuan qing ta$_i$ lai   yanjiang de] zuojia$_i$]
          who like   who plan   ask   him come talk   DE author
          'Who likes the author that who planned to ask him to come to talk?'

     c. shei xihuan [[zhangsan dasuan qing ta$_i$ lai   yanjiang de]
          who like   Zhangsan plan   ask   him come talk   DE
          zuojia$_i$]
          author
          'Who likes the author that Zhangsan planned to ask him to come to talk?'

(29) a. shei kandao-le [[shei shuo $\emptyset_i$ mingtian yao biaoyan de]
          who saw   who say   tomorrow will perform DE
          yanyuan$_i$]
          actor
          'Who saw the actor that who said would perform tomorrow?'

     b. *shei kandao-le [[shei shuo ta$_i$ mingtian yao biaoyan de]
          who saw   who say he tomorrow will perform DE
          yanyuan$_i$]
          actor

'Who saw the actor that who said he would perform
tomorrow?'

   c.   shei kandao-le [[zhangsan shuo ta$_i$ mingtian   yao biaoyan de]
       who saw   Zhangsan say   he tomorrow will perform DE
       yanyuan$_i$]
       actor
       'Who saw the actor that Zhangsan said he would perform
       tomorrow?'

We therefore conclude that when a resumptive pronoun occurs, the
structure is base-generated and involves a (base-generated) operator;
when a gap occurs, the structure is derived by movement of the Head.
The distinction is supported by reconstruction possibilities. Is this correlation always true? For instance, we noted in chapter 4 that a gap can be
the result of operator movement in LA and English. The operator is in a
predication/agreement relation with a base-generated Head. In such
structures, reconstruction of the Head is not available although a gap
appears in the relative clause. We showed above that sentences like those
in (28) and (29) containing resumptive pronouns support the existence of
a relative operator. In the next section, we show further that operator
movement must be available to derive relative constructions in Chinese,
on the basis of evidence from relativization of an adjunct.

6.3 NP versus Adjunct

In Chinese relative constructions, an adjunct as well as an argument can
be relativized. Chinese has the same relativization possibilities as English
(see (30)–(31)). That is, Chinese has all the counterparts of English *wh*-
relatives.

(30) a. the man *who* came here
      b. the work *which* he did
      c. the way (?*)*how*/*that* he fixed the car[15]
      d. the reason *why* he left

(31) a. lai   zher de ren
         come here DE man
         'the man who came here'

      b. ta zuo de gongzuo
         he do DE work
         'the work which he did'

   c. ta xiu che de fangfa
     he fix car DE way
     'the way that he fixed the car'
   d. ta likai de yuanyin
     he leave DE reason
     'the reason why he left'

For argument relativization, we demonstrated that (31a–b) can be derived by NP movement to the Head position. For adjunct relativization, however, what is relativized is not an NP category. Rather, it is a PP or Adv, as indicated by the following corresponding nonrelative cases:[16]

(32) a. ta *yong na   fangfa* xiu che
      he with that method fix car
      'He fixed the car in that way.'
   b. ta *yinwei   na-ge   yuanyin* likai
     he because that-CL reason   leave
     'He left because of that reason.'

Note that the Head in the adjunct relativization examples is a nominal expression, not an Adv or a PP (see section 4.5). An Adv cannot become an NP after movement. Moreover, a PP cannot be moved directly to the NP Head position. It cannot be correct that the object of P is moved directly to the Head position and the P is subsequently deleted. As Ning (1993) points out, there is an interesting contrast between topicalization and relativization in Chinese with respect to the distribution of prepositions.[17] In contrast to relativization of the object of P in cases like (31c–d), which is acceptable (see (33)), topicalization in the same cases is not acceptable without the P (cf. (34) and (35)).

(33) a. ta xiu hao na-bu che de fangfa
      he fix well that-CL car DE way
      'the way he fixed that car'
   b. ta bu xiu che de yuanyin
     he not fix car DE reason
     'the reason he does not fix cars'

(34) a. *na-ge   fangfa, ta xiu hao na-bu che
      that-CL way   he fix well that-CL car
      'That way, he fixed that car.'
   b. *na-ge   yuanyin, ta bu xiu che
     that-CL reason   he not fix car
     'That reason, he does not fix cars.'

(35) a. wei na   yuanyin, ta bu xiu che
         for that reason   he not fix car
         'For that reason, he does not fix cars.'
     b. yong na-ge   fangfa, ta xiu hao na-bu   che
         use   that-CL way   he fix well that-CL car
         'In that way, he fixed that car.'

Because of this contrast between relativization and topicalization, Ning (1993) argues that topicalization is derived by directly raising the topic phrase, which can be a PP, to the peripheral position. When the adjunct is a PP, adjunct topicalization requires the entire PP to appear in the peripheral position. Relativization, on the other hand, is not derived by direct XP movement. Instead, it is derived by movement of a null operator as proposed by Chomsky (1977b). The operator is equivalent to a *wh*-operator in English. That is, with respect to adjuncts, the operator can be the equivalent of a PP, as is evident in English question/answer pairs involving *how* and *why*.[18]

(36) a. *How* did you do it? *With care.*
     b. *Why* did you do it? *For you.*

The operator is moved to the Spec of Comp of the relative clause and the Head is base-generated in its surface position. The operator is then interpreted with the Head via some interpretive mechanism, such as predication. Alternatively, the operator is licensed by being in an agreement relation with the Head: the two agree in ϕ-features and, most likely, some substantive features such as [+human], [+place], [+time]. This process captures the strict co-occurrence between matching Head and operator expressions: *the person who, the thing which, the reason why*, and so on (see section 4.4).

(37) [[$_{CP}$ Op$_i$ [$_{IP}$ ... t$_i$ ...]] Head$_i$]

In this representation, the trace is derived by movement of a null operator, not by movement of the Head, which is base-generated in its surface position.

   In short, if the Head is directly moved from the relative clause, the Head and the gap in the relative clause must be of the same category. The fact that the Head is an NP indicates that what is moved is an NP, and consequently the gap is an NP. Clearly, an NP is not a PP or Adv. In contrast, an operator moved to the Spec of Comp can be the equivalent of a PP or Adv. Accordingly, when the gap is equivalent to a PP or Adv, it cannot be derived by NP movement to the Head position. Instead, it is derived by operator movement to the Spec of Comp (see sections 4.4–4.5). That is, even though NP relativization and PP/Adv relativization both derive a gap in the relative clause, and even though in both cases the Head is an NP, the two gaps behave differently with respect to reconstruction. In the NP relativization cases, the gap in the relative clause is the trace derived by NP movement to the Head position.[19] Reconstruction of the relative Head is possible. In contrast, the gap in the PP/Adv relativization cases is not a trace derived by NP movement to the Head position, but a trace of the moved *wh*-operator. Therefore, reconstruction of the Head to the gap position should not be possible. In brief:

(38) a. *NP relativization*

$[[_{CP}[_{IP} \dots [_{NP} t_i] \dots]] [_{Head} NP]_i]$

- direct NP movement to Head
- reconstruction of Head to t possible

b. *Adjunct relativization*

$[[_{CP} Op_i [_{IP} \dots [_{PP} t_i] \dots]] [_{Head} NP]]$

- Head base-generated, operator movement to the Spec of Comp
- reconstruction of Head to t impossible

The distinction with respect to the availability of reconstruction is indeed true. In contrast to the argument relativization cases in (39) and (40), which allow reconstruction, the adjunct relativization cases in (41a) and (42a) do not show reconstruction effects. That (41a) and (42a) are unacceptable owing to lack of reconstruction is supported by the contrast between these sentences and (41b), (42b), which show that binding into a 'how'/'why' expression is possible in appropriate contexts, and (41c), (42c), which show that, when the Head is a method or reason expression, it can have a modifier (a *de* phrase).

(39) *Relativization from subject position*

wo yijing   kandaole [[meige xuesheng$_i$ dou renwei zui   hao de]
I   already saw   every student   all   think most good DE
ni gei ta$_i$ de liwu]
you give him DE present
'I already saw the present that you gave to him that everyone thought was the best.'

(40) *Relativization from object position*
      ni   hui kandao [[wo xiwang meige xuesheng$_i$ dou neng dai   lai
      you will see   I   hope   every student   all can bring come
      de] wo gei ta$_i$ de liwu]
      DE I   give him DE present
      'You will see the present that I gave to him$_i$ that I hope every
      student$_i$ will bring.'

(41) a. *Relativization of 'how' expressions*
         *[[wo xiwang meigeren$_i$ dou neng xiu-hao che de] wo jiao   ta$_i$
           I ` hope   everyone all can fix-well car DE I   teach him
         de fangfa]
         DE method
         'the way that I taught him that I hope everyone can fix the
         cars'
     b. wo xiwang meigeren$_i$ dou neng yong wo jiao ta$_i$ de fangfa
         I   hope   everyone all can use   I   teach him DE method
         xiu-hao che
         fix-well car
         'I hope everyone will use the method that I teach him to fix
         cars.'
     c. [[wo xiwang ta neng xiu-hao che de] (na-ge) wo shi-guo de
           I   hope   he can fix-well car DE that-CL I   try-ASP DE
         fangfa]
         method
         'the way that I tried before that I hope he can fix the cars'

(42) a. *Relativization of 'why' expressions*
         *[[wo yiwei   meigeren$_i$ dou bu neng lai   de] ni   gaosu ta$_i$
           I   thought everyone all not can come DE you tell   his
         mama de yuanyin]
         mother DE reason
         'the reason that you told his mother that I thought everyone
         cannot come'
     b. meigeren$_i$ dou yiwei wo yinwei ta$_i$ mama bu yunxu mei
         everyone   all think I   because his mother not permit not
         lai
         come
         'Everyone thought I did not come because his mother did not
         permit (me) to.'

    c. [[wo yiwei   ta bu neng lai   de] (na-ge) ta mama zhidao
         I   thought he not can   come DE   that-CL he mother know
         de yuanyin]
         DE reason
         'the reason that his mother knows that I thought he cannot
         come'

On the other hand, we expect the derivations in (38) to be subject to island conditions because they are derived by movement. This is also true. The following examples show that adjunct relativization cannot leave a gap inside an island, even though a long-distance dependency is allowed:

(43) a. zhe jiu   shi [[ta renwei [ni   yinggai t_i/(zenme$_i$) zuo zhejian
       this exactly is   he think you should   how   do this
       shi   de]] fangfa$_i$]
       matter DE method
       'This is the way that he thinks you should do this work.'
    b. zhe jiu   shi [[ta renwei [nimen t_i/(weishenme$_i$) yinggai likai]
       this exactly is   he think you   why   should leave
       de] yuanyin$_i$]
       DE reason
       'This is the reason why he thinks you should leave.'

(44) a. *zhe jiu   shi [[[[ta xihuan [t_i zuo zhejian shi]   de] ren]
       this exactly is   he like   do this   matter DE person
       de] fangfa$_i$]
       DE method
       'This is the way that he likes the person that does the work
       (how).'
    b. *zhe jiu   shi [[[[ruguo ta t_i shengqi] ni hui bu gaoxing] de]
       this exactly is   if   he angry   you will not happy   DE
       yuanyin$_i$]
       reason
       'This is the reason(x) that you will not be happy if he gets
       angry (because of) x.'

For cases with an argument gap, even though there are instances that may suggest that relativization does not obey island conditions, the violation always involves an island in the subject position (or a topic position; see Gasde and Paul 1996); see Huang 1982.

(45) [[[t$_i$ chuan de] yifu]   hen piaoling de] na-ge   ren$_i$
        wear DE clothes very pretty   DE that-CL person
      'the person$_i$ that the clothes he$_i$ wears is pretty.'

When the island is in the object position, the effect of island conditions reappears.

(46) *[wo xihuan [[t$_i$ chuan de] yifu]   de] na-ge   ren$_i$
         I   like   wear DE clothes DE that-CL person
      'the person$_i$ that I like the clothes he$_i$ wears'

Certainly, we do not want to claim that island conditions are relevant in some cases but not in others. The acceptability of (45) should be due to some derivation other than movement. This is exactly what Huang (1982) argues. He claims that Chinese allows an empty pro, which is subject to an identification condition: namely, it must be identified by the most local c-commanding antecedent. In (45), the most local c-commanding antecedent is the relative Head. In (46), the most local c-commanding antecedent is the subject of the relative clause. Thus, a pro is properly identified in (45) but not in (46). The contrast between (45) and (46) argues for the relevance of island conditions when movement applies and the existence of a properly bound pro when movement does not apply.

Furthermore, a pro is a nominal element, not a PP/Adv. It is not surprising that adjunct relativization does not allow an empty form in any island context, including a position that falls under the Subject Condition.

(47) a. *zhe jiu   shi [[[ta e$_i$ xiu che] hen rang women gaoxing] de
         this exactly is   he   fix car very let   us   happy   DE
         fangfa$_i$]
         method
         'This is the method that it makes us happy that he fixed the car
         (with it).'
      b. *zhe jiu   shi [[[ta e$_i$ nian-wan shu] hen zhongyao de]
         this exactly is   he   read-finish book very important DE
         yuanyin$_i$]
         reason
         'This is the reason that it is important that he finishes his
         studies (there).'

In brief, relativization can be derived by movement of an NP directly to the Head position. Reconstruction of the Head is possible in such cases. In the case of adjunct relativization, direct movement to the Head is not possible because of categorial mismatch. Such a structure is derived by operator movement to the Spec of Comp, which is interpreted with the Head via some interpretive mechanism (such as predication/agreement). There is no movement relation between the Head and the gap in the relative clause. Reconstruction of the Head to the gap position inside the relative clause therefore is not possible. The NP and adjunct relativization cases in (38) do share one similarity, however: they are subject to island conditions, because they are both derived by movement.

6.4 Null Operator, Null Head

The different relative constructions and their properties can be summarized as follows:

(48) *NP relativization*
   a. $[[_{CP}[_{IP} \ldots [_{NP} t_i] \ldots]] [_{Head} NP]_i]$
      - direct NP movement to Head
      - reconstruction of Head to t possible
      - sensitive to island conditions
   b. $[[_{CP} Op_i [_{IP} \ldots [_{NP} pronoun_i] \ldots]] [_{Head} NP]_i]$
      - Head base-generated, operator in the Spec of Comp coindexed with a resumptive pronoun
      - reconstruction of Head to resumptive pronoun impossible
      - resumptive pronoun acceptable within an island

(49) *Adjunct relativization*
   $[[_{CP} Op_i [_{IP} \ldots [_{PP} t_i] \ldots]] [_{Head} NP]]$
   - Head base-generated, operator movement to the Spec of Comp
   - reconstruction of Head to t impossible
   - sensitive to island conditions

Although we draw the main distinction between NP relativization and adjunct relativization according to what is relativized, another possible distinction is between (48a) on the one hand and (48b) and (49) on the other. The former involves direct movement of the relativized expression to the Head position (Head raising) and the latter involve an operator. This distinction is supported by three quite interesting facts that have not previously been discussed. First, (48a) and (48b)/(49) can be distinguished by the availability of reconstruction, as shown earlier. Second, they can also be distinguished by the relevance of an island effect. Thus, just as the use of a resumptive pronoun creates an island, in contrast to the lack of an island when a relative construction is derived by Head movement, as illustrated in (28) and (29), adjunct relativization also exhibits island effects. This is illustrated by the not-quite-acceptable (50a) and (50c), adjunct relativization cases where a *wh*-phrase occurs inside a relative clause, contrasting with the acceptable (50b) and (50d), argument relativization cases where a *wh*-phrase occurs inside a relative clause.

(50) a. ??ta zhidao [[ni   zai nar   xiu che de] yuanyin]
         he know   you at where fix car DE reason
         'He knows the reason you fixed the car where?'

     b. ta xihuan [[ni   zai nar   xiu de] che]
         he like   you at there fix DE car
         'He likes the car you fixed where?'

     c. ??shei tingdao-le [[ni   jiao shei   xiu che] de yuanyin]
         who heard   you ask whom fix car DE reason
         'Who heard the reason you asked whom to fix the car?'

     d. shei kandao-le [[ni   jiao shei   xiu] de che]
         who saw   you ask whom fix   DE car
         'Who saw the car you asked whom to fix?'

A third interesting difference is reflected in a contrast that has important implications with respect to how null Heads of relative constructions should be analyzed: relative constructions derived by Head movement allow the Head to take a null form but those involving an operator do not.[20] That is, cases of adjunct relativization and resumption do not allow a null Head. The following examples illustrate the NP/adjunct contrast:

(51) a. lai   zher de Ø
         come here DE
         '(the one) that came here'

     b. ta zuo de Ø
         he do DE
         '(the thing) that he did'

     c. *ta xiu che de Ø
         he fix car DE
         '(the way) that he fixed the car'

     d. *ta likai de Ø
         he leave DE
         '(the reason) that he left'

The following examples illustrate the unacceptability of a null Head in relatives with resumption:

(52) *wo xiang kan [[ni   shuo zhang hui dai   ta$_i$ huilai de] Ø$_i$]
     I   want see   you say   Zhang will bring him back   DE
     'I want to see (the one) that you said that Zhang would bring back.'

(53) a. *wo xiang kan [[ni   [yinwei ta$_i$ bu lai]   hen shengqi de] Ø$_i$]
         I   want see   you because he not come very angry   DE
         'I want to see (the one) that you are angry because he would not come.'

   b. *wo xiang kan [[ni   yaoqing [dai   ta$_i$ lai   de ren]   lai
      I   want see   you invite   bring him come DE person come
      zher de] Ø$_i$]
      here DE
      'I want to see (the one) that you invited the person that brought him over.'

Note that it is not the case that 'how' and 'why' expressions (see (51c–d)) cannot take a null form. As long as a relative clause does not occur, a modifier can precede an empty Head.[21]

(54) a. [[ta xiu che de] fangfa] bi   [[wo xiu che de] fangfa] hao
         he fix car DE method compare I   fix car DE method good
         'The way he fixes cars is better than the way I fix cars.'

   b. *[[ta xiu che de] fangfa] bi   [[wo xiu che de] Ø] hao
      he fix car DE method compare I   fix car DE   good
      'The way he fixes cars is better than (the way) I fix cars.'

   c. [[ta xiu che de] fangfa] bi   [[wo de] Ø] hao
      he fix car DE method compare I   DE   good
      'The way he fixes cars is better than mine.'

The acceptability of (54c) contrasts with the unacceptability of (54b): when the modifier is a nominal phrase, not a relative clause, the modified Head can take a null form. The following examples further illustrate this point:

(55) a. [[ta bu neng lai   de] yuanyin] wo zhidao; [[ni   bu neng
         he not can come DE reason   I   know   you not can
         lai   de] yuanyin] ne
         come DE reason   Q

'The reason that he cannot come, I know; how about the
reason you cannot come?'
   b. *[[ta bu neng lai   de] yuanyin] wo zhidao; [[ni   bu neng
        he not can   come DE reason I   know   you not can
      lai   de] Ø] ne
      come DE   Q
      'The reason that he cannot come, I know; how about (the
      reason) you cannot come?'
   c. [[ta bu neng lai   de] yuanyin] wo zhidao; [[ni   de] Ø] ne
        he not can   come DE reason I   know   you DE   Q
      'The reason that he cannot come, I know; how about yours?'

Because the unacceptable cases are those involving an operator, it is possible that this contrast is due to requirements on the relative operator: a
relative operator needs to be identified, in the sense that some content
(restriction) needs to be provided for it to be interpreted. A null form
does not have enough content to identify the null operator. Alternatively,
under the matching analysis, the operator needs to match the Head with
respect to features, such as [person], [number], [human], [place], [time].
However, an empty Head, lacking lexical content, does not have all of
these features. In contrast, for relatives derived by NP movement, a null
form (not an operator) can be base-generated and moved to the Head
position. No operator needs to be identified. A null Head, therefore, is
acceptable in such cases. Similarly, a null Head is acceptable in cases
where the modifier is not a relative clause; hence, no operator is involved
and no matching/identification of the operator is required, as shown in
(54)–(55).

6.5   Resumptive Adjuncts

There is further evidence showing that relativization in Chinese indeed
can be derived by operator movement. This comes from relative clauses
containing an in-situ 'why', the relative Head being the noun 'reason'. To
a certain degree, 'how' behaves the same way.[22]

Weishenme 'why' and *zenme* 'how' exhibit interesting behavior in Chinese relatives. They can occur "resumptively" within the relative clause
when the Head is *yuanyin/liyou* 'reason' for 'why', *fangfa* 'method'/*yangzi*
'manner' for 'how'. Other *wh*-words cannot be used this way.

(56) a. ?ta *ruhe/zenme*$_i$ xiu che de fangfa$_i$, meiren zhidao
he how   fix car DE method nobody know
'Nobody knows the way (how) he fixed the car.'

b. ta *weishenme*$_i$ bu lai   de yuanyin$_i$, meiren zhidao
he why   not come DE reason   nobody know
'Nobody knows why he didn't come.'

c. ni   kandao ta$_i$/*shei$_i$ mama de xiaohai$_i$
you see   he/who   mother DE child
'the child whose mother you saw'

d. *ni   zai shenme shihou$_i$ lai   de shihou$_i$
you at what   time   come DE time
'the time when you came at what time'

These in-situ *wh*-words can be related to the Head noun across clausal
boundaries.

(57) a. ?zhe jiu   shi [[ta juede [ni   yinggai *ruhe/zenme*$_i$ xiu che] de]
this exactly is   he feel   you should how   fix car DE
fangfa$_i$]
method
'This is the way$_i$ (how$_i$) he feels you should fix the car t$_i$.'

b. zhe jiu   shi [[women yiwei   [ta *weishenme*$_i$ mei lai]   de]
this exactly is   we   thought he why   not come DE
yuanyin$_i$]
reason
'This is the reason$_i$ why$_i$ we thought he did not come t$_i$.'

However, they cannot occur inside an island.

(58) a. *zhe jiu   shi [[[ruguo ta *weishenme*$_i$ shengqi] ni   hui bu
this exactly is   if   he why   angry   you will not
gaoxing de] yuanyin$_i$]
happy DE reason
'This is the reason that you will not be happy if he gets angry
why.'

b. *zhe jiu   shi [[[ruguo ta *zenme*$_i$ xiu che] ni   hui bu gaoxing
this exactly is   if   he how   fix car   you will not happy
de] fangfa$_i$]
DE method
'This is the way that you will not be happy if he fixes cars
how.'

What is such an in-situ *wh* and why is it restricted to 'why' and, to a certain extent, 'how'? We suggest below that the *wh*-words that can stay in situ are those that less easily behave like indefinite pronouns (or indeterminates—Kuroda 1965; Nishigauchi 1990; Cheng 1991; Li 1992; Tsai 1994).[23]

As mentioned in sections 3.4 and 6.1.2, in Chinese a *wh*-word generally is not inherently an interrogative. It can have noninterrogative interpretations, such as existential or universal readings depending on context. We therefore proposed that a Chinese *wh*-word is interpreted according to its licenser, which can be a universal quantifier, an existential quantifier, or an interrogative. The following sentences illustrate the versatility of *shenme* 'what' in various contexts:

(59) a. ta mei zuo shenme
    he not do what
    'He did nothing.'

  b. ni   zuole shenme ma
    you did   what   Q
    'Did you do something?'

  c. wo yiwei   ta zuole shenme
    I   thought he did   what
    'I thought he did something.'

  d. ruguo ni   xihuan shenme, wo jiu   ba ta mai-xialai
    if   you like   what   I   then BA it buy-down
    'If you like something, I will buy it.'

  e. ni   xihuan shenme, wo jiu   mai shenme
    you like   what   I   then buy what
    'I will buy what you like.'

However, 'why' and to a certain extent 'how' do not occur in such contexts as easily.[24]

(60) a. *ta hui weishenme hen hao ming   ma
     he will why   very good fortune Q
     'Will he get lucky for some reason?'

  b. ??ta hui zenme xiu che ma
     he will how   fix car Q
     'Will he fix cars in some way?'

(61) a. *ruguo ta weishenme hao ming, ni   jiu   hui yinwei
        if   he why   good fortune you then will because
        na-ge   yuanyin hao ming
        that-CL reason   good fortune
     b. *ruguo ta zenme xiu che, ni   jiu   yinggai yong na-ge   fangfa
        if   he how   fix car you then should use   that-CL method
        xiu che
        fix car

The *wh*-phrases in cases like (59a–e) are viewed as variables or polarity items bound/licensed by some quantifier in the context. The much narrower distribution of 'why' ('how') indicates that these are the least variable-like of the *wh*-words in Chinese. That is, they are more like operators and can function as relative operators in this language. As such, they undergo movement at LF to the Spec of Comp of the relative clause (the *wh*-operator movement analysis).[25] This accounts for the locality condition on the distribution of *wh*-words such as those in (57)–(58). The other *wh*-phrases (except 'how', which seems to fall between the two groups) are never operators themselves. They therefore do not have the same distribution as 'why' and 'how' and do not undergo movement at LF. 'Why' and 'how' inside a relative clause are therefore more like in-situ relative operators, like those found in Hindi.

The existence of such constructions provides clear evidence that operator movement can derive relative clauses in Chinese. The locality condition is indicative of movement. The lack of reconstruction in such cases argues that movement does not take place directly to the Head position.

(62) *[[wo yiwei meigeren$_i$ dou yijing   zhidao ni   weishenme$_j$ likai de]
      I   think everyone all   already know you why   leave DE
      [gen ta$_i$de yiyang de yuanyin]$_j$]
      with his   same   DE reason
      'the reason that was the same as his that I thought everyone
      already knew you left why'

Moreover, the Head in these *wh*-operator cases cannot be null. The operator needs to be identified/agree with a head in all relevant features.

(63) a. ?ta *ruhe/zenme*$_i$ xiu che de Ø, meiren zhidao
        he how   fix car DE   nobody know
        'Nobody knows the (way) (how) he fixed the car.'

    b. *ta *weishenme*ᵢ bu lai   de Ø, meiren zhidao
       he why   not come DE   nobody know
       'Nobody knows the (reason) why he didn't come.'

Therefore, this pattern is just like the adjunct relativization cases discussed in the previous sections. Both are derived by operator movement
to the Spec of Comp.

6.6 Gapless Structures

To complete our discussion of the strategies used to derive relative constructions, we would like to briefly look at so-called gapless relative
structures in Chinese—those without a gap or a resumptive pronoun in
the relative clause. Consider the following examples:

(64) a. zhe jiu   shi [[ta kao-shi   de] jieguo]
       this exactly is   he take-exam DE result
       'This is the result of his exam-taking.'
    b. zhe jiu   shi [[ta chang-ge de] shengyin]
       this exactly is   he sing-song DE voice/sound
       'This is his singing voice/sound.'
    c. zhe jiu   shi [[ta zuo-e de] houguo]
       this exactly is   he do-evil DE consequence
       'This is the consequence of his evildoing.'
    d. zhe jiu   shi [[ta sha zhe-ge xiaohai de] jiama]
       this exactly is   he kill this-CL child   DE price
       'This is the price for his killing the child.'

In such instances, the relative Head cannot be related to any position
within the relative clause. Specifically, the Head noun must be related to
the entire relative clause; it cannot be related just to an embedded clause.
Therefore, (65a) and (65b) are unacceptable because 'the voice' and 'the
consequence', respectively, cannot be related to the embedded clause
within the relative clause.

(65) a. *zhe jiu   shi [[wo xihuan [ta chang-ge] de] shengyin]
       this exactly is   I like   he sing-song DE voice
       'This is the voice of my liking him singing.'
    b. *zhe jiu   shi [[wo ting-shuo [ta zuo-e] de] houguo]
       this exactly is   I   hear-say he do-evil DE consequence
       'This is the consequence of my hearing him do evil.'

This type of "relative clause" in fact may not be the typical relative clause that linguists are familiar with. More concretely, we note that this pattern, rather than being a counterpart of the English [Head + Relative Clause], is more like the English Head noun + preposition + XP (a PP) (i.e., [NP [P XP]]), such as [*the price* [*for his killing the boy*]], [*the sound* [*of his singing*]], [*the consequence* [*of his evildoing*]]. Just as in these English cases, where the entire PP bears a direct relation to the Head noun, so in (64)–(65) the Head noun must be related to the entire "relative clause," rather than a subpart of it (such as an embedded clause, as in (65)).[26] (65a–b) can be contrasted with (66a–b), which also contain embedded clauses but are acceptable. They are acceptable because the voice/sound is related to the voice/sound of my imagination (of his singing) and the consequence is related to my liking him to do evil.[27]

(66) a. zhe jiu   shi [[wo xiangxiang ta chang-ge de] shengyin]
        this exactly is   I   imagine   he sing-song DE voice
        'This is the sound of my imagining him singing.'
     b. zhe jiu   shi [[wo xihuan ta zuo-e de] houguo]
        this exactly is   I   like   he do-evil DE consequence
        'This is the consequence of my liking him to do evil.'

6.7 Chain Binding?

Having discussed the properties of different types of relative constructions, we are now ready to show that the reconstruction facts manifested in Chinese relative constructions must be correlated with NP movement (vs. DP movement) and cannot be due to other nonmovement strategies such as chain binding (Barss 1986; Cecchetto and Chierchia 1999).

Recall that Chinese relative constructions exhibit reconstruction effects with respect to binding but not scope. The same discrepancy has been noted for different constructions in other languages, and an account based on the notion of chain binding has been proposed. For example, Cecchetto and Chierchia (1999) note a certain inconsistency in reconstruction effects in clitic left-dislocation constructions in Italian.

(67) *A casa   di *Leo*, *pro* (ci)   va   volentieri.
      to the.house of Leo (he) (there) goes with.pleasure

(68) In qualche cassetto, Leo ci   tiene ogni carta
     in some   drawer   Leo there keeps every paper
     importante. (∃∀ *but* *∀∃)
     important
     'Every important document Leo keeps in some drawer.'

(67) shows that reconstruction must take place since it interacts with binding theory (Principle C in this case), and (68) shows that reconstruction does not take place for scope interaction. Cecchetto and Chierchia's account for PP dislocation in such cases involves base-generating the PP in its surface position, which is related to a clitic. The distribution of the clitic is subject to certain locality conditions in relation to the PP. The clitic must move to sentence-initial position in order to be interpreted. This is what derives the locality constraints on the distribution of such clitics. To account for the Principle C effects with PP dislocation, Cecchetto and Chierchia appeal to the concept of chain binding, adapting ideas developed by Barss (1986). *Chain* as adopted by Cecchetto and Chierchia is defined as in (69) and chain binding as in (70).

(69) A chain $\langle \beta_1, \ldots, \beta_n \rangle$ is a sequence of nodes sharing the same θ-role such that for any i, $1 \leq i \leq n$, β_i c-commands and is coindexed with β_{i+1}. (p. 140)

(70) In a chain $\langle XP_1, \ldots, XP_n \rangle$ when a phrase YP c-commands a link XP_i of the chain, it counts for the purposes of binding theory as if it c-commanded every link of the chain. (p. 139)

Cecchetto and Chierchia account for the contrast between (67) and (68) by appealing to the assumption that chain binding interacts with binding theory but not with scope. If this were true, the reconstruction facts concerning Chinese relative constructions would not argue for the distinction between NP movement and DP movement, as we proposed.

Choueiri (2002, chap. 3), however, argues that Cecchetto and Chierchia's generalizations are not quite correct. She observes that the cases where chain binding seems to interact with binding theory are actually based on incorrect assumptions about the structural position of the relevant elements. When the correct structural positions are clarified, chain binding in fact does not interact with binding theory. For reasons of space, we do not repeat Choueiri's arguments and examples here (but see her section 3.3.2). Instead, we would like to claim that different reconstruction effects manifested in various Chinese relative constructions provide strong empirical evidence against a chain-binding account.

Recall that relative constructions derived by different processes exhibit different reconstruction effects. Whereas relative constructions in Chinese derived by Head raising exhibit reconstruction effects with respect to binding but not scope, those derived by operator movement (such as those involving adjuncts or resumptive pronouns) show no reconstruction effects at all. Nonetheless, a chain is still formed in cases derived by operator movement, according to Barss and to Cecchetto and Chierchia, as well as in cases where movement applies. Were chain binding to interact with binding theory, the contrast in reconstruction effects between relatives derived by Head raising and those derived by operator movement could not be accounted for.

6.8   Summary

In this chapter, we have argued that an NP-raising relativization process operating on an adjunction structure is licit if the condition on movement applies derivationally, an account that has the advantage of not making adjunction an exception to the extension condition governing movement. This derivational view of movement constraints argues that derivation must play a role in grammar, in addition to representations. In other words, some conditions apply in the process of derivation and others apply to representations. Both are necessary to the grammar.

Moreover, our analysis demonstrates that an NP (Restriction) in Chinese can be generated in an argument position. This possibility is supported not only by reconstruction facts concerning relative constructions but also by the behavior of *wh*-phrases and the distribution of the plural marker *-men* in this language. The relativized NP is interpreted when it is associated with the external D, as in English, and Cl or a quantifier outside the relative construction, as in Chinese.

The types of derivations available can be summarized according to what is relativized: NP relativization versus adjunct relativization. We have also established that gapless structures differ from NP and adjunct relativization structures with respect to locality conditions.

(71) *NP relativization*

    a. $[[_{CP}[_{IP} \dots [t_i] \dots]] [_{Head} NP]_i]$

        · direct NP movement to Head

        · reconstruction of the Head to t possible

        · sensitive to island conditions

b. [[$_{CP}$ Op$_i$ [$_{IP}$ ... [pronoun$_i$] ...]] [$_{Head}$ NP]$_i$]
  - Head base-generated and coindexed with an operator related to a base-generated pronoun
  - reconstruction of the Head impossible
  - occurrence of the pronoun within an island acceptable

(72) *Adjunct relativization*

[[$_{CP}$ Op$_i$ [$_{IP}$ ... [t$_i$] ...]] [$_{Head}$ NP]$_i$]
  - Head base-generated, operator movement to the Spec of Comp
  - reconstruction of the Head to t impossible
  - sensitive to island conditions

(73) *Gapless structures*

[[gapless clause] *de* Head]
  - no gap or pronoun
  - strict locality conditions (Head cannot be related only to an embedded clause)

Among these patterns, NP movement to the Head directly contrasts with relative constructions involving an operator, in terms of reconstruction (un)availability, the (lack of) manifestation of *wh*-island effects, and the (un)acceptability of a null Head (section 6.4). The contrast in reconstruction effects also argues against a chain-binding approach to the difference in the availability of reconstruction with respect to binding and scope.

The available patterns and derivations also demonstrate that Chinese relativization confirms the conclusion reached in chapter 4: both a Head-raising process and an operator movement process must be available to derive relative constructions. That is, this conclusion holds in both Head-initial languages with a complementation structure, such as English, and Head-final languages with an adjunction structure, such as Chinese. Nonetheless, there are significant differences between Chinese and English: Head raising is NP movement in the former but DP movement in the latter. Clearly, both options cannot apply equally in these two types of languages; if they did, the differences in reconstruction effects discussed in chapters 4 and 5 would not be accounted for. Why is there such a difference between NP and DP movement? How does a language choose which option to take? How should language variation be defined? We now turn to these issues regarding language universals and language variation.

Chapter 7

Typology of Relativization

We have discussed the structures and derivations of various types of relative constructions in English, LA, and Chinese. We noted that relative constructions in different languages and even within a single language exhibit different reconstruction effects: DP reconstruction, NP reconstruction, or no reconstruction at all. Such empirical differences require different analyses: relative constructions can be derived differently both within a language and crosslinguistically. They differ in the presence or absence of movement; they differ in what is moved; and they differ in where the moved element lands. Moreover, as we have shown, Head-initial relative constructions in English and LA have a complementation structure, [$_{DP}$ D CP], and the Head-final relative construction in Chinese has an adjunction structure [$_{NP}$ CP NP].

Clearly, the structures and mechanisms needed to derive relative constructions are not uniform across languages or within a language. The following theoretical questions arise: Is there a universal relative construction in Universal Grammar? If so, what are its properties? How and/or why does a language choose among the available options (complementation vs. adjunction, the variations on what moves where)? In this chapter, we seek to answer these questions. We will approach them from the two domains we have been focusing on: structure and derivation. We will show that, at least with the theoretical mechanisms currently available, some further refined analyses are yet to come. Moreover, the empirical differences among relative constructions cannot be captured either by a uniform structure (section 7.1) or by a uniform derivational process (section 7.2). The variations, however, are not random. They follow from the general morphological and syntactic properties of the individual languages and constructions, which are also reflected in the variations in forming *wh*-interrogatives. At this point, to help define the range of variation, we will consider more languages of different types.

7.1   Universal Structure?

As mentioned, English and LA relative constructions have been argued to instantiate a complementation structure: D taking a CP complement. However, for Chinese relative constructions, not only is there no positive evidence for the complementation structure, there is in fact direct evidence for the need to adopt an adjunction structure.

Now, if Chinese cannot simply adopt the complementation structure, can we address the issue of universal structures from the reverse perspective and claim that all languages adopt the adjunction structure for relative constructions? This is, in fact, what Fukui and Takano (2000) attempt to do, arguing that a language with a Head-initial relative construction (English) and a language with a Head-final relative construction (Japanese) both have the same structure for relative constructions. They purportedly differ only in the presence or absence of N-to-D movement. Below, we first outline Fukui and Takano's proposal and then show that even if certain mechanisms are modified to implement their analysis, a universal adjunction structure faces challenges when the full range of variation in English, LA, and Chinese relative constructions is considered.

7.1.1   Universal Adjunction Structure?

Fukui and Takano (2000) claim that the ordering between a relative clause and the Head it modifies is determined by the absence or presence of D and the subsequent movement of N to D when D is present. Adopting Kayne's (1994) proposal that only left-adjunction is allowed in the grammar, Fukui and Takano claim that a relative clause is always left-adjoined to its Head: [CP N].[1] A Japanese relative construction like (1) has the structure in (2) after the relative clause is left-adjoined to the Head.

(1) john-ga   kinoo   mita syasin
    John-NOM yesterday saw picture
    'the/a picture that John saw yesterday'

(2)

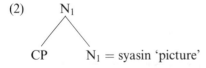

N_1

CP N_1 = syasin 'picture'

Because a Japanese nominal phrase does not contain a D projection or other functional category according to Fukui and Takano, (2) will not merge further, and it is the full representation for the relative construction illustrated in (1). (Fukui and Takano (2000) have modified (2) slightly: the relative clause should be an IP ('I'P'), not a CP, a claim to which we will return shortly.)

In contrast, an English nominal phrase must project a D. A phrase marker like (2) must merge further with a D in order to generate a well-formed nominal structure in English. After D merges with the phrase markers, N-to-D raising must take place in order for the N to check the features in D. An English relative construction like (3), therefore, has the structure in (4).

(3) a picture which John saw yesterday[2]

(4)

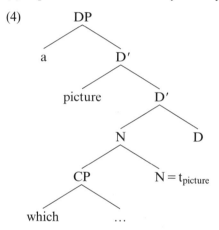

The following generalization thus emerges given Fukui and Takano's theory: the order [Relative Clause + Relative Head] indicates that N-to-D raising has not applied, and the reverse order [Relative Head + Relative Clause] indicates that N-to-D raising has applied. The former is illustrated by Japanese and the latter by English.

Fukui and Takano note further that there is a cluster of differences between English-type and Japanese-type languages that "fall out in a simple and elegant fashion, based solely on the single parametric difference between the languages: English exhibits N-to-D raising, while Japanese does not (simply because the latter language lacks the category D)" (p. 219).[3] The differences involve relative pronouns, operator movement, complementizers, and internally headed relative clauses.

Relative pronouns. According to Fukui and Takano, the absence of a relative pronoun (as in Japanese) or its potential presence (as in English) can be derived from the structural contrast between (2) and (4). Assuming that a relative pronoun must be bound by a relative Head, Fukui and Takano claim that a relative pronoun in a structure like (4) is legitimate because in this structure, the relative Head (the raised N) c-commands the relative pronoun *which*. The relative pronoun *which* is therefore properly bound; hence, English allows a relative pronoun in a relative clause. In contrast, because N_1 has two segments in (2), the relative Head does not c-command CP, if the definition of c-command proposed by May (1985), Chomsky (1986a), and Kayne (1994) is adopted, which incorporates the notions of segments and exclusion.[4] If the relative Head does not c-command the relative clause CP, it cannot c-command a relative pronoun in the CP. In order for (2) to be well formed, the relative clause cannot contain a relative pronoun, since such a relative pronoun would not be c-commanded and properly bound by the relative Head. Consequently, Japanese does not and cannot have a relative pronoun in its relative clause. The contrast between the structures in (4) and (2) captures the contrast between the existence of a relative pronoun in English and the lack of one in Japanese.

Operator movement. According to Fukui and Takano, the lack of a relative pronoun indicates that a Japanese relative clause is not "operator-oriented"; in other words, it is not licensed as a modifier of the relative Head through the mediation of a relative pronoun functioning as an operator creating an open position within the relative clause. Instead, attributing the insight to Kuno (1973) and Murasugi (1991), Fukui and Takano argue that a Japanese relative clause is licensed by an "aboutness" relation between itself and the relative Head. For example, the relative clause in (5) can be interpreted as being about a picture; therefore, being in an aboutness relation with its relative Head, it is properly licensed.

(5) john-ga   kinoo   mita syasin
    John-NOM yesterday saw picture
    'the/a picture John saw yesterday'

Fukui and Takano claim that such an aboutness condition is not peculiar to the licensing of the Japanese relative clause. It is also evident in the licensing of certain topic constructions in Japanese and English.

(6) sakana-wa tai-ga   ii
    fish-TOP   red.snapper-NOM good
    'As for fish, a red snapper is the best.'

(7) As for sports, I like baseball best.

Because there is no operator movement in Japanese relativization and an aboutness condition is sufficient to license a relative clause, it follows that gapless relative clauses are possible in this language, as in (8); moreover, relativization is not subject to island conditions, as demonstrated in (9), where the relativized nominal has originated from within a complex NP.

(8) [syuusyoku-ga   taihen   na] buturigaku
    employment-NOM difficult is   physics
    'physics (that) finding a job is difficult'

(9) [pro$_i$ kiteiru   yoohuku-ga yogoreteiru] sinsi$_i$
        is.wearing suit-NOM   is.dirty   gentleman
    'a gentleman who the suit that (he) is wearing is dirty'

Complementizers. Another contrast following from the proposed structural and movement differences is that a relative clause in Japanese, unlike one in English, has a TP structure, rather than a CP structure. Japanese relative clauses do not need a CP: because of the lack of N-to-D raising, Japanese relative clauses must not be operator-oriented. The fact that an operator is not needed makes the Spec of CP unnecessary. Following Diesing's (1990) suggestion that a functional category is present in a structure only when it is necessary, Fukui and Takano claim that a CP is not necessary in a Japanese relative clause and thus is not projected. The lack of a CP projection means the lack of a C to host a complementizer. This captures the fact that Japanese does not have the counterpart of the complementizer *that* in the English relative clause *a picture **that** John saw yesterday.*[5] A relative clause, accordingly, is not a CP in Japanese. It is an IP/TP (Murasugi 1991).

Internally headed relative clauses. Finally, Fukui and Takano note that only languages of the Japanese type allow internally headed relative clauses (IHRCs). Following Cole's (1987) proposal that an IHRC has a Head that is a null pronominal coreferential with the internal Head, they note that if the English structure (4) were to instantiate an IHRC, it would violate Principle C because the Head pro would be coindexed with, and c-command, the internal Head. In contrast, a pro in the relative Head position does not c-command the internal Head in (2), the proposed structure for Japanese. Consequently, only Japanese allows an IHRC.

In brief, the contrast between the English structure (4) and the Japanese structure (2), as manifested in the different ordering between a relative clause and a relative Head, derives the different properties of English and Japanese relative clauses with respect to the availability of a relative pronoun, operator movement, a complementizer, and an internally headed relative clause. The lack of operator movement is related to the availability of an aboutness condition licensing a relative clause, which does not obey island conditions. The lack of operator movement and the availability of licensing by an aboutness condition also make a gapless relative clause possible.

A number of other Japanese linguists have also noted that Japanese relative clauses do not involve operator movement. Saito (1985), for instance, shows that the lack of operator movement is manifested in the absence of long-distance relativization of reason/manner adjuncts. Such relativization is clause-bound (Murasugi 2000a,b).

(10) a. [[mary-ga   e$_i$ kaetta] riyuu$_i$]
         Mary-NOM   left   reason
         'the reason$_i$ Mary left e$_i$'

    b. *[[mary-ga   [john-ga   e$_i$ kaetta to]   omotteiru] riyuu$_i$]
         Mary-NOM   John-NOM   left   COMP think   reason
         'the reason$_i$ Mary thinks [that John left e$_i$]'

    c. [[mary-ga   e$_i$ mondai-o   toita] hoohoo$_i$]
         Mary-NOM   problem-ACC solved method
         'the method$_i$ Mary solved the problem e$_i$'

    d. *[[mary-ga   [john-ga   e$_i$ mondai-o   toita to]
         Mary-NOM   John-NOM   problem-ACC solved COMP
         omotteiru] hoohoo$_i$]
         think   method
         'the method$_i$ Mary thinks [that John solved the problem e$_i$]'

Murasugi (1991) argues that the relativization of manner/reason adjuncts is not true relativization given that a true relative clause contains a gap. She argues that the expressions in (10) do not contain a gap and that the acceptable expressions in (10a) and (10c) are just like other gapless cases.

(11) [[sakana-ga yakeru] nioi]
     fish-NOM burn   smell
     'the smell that a fish burns (the smell of fish-burning)'

The interpretation of (10a), for instance, parallels the interpretation of English (12) (see the relevant discussion on gapless relatives in Chinese in section 6.6). Such examples are derived by base-generation.

(12) the reason for John's leaving

The unacceptable examples in (10b) and (10d) cannot be base-generated with a pro in place of the adjunct gap e in the embedded clause, because a pro appears only in argument positions. Indeed, a stronger claim has been made: Japanese relative clauses simply are not derived by any type of movement. The following example from Hoji (1985, discussed in Murasugi 2000a,b) shows the lack of reconstruction in cases involving an anaphor:[6]

(13) *$[_{NP}[$john$_i$-ga e_j taipu-sita] [zibun$_i$-no ronbun]$_j$]
           John-NOM   typed   self-GEN   paper
      'self$_i$'s paper that John$_i$ typed'

Cases containing bound pronouns and scope interaction also demonstrate the lack of reconstruction in relative structures. According to Hajime Hoji (personal communication), the relative construction in (14) does not allow the reconstructed bound pronoun interpretation, in contrast to its scrambling and cleft counterparts in (15).

(14) [[toyota-sae]-ga$_i$ e_j uttaeta] [so-ko-o$_i$ uragitta
         Toyota-even-NOM   sued   that-placed-ACC betrayed
         kaisya]$_j$]-ga   tubureta
         company-NOM bankrupt
      '[(The) company/nies that had betrayed it$_i$ that [even Toyota]$_i$ sued] went bankrupt.'

(15) a. [so-ko-o$_i$ uragitta kaisya-o]$_j$ toyota-sae-ga$_i$ e_j
             that-place-ACC betrayed company-ACC Toyota-even-NOM
             uttaeta (koto)
             sued   (fact)
             '(the) company/nies that had betrayed it$_i$, [even Toyota]$_i$ sued'
      b. [toyota-sae-ga$_i$ uttaeta] no-wa [so-ko-o$_i$ uragitta
             Toyota-even-NOM sued   TOP   that-place-ACC betrayed
             kaisya-o]   da
             company-ACC be
             'It is [(the) company/nies that had betrayed it$_i$] that [even Toyota]$_i$ sued.'

A sentence like (16) does not allow reconstructed scope interpretation, either, unlike its scrambling counterpart.

(16) [[toyota-sae]-ga   e$_j$ uttaeta] [hutatu-no kaisya]$_j$]-ga   tubureta
     Toyota-even-NOM   sued   two-GEN company-NOM bankrupt
     '(The) two companies that even Toyota sued went bankrupt.'

These observations support the claim that Japanese relative clauses are not derived by movement and do not contain an operator.

7.1.2   Problems with the Universal Adjunction Structure

Fukui and Takano's (2000) proposal relating word order differences to differences in N-to-D raising, which is the result of projecting or not projecting a D for a nominal phrase, appears to be quite elegant. Under their proposal, both Head-final and Head-initial languages have an adjunction structure for relative constructions. Fundamentally, the presence or absence of D plays the crucial role in determining which languages are Head-initial and which are Head-final with respect to order in relative constructions. If D is projected, N-to-D raising takes place and a Head-initial relative construction is derived. If D is not projected, N-to-D raising is not available and a Head-final relative construction is derived. The absence or presence of N-to-D raising is correlated with other properties concerning the derivation of relative constructions. The universal adjunction structure, coupled with N-to-D raising, describes different types of relative constructions.

We demonstrate below that a universal adjunction structure faces challenges when a wider range of data from English, LA, and Chinese is considered. Nonetheless, Fukui and Takano's insight regarding the importance of D in determining the structure of relative constructions will play a significant role when we consider the projection and properties of D in relation to the relative clause.

7.1.2.1   Problems with Chinese Relative Constructions   As Li (2001) discusses, despite its attractiveness, Fukui and Takano's (2000) account for the distinction between Japanese and English relative constructions does not seem to extend to Chinese relatives. At first glance, Chinese relative constructions look exactly like their Japanese counterparts on the surface: neither requires a determiner; both are Head-final; neither appears to have complementizers or relative pronouns; and both include gapless variants. Chinese even has a well-formed sentence corresponding to (8),

the Japanese example used by Fukui and Takano to argue for the irrelevance of island constraints in relative constructions and hence for the lack of movement.

Closer examination of Chinese relative constructions, however, reveals a different picture.

Let us begin with the issue of whether locality conditions are relevant in the derivation of Chinese relative constructions. As discussed in section 6.5, even though there appear to be some instances where an empty category related to the Head noun occurs inside an island, it is the presence of an empty pronoun (a pro) that makes the relative structure acceptable. A pro needs to be identified. When it is not properly identified by the Head noun, the relative structure manifests island condition effects. We therefore claimed that relativization in Chinese obeys island conditions. We concluded that, other than the instances involving a properly identified pro, a relative clause containing a gap is derived by movement in Chinese. The movement can be NP movement to the Head, as evidenced by reconstruction effects, or operator movement to the Spec of CP, as in the cases of (long-distance) adjunct relativization. The latter is supported by the facts concerning the failure of reconstruction of the relative Head, the distribution of in-situ *wh*-phrases such as *weishenme* 'why' and *zenme* 'how', and the relevance of locality conditions.[7]

When operator movement applies to derive relative constructions in Chinese, the relative clause must still be a CP, rather than a TP, in order for the operator to occupy the Spec of CP. Because relative operators are available, the licensing of a relative clause need not resort to a vague "aboutness" relation. Not resorting to this relation to license a relative structure and not equating topicalization with relativization have several merits.

First, relativization and topicalization *are* different in Chinese. Licensing both constructions by an "aboutness" condition fails to account for the contrasts between them. As shown in section 6.5, topicalization requires the presence of P when a PP is topicalized, whereas relativization allows the "disappearance" of the P. That is, as the following contrasts show, there are instances where relative constructions are allowed, but their topicalization counterparts are not:

(17) a. *zhe chechang, ta xiu che
          this garage   he fix car
          'This garage, he fixes cars.'

    b. ta xiu che de chechang
       he fix car DE garage
       'the garage where he fixed cars'

(18) a. *nage fangfa, ta xiu hao le na-bu che
        that way   he fix well ASP that-CL car
        'That way, he fixed that car.'
     b. ta xiu hao na-bu che de fangfa
        he fix well that-CL car DE way
        'the way he fixed that car'

(19) a. *na-ge   yuanyin, ta bu xiu che
        that-CL reason   he not fix car
        'That reason, he does not fix cars.'
     b. ta bu xiu che de yuanyin
        he not fix car DE reason
        'the reason he does not fix cars'

Many of the so-called gapless relatives also do not have a topicalization counterpart.

(20) a. ta bu nian shu de houguo
        he not read book DE consequence
        'the consequence of his not reading books'
     b. *zhe-ge houguo,   ta bu nian shu
        this-CL consequence he not read book
        'This consequence, he does not read books.'

(21) a. ta chang liuxing ge   de shengyin
        he sing popular song DE voice
        'the voice/sound of him singing popular songs'
     b. *zhe-ge shengyin,   ta chang liuxing ge
        this-CL voice/sound he sing   popular song
        'This voice/sound, he sings popular songs.'

There are also instances where topicalization is possible but relativization is not.

(22) a. yu, wo xihuan chi xian yu
        fish I   like   eat fresh fish
        'Fish, I like to eat fresh fish.'
     b. *wo xihuan chi xian yu de yu
        I   like   eat fresh fish DE fish
        'the fish that I like to eat fresh fish'

As mentioned in note 17 of chapter 6, the following sentences further illustrate the fact that a topic structure can be acceptable whereas its relativized counterpart is not. The verb *fasheng* 'happen' has both an unaccusative and a transitive use. (23) illustrates its unaccusative use with one argument (Theme), and (24) its transitive use with an additional argument (Experiencer).

(23) a. yiwai   fashengle
       accident happened
       'An accident happened.'
   b. tamen fashengle yiwai   le
       they   happened accident LE
       'They had an accident.'

Both (23a) and (23b) can occur in construction with a topic, with or without a chain.

(24) a. tamen, yiwai   fasheng le
       they   accident happen LE
       '(As for) them, an accident happened.'
   b. $tamen_i$, e_i fashengle yiwai   le
       they   happened accident LE
       'As for them, they had an accident.'

But only (24b) has a well-formed relativized counterpart; (24a) does not.

(25) a. *[$_{NP}$[$_{S'}$ yiwai   fashengle de] neixie ren]
               accident happened DE those person
       '*the people such that an accident happened'
   b. [$_{NP}$[$_{S'}$ e_i fashengle yiwai   de] neixie ren_i
              happened accident DE those person
       'the people who had an accident'

Moreover, within relative constructions, the proposal based on "aboutness" licensing fails to account for an observed difference in distribution between gaps and resumptive pronouns: the distribution of gaps is sensitive to islands but the distribution of resumptive pronouns is not (modulo the distribution of pro). In addition, as noted in chapters 5 and 6, the availability of reconstruction differs among the various patterns, a fact the "aboutness" approach fails to account for. Relative constructions with gaps in an argument position exhibit the effects of reconstruction. Those with gaps in an adjunct position or a resumptive pronoun do not

allow reconstruction. Were the "aboutness" condition the only requirement for licensing a relative clause, it is not clear why there would be such
differences among these different relative constructions.

Finally, evidence for Fukui and Takano's analysis based on internally
headed relative clauses is absent in Chinese. Such a construction simply
does not exist in this language.[8] It can only be assumed that a language with a Head-final relative construction can, but need not, have
an internally headed relative construction. The absence of this construction in Chinese does not help in determining the structure of relative
constructions.

In brief, the seemingly very appealing correlation of properties that
would result from the projection of a D and the accompanying N-to-D
raising, and that distinguishes English (illustrating Head-initial relative
constructions) from Japanese (illustrating Head-final relative constructions), does not exist in Chinese.[9] In fact, Chinese seems to share more
important characteristics with English than it does with Japanese even
though Chinese and Japanese both have Head-final relatives. Chinese and
English, but not Japanese, can derive relative structures by movement. In
both these languages, the distribution of gaps is sensitive to island conditions and internally headed relative clauses do not exist. Is it possible,
then, to extend Fukui and Takano's proposal and claim that Chinese is
indeed more like English along the lines predicted by their approach?
Suppose, for instance, that N-to-D raising somehow also applies in Chinese, and that as a result Chinese allows operator movement, in contrast
to Japanese, which does not allow such movement. This revised proposal can be articulated as follows: English requires overt N-to-D raising;
therefore, operator movement is allowed and the word order is Head-
initial. Chinese is like English in allowing N-to-D movement but differs
from English in word order. Therefore, Chinese requires N-to-D raising
(which licenses operator movement under this proposal) to apply covertly, placing the N in a position c-commanding the relative clause. This
allows operator movement to apply in Chinese while maintaining its
Head-final word order. Japanese, on the other hand, does not allow N-to-
D raising either overtly or covertly. Therefore, N never occurs in a position c-commanding the relative clause and operator movement is never
available. This revised proposal would keep Fukui and Takano's analysis
for Japanese and English and extend it to Chinese.

This alternative, unfortunately, is inadequate, quite apart from forfeit-
ing the advantage that Fukui and Takano's analysis correlates N-to-D

movement with word order. First of all, it has been argued that N-to-D raising is not always available in Chinese. As briefly presented in section 6.3 regarding nominal structures in Chinese, there is evidence that N-to-D raising exists in Chinese in some instances. However, this process necessarily derives a definite bare noun (a noun without a demonstrative, number, and classifier). For indefinite nominals and those with a demonstrative or a classifier expression, N-to-D raising is not available, owing to the Head Movement Constraint in cases containing classifiers and the lack of a D projection in cases of indefinites. If N-to-D raising is not available in such cases, the revised version of Fukui and Takano's analysis would predict that such relative clauses should be just like their Japanese counterparts in allowing only base-generated Heads. However, this is false. For instance, a phrase can contain a classifier, and a relative construction can still be derived by movement. We list two examples here: one involving NP reconstruction and the other, long-distance relativization of reason adjuncts. The only possible word order is Head-final.

(26) wo zai zhao [na-ben [[zhangsan$_i$ xie   e de] [e miaoshu   ziji$_i$
     I   at seek that-CL Zhangsan write DE   describe   self
            fumu parents
     de] shu]]
     DE book
     'I am looking for the book that describes self's parents that
     Zhangsan wrote.'

(27) [na-ge   [[ni   yiwei zhangsan (weishenme) bu neng lai   de]
        that-CL you think Zhangsan (why)   not can   come DE
     liyou]]
     reason
     'the reason that you thought Zhangsan could not come (why)'

In short, relative constructions in Chinese can be derived by movement even in contexts where N-to-D raising does not take place, contrary to the predictions made by an analysis based on Fukui and Takano's (2000).

There are also other differences between English and Chinese relative constructions that are too significant to allow us to group the two languages in the same category and say that they differ only in when N-to-D raising takes place (i.e., overtly or covertly). Recall that Chinese does not require a relative construction to be projected as a DP, while English does. This is illustrated by the following contrast:

(28) a. *He is an actor that wants to do everything and producer that
        wants to please everyone.

    b. He is an actor that wants to do everything and a producer that
       wants to please everyone.

(29) a. wo xiang zhao yi-ge   fuze   yingwen de mishu   *jian* jiao
        I   want find one-CL charge English DE secretary and teach
        xiaohai de jiajiao
        kid   DE tutor
        'I want to find a secretary that takes care of English (matters)
        and tutor that teaches kids.'

    b. wo yao dang yi-ge   neng yin shi   de shiren *jian* neng hua
       I   want be   one-CL can sing poem DE poet   and can   draw
       huar   de huajia
       picture DE artist
       'I want to be a poet that can sing poems and artist that can
       draw pictures.'

This contrast suggests a fundamental structural difference between relative constructions in the two languages. Yet another indicator of important differences is that, as noted in chapter 4, English shows the full range
of reconstruction effects of the relative Head, while Chinese does not
reconstruct for the interpretation of scope.

In brief, there are substantial differences between English and Chinese
relative constructions. If both languages allow N-to-D raising, which in
turn licenses operator movement to derive relative constructions, it is not
clear why English would require a DP for a relative construction but
Chinese would not and why English exhibits the full range of reconstruction effects but Chinese is more limited. In light of the facts and analyses
presented for English and Japanese, Chinese challenges the proposal that
language variation can be captured by a universal adjunction analysis
coupled with N-to-D raising.

**7.1.2.2 Problems with English and Lebanese Arabic Relative Con-
structions** Besides failing to account for Chinese-type languages, the
analysis described above fails to account for other generalizations. In this
section, we consider the challenges posed by English and LA.

First of all, the adjunction analysis for Head-initial relative constructions fails where the complementation structure succeeds—namely,
it is unable to capture the close dependency between the external D and

the relative clause. A very close relation exists between D and the relative clause in both English and LA (see section 4.1; Choueiri 2002, chap. 4). The close relation is expressed in terms of selection in a complementation structure: D selects the relative clause. This contrasts with the Head-final relatives in Chinese (as well as in Japanese), which do not show a dependency between D and the relative clause. Moreover, a universal adjunction analysis fails to account for why English and LA complex nominals must be projected as DPs, in contrast to their Chinese counterparts, which can be NPs.

In addition, contrary to the claim of an adjunction analysis that a Head-initial relative clause necessarily involves N-to-D movement, some relative constructions in English and LA do not move N to D overtly. This observation is based on the empirical evidence adduced for those languages that do allow N-to-D raising overtly. It has been widely shown that an analysis of overt N-to-D raising can be supported by the order of N relative to determiners or adjectives. The relevant observations and proposals have been made, for example, for Semitic (e.g., Ritter 1986, 1989; Ouhalla 1988; Fassi Fehri 1989; Siloni 1989, 1990; Borer, to appear), Scandinavian (e.g., Delsing 1988; Taraldsen 1990; Holmberg 1992), and Romance languages (e.g., Longobardi 1994). As Longobardi (1994, 611) notes, Taraldsen (1990) analyzes the Norwegian paradigm in (30) in terms of N raising: the noun can occur before the determiner.

(30) a. hans bøker om   syntaks
        his   books about syntax
     b. bøkene   hans om   syntaks
        book.s.the his   about syntax

Indeed, a common alternation in Scandinavian languages and Romanian (see Dobrovie-Sorin 1987; Grosu 1988) is for an indefinite article to precede a noun and a definite article to be suffixed to a noun: 'a book' versus 'book-the' (Longobardi 1994, 611). That is, N can be raised to D in definite expressions, whereas raising does not take place in indefinite expressions (at least not overtly).

In Italian, common nouns do not normally raise to D overtly, whereas pronouns and proper names may be base-generated in D or generated in N and raised to D (Longobardi 1994, 637). The raising of proper names is illustrated in (31) (Longobardi's (29)): when the definite article does not occur, the proper name must be raised to fill the D position.

(31) a.   E' venuto il   vecchio Cameresi.
          came   the older   Cameresi
     b. *E' venuto vecchio Cameresi.
          came   older   Cameresi
     c.   E' venuto Cameresi vecchio.
          came   Cameresi older

More generally, on the basis of extensive data from Semitic, Scandinavian, and Romance languages, Longobardi (1994, 640) proposes the
following generalization:

(32) *N-raising generalization*
     In languages and constructions where raising of the head noun to
     the D position substitutes it for the article, only proper names are
     allowed to raise; in languages and constructions where raising
     adjoins (prefixes) the noun to the article, common nouns also may
     be allowed to raise to D.

This generalization highlights the role of the distribution and ordering of
articles and nouns in establishing the empirical basis for N-to-D raising.
Importantly, N-to-D raising does not occur across the board in languages
with articles: not all Ns are raised to D even in languages with consistently Head-initial relative constructions.

    With this discussion in mind, note that English differs from Italian in
the availability of N-to-D raising. (31) in Italian contrasts with (33) in
English (Longobardi's (37)).

(33) a.   Old John came in.
     b. *John old came in.

Accordingly, Longobardi (1994, 641) concludes:

(34) N raises to D (by substitution) in the Syntax in Italian but not in
     English.

    In short, the distribution of elements like common nouns and proper
names in relation to articles in a wide range of languages reveals generalizations such as (32) and (34). These conclusions contradict Fukui
and Takano's claim that N-to-D raising always occurs overtly in English, even with common nouns and indefinite nominals, which allows
them to derive the consistently Head-initial relative construction in this
language.[10]

The proposal that combines adjunction with N-to-D raising fails to accommodate not only the English facts but also the relevant facts in other languages, such as certain Semitic and Scandinavian languages that show evidence of overt N-to-D raising only in some cases but where relative constructions are consistently Head-initial. For example, LA has definite and indefinite relative constructions. Both are consistently Head-initial. Definite relatives can occur in construct state nominals, where N-to-D raising can apply. However, relatives can also occur in free state nominals. It is not clear that N-to-D raising must apply in such nominals.

7.1.3 Complementation and Adjunction Structures

The discussion so far has shown that a universal adjunction structure [Relative Clause + Head], coupled with a parametric difference in N-to-D raising, cannot account for all relative constructions. There are languages with exclusively Head-initial relative constructions where N-to-D raising nonetheless applies only in some nominal expressions. Indeed, English, which has been used to argue for the correlation between overt N-to-D raising and Head-initial relative constructions, crucially does not have overt N-to-D raising.

Is it possible, then, to decouple the notion of a universal adjunction structure and the application of N-to-D raising in order to account for the varieties of relative constructions? An alternative, for instance, would be to revise the parametric difference while retaining a universal adjunction structure. The parameter would not encompass the presence or absence of N-to-D raising but, for example, the direction of adjunction: left-adjunction for Head-final languages and right-adjunction for Head-initial languages. Although this approach would have significant implications for how universal phrase structures should be formulated (recall the prohibition against right-adjunction proposed by Kayne (1994)), its more important drawback is that it misses some important empirical generalizations, such as the close dependency between D and the relative in English but not in Chinese and the fact that a relative construction is necessarily a DP in the former language but not the latter. A universal adjunction structure, no matter how the ancillary parameters are formulated, seems difficult to maintain.

In summary, then, let us recapitulate the problems facing a typology of relative clauses and further discuss some issues of adopting universal structure(s), either an adjunction structure or a complementation structure or both, for all languages. The syntax of Chinese relative constructions provides evidence against adopting a complementation structure as a necessary or sufficient universal structure for relative constructions. In Chinese, an adjunction structure should be adopted for relative constructions because there is no evidence for the complementation structure but there *is* direct evidence, based on coordination and reconstruction, that favors an adjunction structure (see chapter 5). On the other hand, adopting a complementation structure for English is well justified. Assuming an adjunction structure for English or LA misses important empirical generalizations in these languages such as the close dependency between D and the relative and the fact that a relative construction is necessarily a DP. We must conclude, then, that both an adjunction structure and a complementation structure are needed to account for relative constructions crosslinguistically. (35)–(36) summarize the main structural properties of relative constructions in these two types of languages.

(35) *English (Head-initial relative constructions)—complementation structure*
   a. The external determiner and the relative clause enjoy a close dependency, which is expressed as a selectional relation in a complementation structure.
   b. The complex nominal must be projected as a DP.
   c. N-to-D raising does not always apply, if indeed it does at all. Nonetheless, a relative construction is consistently Head-initial.
   d. A complementation structure [D + Relative Clause] is adopted.

With respect to the properties in (35), LA behaves like English (see section 4.3 and Choueiri 2002).[11]

(36) *Chinese (Head-final relative constructions)—adjunction structure*
   a. No evidence exists for a close relation between a relative clause and a determiner (such as a demonstrative).
   b. The complex nominal can be projected as an NP.
   c. N-to-D raising does not always apply, although it does in cases of definite bare nouns. Nonetheless, a relative construction is consistently Head-final.
   d. An adjunction structure [Relative Clause + Head] is adopted.

Japanese is a language of this type. Following Fukui and Takano (2000).

Clearly, then, both complementation and adjunction structures should exist in Universal Grammar, and languages choose one or the other: for example, there is evidence for adjunction but not complementation in Chinese, and for complementation but not adjunction in English. What determines a particular language's choice between the two structures?

The discussion of English and LA in chapter 4 documented the role played by the determiner in the formation of relative constructions. By contrast, the determiner plays no role in the formation of relative constructions in Chinese. It has also been proposed that a relative clause is generated as part of a determiner in English (Smith 1964): a D node is expanded to an article (determiner) and a relative clause. For instance, the following phrase structure and transformation (in the framework of the time) were proposed for English relatives:

(37) $[_{NP}[_{Det}$ the $+$ S$]$ N$]$ $\rightarrow$ $[_{NP}[_{Det}$ the$]$ N S$]$

The insight here is that the structure of a relative clause and the existence and choice of an article (determiner) are closely related. A determiner selects a relative clause. It is, therefore, quite plausible to speculate that the obligatory projection of a D within a nominal phrase provides a clue that a complementation structure should be chosen: a relative clause is a complement that bears a relation to D. This is the case with English and LA.[12]

The absence of an obligatory D projection (especially for indefinite nominal expressions) in a language like Chinese (and Japanese) provides a clue to an adjunction structure. The difference in word order can be derived from the difference between complementation and adjunction structures. If only left-adjunction is available (Kayne 1994), then an adjunction structure, without further complications, derives head-final relatives, whereas a complementation structure derives head-initial relatives. This speculation entails that the following type of language should be impossible: one that obligatorily projects a D for all its nominal expressions, requires a dependency relation between the relative clause and D, and has head-final relative constructions.[13] Hindi might provide some support for this speculation. In Hindi, according to Mahajan (2000 and personal communication), a definite relative generally requires a demonstrative (which can be considered an obligatory projection of D)[14] and an indefinite relative has a number expression (which is also projected as a DP; cf. LA definite and indefinite relatives). In other words, the occurrence of a relative clause requires a DP to be projected.

Significantly, even though this language requires objects to occur before the verb (it is Head-final within VPs), the relative construction is essentially Head-initial.[15] Further research, however, is needed in order to establish the reliability of such predictions.

7.2 Derivation

We have entertained and rejected the possibility of a universal structure for relative constructions. Languages may adopt different structures for their relative constructions. Head-initial languages and Head-final languages differ from each other and among themselves. Head-initial English and LA relatives are quite different from Head-final Chinese and Japanese relatives. Chinese also differs significantly from Japanese. The relevant facts can be summarized as follows:

(38) *English (Head-initial)*
   a. Full range of reconstruction effects exhibited in non-*wh*-relatives
       (DP reconstruction)
   b. No reconstruction exhibited in *wh*-relatives or adjunct relatives

(39) *LA (Head-initial)*
   a. Full range of reconstruction effects exhibited in definite relatives
   b. No reconstruction exhibited in indefinite relatives

(40) *Chinese (Head-final)*
   a. Reconstruction of the Head (NP reconstruction) for binding but
       not for scope in argument relativization
   b. No reconstruction exhibited in adjunct relativization or
       relativization with resumption
   c. Long-distance relativization of adjuncts acceptable

(41) *Japanese (Head-final)*
   a. Reconstruction unavailable
   b. Long-distance relativization of adjuncts unacceptable

The following derivations have been proposed for relatives in these languages. In English, relative constructions containing gaps but not exhibiting reconstruction effects are derived by operator movement (see chapter 4). In LA, indefinite relatives are base-generated (Aoun and Choueiri 1997; Choueiri 2002). However, the absence of reconstruction is compatible with an analysis that assumes that operator movement is available if a gap exists. In Chinese, relative constructions containing

Table 7.1
Relativization strategies. (*DP movement* abbreviates *movement of a DP with an empty D.*)

	English	LA	Chinese	Japanese
NP movement	no	no	yes	no
DP movement	yes	yes	no	no
Operator movement	yes	(yes)[a]	yes	no
Base-generation	yes	yes	yes	yes

[a] No direct evidence exists for operator movement in LA, although there is no evidence against it, either. See note 19.

gaps but not exhibiting reconstruction effects also involve operator movement (chapters 5 and 6). In Japanese, the lack of long-distance relativization of adjuncts shows that operator movement does not take place. Base-generation is available in all languages, especially in contexts that disallow movement and contexts that involve resumptive pronouns. Table 7.1 summarizes the strategies each language uses.[16]

Why do these languages behave the way they do, and why do they have or lack the various patterns? What are the factors that determine the similarities and differences among these relative constructions? We have touched on these issues in previous chapters. Here, we will focus on the point made earlier that, in principle, all strategies are available to each language. However, some option(s) many not be realized because of independent morphosyntactic considerations. Specifically, as we will show by examining all the options in the languages in question, the availability of Head raising, operator movement, and base-generation is dictated by the morphosyntactic properties of the phrases to be relativized. These morphosyntactic factors are reflected in *wh*-interrogatives; that is, the properties of *wh*-interrogatives are indicative of the strategies available for relativization. In what follows, we will first focus on the behavior of *wh*-expressions in these languages and then discuss the availability of the various options, basing our inquiry on the parallelism between the formation of *wh*-interrogatives and relative constructions.

7.2.1 *Wh*-Interrogatives

With respect to morphological composition, *wh*-expressions divide into three different types, manifested in English/LA, Japanese, and Chinese, respectively. As shown in section 3.4, the traditionally understood *wh*-

words should be decomposed into three parts: Question, Quantification, and Restriction. What separates English and LA from Chinese is that a *wh*-word generally represents only the Restriction in Chinese but contains the Quantification and Restriction in English and LA. Accordingly, even though Chinese and LA both allow *wh*-phrases to remain in situ in *wh*-interrogatives (in English, this is true for multiple *wh*-questions only), such in-situ *wh*-phrases have different makeups: in Chinese, they do not have a Quantification, but in LA, they do. The three languages also differ in the availability of overt *wh*-movement: *wh*-phrases can undergo overt *wh*-movement to form questions in English/LA but not in Chinese. This possibility in English/LA can be understood as the result of generating Question, Quantification, and Restriction all as one unit, undergoing movement to form questions.

Regarding Japanese, according to Watanabe (1992), Hagstrom (1998), Miyagawa (2001), and others, a question particle is generated together with the *wh*-expression, but it undergoes overt movement independently to check the appropriate feature in C. More precisely, a *wh*-question in Japanese typically contains a *wh*-phrase in situ and a question/quantification (Q) particle at the end.[17]

(42) taroo-ga   nani-o   katta   no
     Taroo-NOM what-ACC bought Q
     'Taroo bought what? = What did Taroo buy?'

The Q-particle may take "the form of *no*, ... or *ka*, in formal style and in all indirect questions" (Miyagawa 2001, 311). In a *wh*-question, the Q-particle, which is an existential quantification according to Miyagawa, originates within the same constituent as the *wh*-phrase and "is raised to C, being attracted by the Q-feature on C. ... Q-particle movement in Japanese ostensibly unifies Japanese *wh*-questions with English *wh*-questions: both exhibit overt movement, to C (Japanese) or to [Spec, CP] (English)" (Miyagawa 2001, 314). That is, English and Japanese differ in the fact that in Japanese, the Q can be moved away from the Restriction but English requires the two to move as a unit.

Miyagawa notes further that all *wh*-phrases in Japanese are separated from the Q-particle in questions. The in-situ *wh*-phrases in *wh*-interrogatives do not have a *wh*-quantificational interpretation without the clause-final Q-particle. This is supported by the fact that the following interpretations, which are typical of *wh*-quantifiers, are possible only if the Q-particle occurs:

(43) *Exhaustive interpretation*
hanako-ga   pikunikku-ni nani-o   mottekita ???(no)
Hanako-NOM picnic-to   what-ACC brought   Q
'Hanako brought what to the picnic?'
(also see Yoshida and Yoshida 1997)

(44) *Pair-list interpretation*
dare-ga   nani-o   katta   *(no)
who-NOM what-ACC bought   Q
'Who bought what?'

(45) *Functional interpretation*
dare-o$_i$ minna-ga   t$_i$ aisiteiru *(no)
who-ACC everyone-NOM   love   Q
'Who does everyone love?' Answer: 'His mother.'

In addition, 'Why' questions are not well formed without the Q-particle.

(46) hanako-ga   naze iku ?*(no)
Hanako-NOM why go   Q
'Why is Hanako going?'
(also see Yoshida and Yoshida 1997)

In brief, depending on whether a language allows overt movement of the whole *wh*-phrase to form *wh*-interrogatives and whether a language allows the Q-part to move independently, the following three types of languages emerge:

(47) a. Question, Quantification, and Restriction are generated as a unit and move as a unit to form questions: English and LA *wh*-questions formed by overt *wh*-movement.
   b. Quantification and Restriction are generated as a unit: English and LA in-situ *wh*-phrases in *wh*-questions.
   c. Quantification and Restriction are generated within a nominal expression but Quantification can be moved away from Restriction: Japanese *wh*-questions.
   d. Restriction is generated as an independent unit: Chinese *wh*-questions.

With this in mind, we turn to the strategies for relativization, which make use of the same morphosyntactic information as the strategies for *wh*-question formation.

7.2.2 Relativization

In this section, we will examine the strategies that have been proposed for relativization in English, LA, Chinese, and Japanese and determine when they are realized, basing our inquiry on the parallelism between *wh*-interrogation and relativization. First, however, we would like to point out that, inherently, there are differences between the two constructions.

(48) Relative clauses, not *wh*-interrogatives, need to be interpreted in the context of a complex nominal. The interpretation of a relative clause (i.e., the relation between a relative clause and the Head) is established when either (a) or (b) obtains.

  a. The Head is directly moved from within the relative clause (i.e., the Head is an argument within the relative clause). Two subcases exist:

   i. A DP with an empty internal D is moved to the peripheral position of a relative clause that is complement to an external D that licenses the internal empty D. The DP in the CP provides an NP to be interpreted with the external D. *or*

   ii. An NP Head is raised from within a relative clause, forming a complex NP with the relative clause.

  b. An operator is present. An operator in the peripheral position of a relative clause bears a predication/agreement relation to the nominal Head.[18]

(49) In cases where an external D can license an internal D, a DP with an empty internal D can occur in the peripheral position of a relative clause. By contrast, *wh*-interrogatives do not have an external D to license an empty internal D.

These differences play a significant role in the formation of *wh*-questions and relative constructions. They entail that a relative construction can be formed by movement of an NP or a DP with an empty D, whereas a *wh*-interrogative cannot. Instead, a *wh*-interrogative must involve a *wh*-phrase. In the following subsections, we examine the options of NP movement, DP movement, and operator movement in turn.

7.2.2.1 NP Movement It is clear from the generalizations in (47) that only Chinese allows the Restriction alone to be generated in an argument position. Indeed, we suggested in chapters 5 and 6 that NP movement is available only if an NP is allowed to be generated in an argument position. Evidence comes from the formation of *wh*-interrogatives and from the behavior of the plural/collective morpheme *-men*. In contrast, English, LA, and Japanese do not allow the Restriction to be generated apart from the Quantification. Nominal expressions in these languages do not allow NPs in argument positions. The difference in the availability of an NP in an argument position accounts for the differences in the availability of NP movement.[19]

In brief, the composition of *wh*-phrases in different languages is indicative of the applicability of NP raising to form a complex nominal—relativization.[20]

7.2.2.2 Operator Movement Recall that English *wh*-interrogatives allow a *wh*-operator to undergo movement to the Spec of CP to form *wh*-questions. English also allows a process of operator movement, parallel to *wh*-movement in questions, to derive relative constructions.[21] However, because other options exist for deriving the same subpattern (e.g., because DP raising exists for deriving definite relatives), the effect of such a derivation may not be manifested.

Recall also that a *wh*-phrase in LA may stay in situ, licensed by a question complementizer. Is this option, used in forming *wh*-questions, also available for relativization? In principle, the answer should be yes, given our claim that *wh*-interrogation and relativization are essentially derived in the same manner. However, the result of this in-situ option is not well formed for relative constructions. This is due to the licensing condition on relativization, particularly (48b), which states that the operator of the relative clause must be licensed by the Head of the relative construction. The licensing is successful when the Head and the operator are in an agreement relation. This is why in English, for instance, when the Head is *the reason*, the operator must be *why*; when the Head is a place, time, or person expression, the operator must be *where*, *when*, or *who*; and so on. In other words, the operator must contain the appropriate substantive features, expressed in the Restriction. If a *wh*-phrase stays in situ,[22] the Restriction is not moved to the initial position in the relative clause (corresponding to the case of a question complementizer related to a *wh*-in-situ in interrogatives) and an agreement relation cannot hold between the Head and the complementizer in the C of the relative CP. Therefore, the relative clause cannot be properly interpreted. Relativization, thus, does not have the counterpart of interrogation that results from generating a complementizer in C related to a *wh*-phrase in situ (Restriction in situ).

In Japanese, where only the Q-particle moves in *wh*-interrogatives, leaving the Restriction in situ, we expect the same to happen in relativization. However relative constructions in Japanese cannot be derived by operator movement; if they could be, long-distance relativization (of adjuncts) would be possible. Why is such movement not available? Because, as just observed, so-called operator movement in Japanese is movement of Q alone, which does not carry a Restriction. Movement of Q without a Restriction does not derive a well-formed relative construction because the Head and the operator must agree in all features, including the features carried by the Restriction.

The same reasoning would lead us to expect that operator movement in Chinese, when it applies, cannot derive a well-formed relative construction, either. Recall that in Chinese, *wh*-phrases constitute a Restriction separate from the Question/Quantification. If the Question/ Quantification moves, it moves without the Restriction. Why, then, does Chinese allow long-distance adjunct relativization, which can only be derived by operator movement? This, again, can be traced to the behavior of *wh*-words in this language. Even though we have claimed that *wh*-phrases in Chinese generally constitute just a Restriction (in other words, that *wh*-phrases are not operators (quantificational) in this language), there are exceptions, as shown by the existence of operators containing a Restriction such as *weishenme* 'why' and *zenme* 'how' (see section 6.5).

(50) a. ?zhe jiu   shi [ta juede [ni   yinggai (*ruhe/zenme$_i$) xiu che] de]
         this exactly is   he feel   you should how   fix car DE
         fangfa$_i$
         method
         'This is the way$_i$ (how$_i$) he feels you should fix the car t$_i$.'
     b. zhe jiu   shi [women yiwei   [ta (*weishenme$_i$) mei lai]   de]
         this exactly is   we   thought he why   not come DE
         yuanyin$_i$
         reason
         'This is the reason$_i$ why$_i$ we thought he did not come t$_i$.'

Moreover, whereas a Q-particle is obligatory in cases like (46) in Japanese, no such particle is required in their Chinese counterparts. These observations account for the fact that long-distance relativization of adjuncts is acceptable in Chinese (*wh*-operators move covertly). Note that this option is not available for Japanese, as it does not have the counterpart of (50). In other words, with respect to the option of using operator movement to derive relative constructions, Chinese and Japanese differ only in the fact that Chinese, but not Japanese, has lexical items such as *weishenme* 'why' and *zenme* 'how', which are themselves operators with a Restriction.[23]

7.2.2.3 DP Movement DP movement is available because a DP with an empty D can be generated and licensed in relative constructions (in contrast to *wh*-interrogation, which does not have an external D to license an empty D (49)). Recall that the promotion analysis proposed by Bianchi (1999) assumes the following complementation structure:

(51) $[_{DP}$ D $[_{CP}$ DP$_i$ [C $[_{IP}$ ... e$_i$ ...]]]]
     The DP in the Spec of CP (the Head) contains an empty D (the internal D).

It is important that there is an internal D and that the internal D is empty. As discussed in chapter 4, such an empty internal D will be incorporated with the external D because it needs to be licensed. This makes the two Ds into one; and the NP associated with the internal D can also be associated with the external D, satisfying the interpretation requirement of the external D. Some English and LA definite relative constructions are derived by such a strategy. However, this strategy is not always available. It fails to apply when the empty internal D is not properly licensed. An indefinite D of an indefinite relative construction in English and LA, for instance, does not license another D; therefore, a DP with an empty D cannot move to derive an indefinite relative.

On the other hand, the lack of a full range of reconstruction effects in Chinese and the complete lack of reconstruction facts in Japanese indicate that DP movement is simply unavailable to derive relative constructions in these languages. Why is this so? One option is to claim simply that no DP with an empty D is generated in these languages; therefore, movement of a DP with an empty D is not available. This might be understood as follows. As discussed in section 6.1.2, when D occurs in Chinese, it always contains specified features, rather than being empty. We showed that D in Chinese is always [+definite]: either it is filled by a definite expression, or it attracts a bare N, deriving a definite nominal expression. Possibly a D in Japanese is always filled as well. As discussed by Hagstrom (1998) and Miyagawa (2001), a quantificational element can occupy a D when it occurs (see section 7.2.1).

Another option is to consider the licensing condition for an empty D. Recall that an empty D must be licensed. It is licensed when it is adjacent to an external D so that the two Ds can be incorporated. In the complementation structure proposed for English and LA, where the raised DP is in the peripheral position of the complement CP, the adjacency condition is met and the empty internal D is licensed: [D [CP[DP D NP] [IP ...]]]. In Chinese and Japanese, however, relative constructions have a left-adjunction structure. Raising of a DP with an empty D, to be licensed by an external D, would have the structure shown in (52).

(52)
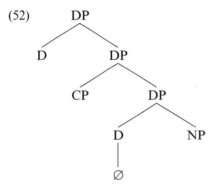

Such a raised DP with an empty D would not be adjacent to an external D because of an intervening relative clause. The empty internal D would not be properly licensed; therefore, such DP movement is not available. The cost of this option, however, is the necessity of stating an adjacency condition. Furthermore, considering that an indefinite nominal is projected as an NP (see chapter 6), it seems that the first option is more likely (see Choueiri 2002, sec. 4.2.5, for the claim that the relativized nominal is indefinite).

Whichever option is chosen, the essence is that in order for DP raising to succeed in relative constructions, a null D must be generated and properly licensed.

7.2.2.4 Summary The different behavior of various subpatterns of relative constructions with respect to reconstruction effects, long-distance relations, island effects, and so on, argues for the existence of different strategies to derive relative constructions. Specifically, the following strategies are, in principle, always available: Head raising (NP or DP raising) and operator movement, in addition to base-generation. In reality, not all options are realized in individual languages. We argue that the choice is not arbitrary. It follows from general morphosyntactic properties of the relevant phrases in the individual languages, which are also reflected in the morphosyntactic structure of *wh*-phrases forming *wh*-interrogatives. That is, the derivation of relative constructions parallels the derivation of *wh*-interrogatives, whatever differences there are between them being traced to their inherent differences (48)–(49). Because each language has its own specific morphosyntactic properties, not all Head-final relative constructions are alike and not all Head-initial relative constructions are alike.

Below, we summarize the similarities and differences between *wh*-interrogative and relative constructions in English and LA (Head-initial), Chinese and Japanese (Head-final), at the same time tabulating how each relativization strategy is realized/not realized, as listed in table 7.1. The strategy of base-generation, however, is not listed, as it must be available in all languages, particularly in cases where movement cannot apply.

(53) *English*
    a. Characteristics
        i. *Wh*-phrases contain a Quantification and a Restriction.
       ii. A DP projection is required in an argument position, even when D is an empty category; an empty D can be licensed by an external D in certain cases.
    b. *Wh*-question formation
        i. Operator movement: available
           Wh-interrogative pronouns undergo movement.
       ii. DP/NP movement: nonapplicable
          Neither a DP with an empty D nor an NP can move because a *wh*-interrogative is not headed by D (49) (it is a clausal, not a nominal expression).
    c. Relativization
        i. Operator movement: available
           Wh-relative pronouns undergo movement.
       ii. DP movement: available
          A DP with an empty D moves in cases where the empty D is successfully licensed (e.g., when the external D is a type I determiner; see Carlson 1977).
      iii. NP movement: nonapplicable
          NPs are not generated in argument positions.

(54) *LA*

   a. Characteristics

      i.   *Wh*-phrases contain a Quantification and a Restriction.

      ii. A question complementizer can be generated in Comp and related to a *wh*-phrase in situ.

      iii. A DP projection is required in an argument position, even when D is an empty category; an empty D can be licensed by an external D in certain cases.

   b. *Wh*-question formation

      i.   Operator movement: available

         Wh-interrogative pronouns undergo movement.

      ii. In-situ strategy: available

         A question complementizer in Comp licenses an in-situ *wh*-phrase.

      iii. DP/NP movement: nonapplicable

         Neither a DP with an empty D nor an NP can move because a *wh*-interrogative is not headed by D (49) and an empty D would not be licensed.

   c. Relativization

      i.   Operator movement: available (but see note 18)

      ii. In-situ strategy: nonapplicable

         (48b) is not satisfied, when the restriction is in situ.

      iii. DP movement: available

         A DP with an empty D moves in cases where the empty D is successfully licensed (e.g., in a definite relative).

      iv. NP movement: nonapplicable

         NPs are not generated in argument positions.

(55) *Chinese*

   a. Characteristics

      i.   *Wh*-phrases generally consist only of a Restriction, except the adjunct *wh* ('why', 'how'), which may contain a Quantification.

      ii. A Restriction-only *wh*-phrase is licensed by a quantifier in a projection separate from the nominal containing the *wh*-phrase.

      iii. An NP (Restriction-only) is allowed in an argument position.

      iv. A DP with an empty D is either not generated at all or is generated but not licensed.

   b. *Wh*-question formation
      i.   Operator movement: available'
           Adjuncts may also undergo movement covertly to form
           questions.[24]
      ii. In-situ strategy: available
           An in-situ *wh*-phrase (Restriction-only) is licensed by a
           question marker.
      iii. DP/NP movement: nonapplicable
   c. Relativization
      i.   Operator movement: available
      ii. In-situ strategy: nonapplicable
           (48b) is not satisfied when the restriction is in situ.
      iii. NP movement: available
           NPs are allowed in an argument position.
      iv. DP movement: not available

(56) *Japanese*
   a. Characteristics
      i.   A *wh*-phrase is always related to a Quantification (Q-
           particle) within the DP projection and the Q-particle is
           moved without the *wh*-phrase.[25]
           A *wh*-phrase itself is not quantificational.
      ii. An NP (Restriction-only) is not allowed in an argument
           position (it contains a trace generated by Q movement).
      iv. A DP with an empty D is either not generated at all or is
           generated but not licensed.
   b. *Wh*-question formation
      i.   Q movement without Restriction and *wh*-phrase in situ
           The Q-particle undergoes movement, leaving a *wh*-phrase in
           situ.
      ii. DP/NP movement: nonapplicable
   c. Relativization
      i.   No Q movement with the Restriction
           (48b) is not satisfied when the Restriction is in situ.
      ii. In-situ strategy: nonapplicable
           (48b) is not satisfied when the Restriction is in situ.
      iii. NP movement: unavailable
           NPs are not allowed in an argument position.
      iv. DP movement: not available

Appendix

In chapters 1 and 3, we discussed two significant lines of analysis for superiority effects, representing a movement approach and a binding/interpretation approach. The movement approach is best represented by Pesetsky's (2000) very refined movement (Attract Closest) account of Superiority. The binding/interpretation approach is best represented by Hornstein's (1995) Weak Crossover account, showing that Superiority should be assimilated to interpretation properties. We showed that the LA data present challenges to both lines of research. However, additional generalizations have been proposed to support either the movement approach or the WCO approach or both—generalizations that seem to give these approaches an advantage over our proposal. In this appendix, we will show that this advantage does not actually exist if more facts are considered.

Two main issues are relevant, one having to do with the rescuing effect of a third *wh*-phrase in cases of Superiority violations discussed by Pesetsky (2000) and Hornstein (1995), the other having to do with the anti-superiority effects discussed by Hornstein (1995).

A1 The Rescuing Effect of an Additional *Wh*-Element

As discussed by Kayne (1983), the addition of a third *wh*-phrase in the right kind of configuration ameliorates Superiority violations.[1] As (1c–d) show, the ungrammatical (1a–b), which involve just two *wh*-phrases, improve when changed to include a third *wh*-phrase.

(1) a. *Who did who persuade to buy books?
    b. *What did who persuade John to buy?
    c. ?Who did who persuade to buy what?
    d. What did who persuade whom to buy?

   Hornstein (1995) notes that the rescuing effect of an additional *wh*-phrase follows from his WCO approach to superiority effects. Recall that the definition of WCO used by Hornstein is cast in terms of the asymmetric notion of linking.

(2) A pronoun cannot be linked to a variable on its right.

>   *Q ... pronoun ... variable ...
> |_____↑

Hornstein cites the following contrast as evidence for a linking approach to WCO: since linking is asymmetric, the pronoun preceding the variable in (3b) can be linked to the pronoun following the variable, as in (4). This is why the WCO effect is suspended.[2]

(3) a. *Who$_i$ did his$_i$ mother introduce x_i to the teacher?
    b. Who$_i$ did his$_i$ mother introduce x_i to his$_i$ teacher?

>   ┌──────────────┐
>   ↓ |
> (4) Q ... pronoun ... variable ... pronoun
> |_____↑

Hornstein (1995, chap. 6) argues that the linking mechanism suspends Superiority violations too: the addition of *where* in (5b) avoids a WCO violation.

(5) a. *What did who buy x at the store?
    b. What did who buy x where?

(6) a. [$_{CP}$ what$_i$ [$_{IP}$[pro$_i$ person](=who) buy t$_i$ at the store]]
    b. [$_{CP}$ what$_i$ [$_{IP}$[pro$_i$ person](=who) buy t$_i$ [[pro$_i$ place](=where)]]]]

(5a), but not (5b), violates WCO. In (5b), represented schematically in (6b), the pronoun to the left of the variable is coindexed with the variable, but not linked to it. Instead, it is linked to the pronoun restricted by *place* (=*where*). In contrast, the pronoun in (6a), the schematic representation of (5a), must be linked to the variable on its right since there is no other possibility, thus violating WCO.

   Pesetsky (2000) indicates that the rescuing effect of an additional *wh*-element follows from his account as well. Again, consider the sentences with three *wh*-phrases.

(7) a. ?Who did who persuade to buy what?
    b. What did who persuade whom to buy?

In such sentences, it is not necessary to phrasally move the first *wh* to satisfy Attract Closest, because the second *wh* and the third *wh* can undergo phrasal movement to satisfy the multiple Spec requirement. Attract Closest is satisfied by moving the feature of the first *wh*. After the "Attract Closest tax is paid," it does not need to be considered again (the Principle of Minimal Compliance). Either the second *wh* (*who*) or the third *wh* (*what*) can undergo phrasal movement.[3]

The rescuing effect of an additional *wh* is not, however, straightforward. Various factors influence this effect. For instance, Kayne (1983, 236–238) observes that the following sentence, which contains three *wh*-phrases, two of which are subjects, is still not acceptable (also see Richards 1997 for discussion of the Principle of Minimal Compliance and Connectedness).

(8) *I'd like to know where who said that what was hidden.

The additional *wh* also seems to be subject to a locality condition. For instance, (9a) and (9b) are not as good as (5b), according to the speakers we have consulted.[4]

(9) a. ?*To whom did who say that John would buy what?
    b. ?*Who did who introduce to guests that came from where?
    c. ?*Who did who ask to tell Mary to dance with whom?

Adding to the complexity of the issue is that the rescuing effect of an additional *wh* is not shared by all native English speakers. There are speakers who do not find improvement even in (5b) (Thomas Ernst, personal communication). Furthermore, in LA an additional *wh* does not ameliorate Superiority violations at all.[5]

(10) a. *miin keen   miin ʔambihke ʔan   saami
        who was.3MS who talk.3MS   about Sami
        'Who did who talk about Sami?'
     b. *miin keen   miin ʔambihke ʔan   miin
        who was.3MS who talk.3MS   about whom
        'Who did who talk about whom?'

We do not know why there are differences among English speakers and differences between LA speakers and some English speakers concerning the rescuing effect of an additional *wh*. We leave this issue to further research.

A2   Antisuperiority Effects

Hornstein (1995) (also see S. Watanabe 1995) extends his WCO analysis of superiority effects to account for the so-called antisuperiority effects (also see, e.g., A. Watanabe 1992; Saito 1994). He argues that the contrast between the following pair of Japanese sentences, where the argument precedes the adjunct in the grammatical (11a) and follows it in the ungrammatical (11b), can also be subsumed under WCO.

(11) a.   john-ga   nani-o   naze katta   no
           John-NOM what-ACC why bought Q
           'Why did John buy what?'
     b. *john-ga   naze nani-o   katta   no
           John-NOM why what-ACC bought Q

'Why', in contrast to argument *wh*-phrases, cannot function as a generator because 'why' does not range over individuals. 'What' must be the generator in such cases, and 'why' is represented as [pro N] when it is dependent on another *wh*-phrase. In (11a), 'what' is the generator and 'why' has the dependent reading, represented as [pro reason]. There is no WCO violation because the pro ('why') is to the right of the variable (the argument position of 'what'): [what … variable … [pro reason] …]. In (11b), there is a WCO violation: 'what' must occupy the Spec of Comp as generator. 'Why' must be represented as [pro N]. The pronoun occurs to the left of the variable bound by the generator 'what': [what … [pro reason] … variable …]. The contrast between (11a) and (11b) follows as an instance of WCO. If this approach is correct, it provides further support for the relevance of WCO to multiple *wh*-questions.

   However, it is not clear that the contrast between (11a) and (11b) should be captured by WCO. First, note that the addition of a c-commanding argument *wh* can rescue sentences like (11b), as noted by A. Watanabe (1992) and further discussed by Saito (1994) and S. Watanabe (1995).[6]

(12) dare-ga   naze nani-o   katta   no
     who-NOM why what-ACC bought Q
     'Why did who buy what?'

The improvement found in (12) initially seems to argue for a WCO approach: the rescuing effect of an additional argument *wh*, whose variable occurs to the left of the pronoun associated with 'why'. Nevertheless, an additional *wh* does not always have a rescuing effect. Saito (1994) (also see A. Watanabe 1992) discusses in detail a locality condition on the additional *wh*: the additional c-commanding *wh* must be close enough to 'why', as shown by the contrast between the unacceptability of (13) and the acceptability of (12).

(13) *dare-ga [john-ga   naze nani-o   katta   to]   omotteru no
     who-NOM   John-NOM why what-ACC bought COMP think   Q
     'Who thinks that John bought what why?'

To capture the locality condition, Saito proposes that the adjunct *wh*-phrase undergoes A-movement and adjoins to an argument *wh*-phrase. That is, adding 'who' to (11b) improves it as in (12) because 'why' can be adjoined to the c-commanding 'who' and piggyback on it. Because the piggybacking movement is an A-movement, it obeys the locality condition on A-movement. The adjunction is necessary in order to derive an LF representation that obeys the Empty Category Principle or some cross-level (S-Structure and LF) condition on relative scope structures (for details, see A. Watanabe 1992; Saito 1994). If Saito's analysis is correct, it shows that the contrast between (11a) and (11b) cannot be fully subsumed under WCO.[7]

Notes

Introduction

1. When reconstruction is available, (part of) the displaced element may be interpreted in the position(s) from which it has been raised. This book discusses and illustrates reconstruction in detail.

2. Capitalized *Superiority* is used to name the constraint and lowercase *superiority effects* is used to describe the linguistic phenomenon.

3. Boeckx (2001) introduces a distinction between Match and Agree. The former, but not the latter, can apply across an island such as an adjunct island. Boeckx further assumes that Move can take place upon Match alone. That is, true resumption as in (6) can be generated by movement. Our notion of Match is a representational notion not related to Move. We discuss the empirical difference between our notion of Match and Boeckx's in chapters 2 and 3.

4. As formulated, the MMC applies to nonargument chains ($\bar{\text{A}}$-chains or non-L-related chains). Chomsky (1995, chap. 4) argues that a minimality constraint regulates argument chains (A-chains or L-related chains) as well. If Chomsky's proposal is adopted, the MMC needs to be formulated to apply to A- and $\bar{\text{A}}$-chains alike. The relation between an anaphor and its antecedent or between a pronoun and its antecedent is not subject to minimality, however.

(i) a. The boys$_i$ introduced the girls to each other$_i$.
    b. The boys$_i$ said that the teachers would talk to their$_i$ parents.

This is not surprising if Chomsky's (1981) analysis is adopted: neither an anaphor nor a pronoun forms a chain with its antecedent; a chain can contain only one θ-role. For different assumptions, see Hornstein 2001 and Kayne 2001.

5. In order to make Attract Closest work, one needs to allow illicit movement and assume that licit and illicit movement compete with each other. This amounts to saying that licit and illicit movement are similar types of processes, which would leave it a mystery why only licit movement allows reconstruction.

6. For convenience, we will use the capitalized term *Head* to refer to the nominal expression that is "modified" by the relative clause, even though in the structures based on the version of the promotion analysis advocated by Kayne (1994) and

Bianchi (1999), the "Head" is in the Spec of the CP, which is not the syntactic head of the projection. More generally, as the discussion on relative structures develops, *Head* will refer to (1) the DP in the Spec of CP of a relative clause when the relative structure is [$_{DP}$ D [$_{CP}$ DP [$_{IP}$ ...]]] (the complementation structure, such as the one adopted by Kayne and Bianchi) or (2) the nominal that the relative clause is adjoined to (the adjunction structure, such as the one in Chinese, to be discussed in chapter 5): [Relative Clause [Head]].

7. Some languages, such as LA, do not use *wh*-words (those appearing in *wh*-interrogatives) as relative pronouns. Instead, a null operator serves the same function, particularly in LA indefinite relative constructions. Other languages use a different series of words that are related to an interrogative *wh*-word (such as Hindi; see, e.g., Mahajan 2000). Nonetheless, such relative operators behave like *wh*-operators syntactically. For ease of presentation, we will refer to a relative operator as a *wh-operator* both when discussing English and when discussing languages that do not use the same form for interrogative pronouns and relative pronouns.

Chapter 1

1. See detailed discussions in chapter 3 on a Weak Crossover approach to Superiority like that proposed by Hornstein (1995).

2. Chomsky (1976) proposes the Superiority Condition, requiring a higher *wh*-phrase to undergo *wh*-movement.

(i) *Superiority Condition*
   a. No rule can involve X, Y in the structure

   ... [... Z ... WYV ...] ...

   where the rule applies ambiguously to Z and Y, and Z is superior to Y.
   b. The category A is superior to category B if every major category
      dominating A dominates B as well but not conversely.

3. Aoun's Generalized Binding approach to Superiority allows it to apply to nonmovement structures as well, given that binding constrains movement as well as nonmovement structures.

4. Analyses based on Connectedness and the Path Containment Condition are not problematic in these cases.

5. This is not a problem for an analysis based on Connectedness or the Path Containment Condition either.

6. Chomsky (1995, 296) states that "*close* is (tentatively) defined in terms of c-command and equidistance." That is, α in (9) cannot be c-commanded by β targeting K. Chomsky later gives the following definition incorporating the notions of domain and chain: "β is closer to HP [a maximal projection headed by H] than α [a feature or X^0 category] if β c-commands α and is not in the minimal domain of CH (the chain containing α—the trivial chain, containing only one member—or α and its trace)" (p. 299).

7. See Simpson 2000, chap. 1, for a review of Superiority and movement.

8. We will provide further evidence in chapters 2 and 4 that an in-situ *wh*-phrase docs not undcrgo covert movement in LA.

9. A gap is also possible in this pattern, where RP_2 is not within an island.

(i) $*wh_2 \ldots [\ldots wh_1 \ldots] \ldots t_2 \ldots$

10. Pesetsky (2000, 17) notes another type of counterexample to the earlier account of Superiority based on language variation: in contrast to English, "In at least the simplest cases, German appears to lack the Superiority contrast entirely." For example:

(i) a. Ich weiss nicht, wer was   gesehen hat.
      I   know not   who what seen   has
      'I don't know who saw what.'
   b. Ich weiss nicht, was wer gesehen hat.
      I   know not   what who seen   has
      'I don't know what who saw.'

We will put aside discussion of the German data, as it is not clear whether German indeed lacks Superiority; see Wiltschko 1998.

11. In order to accommodate the contrast between a language like Bulgarian that requires multiple *wh*-phrases to occur at the beginning of a question and a language like English that allows only one *wh*-phrase in such a position, Pesetsky (2000) proposes different pronunciation rules for the two types of languages. English has the rule stated in (38). Bulgarian has the following rule (p. 8):

(i) *Pronunciation rule (Bulgarian)*
   All *wh*-phrase movement to C is overt, in that *wh* is pronounced in its new position and unpronounced in its trace positions.

12. As will be discussed in chapter 3, negation or a negative polarity item does not affect the acceptability of multiple *wh*-questions in LA. Rather, it affects interpretation: only a single-pair interpretation is available if a negation or negative polarity item intervenes between the two *wh*-phrases. Furthermore, it should be noted that some English speakers also find that the intervention of a negation or negative polarity item blocks a pair-list interpretation, but it does not cause unacceptability in cases like the following (also see note 13):

(i) Which person didn't persuade any student to read which paper?

13. Pesetsky (2000) notes that, for some speakers, (45d) may be acceptable with a single-pair reading in some special contexts. He gives the following scenario:

For example, suppose you pass a classroom and hear the teacher yelling. You know that this teacher only yells at the class when a student has failed to read his or her book for that day. In such a context (and only in such a context), some speakers accept a question like *Which book didn't which person read today?* (pp. 60–61)

LA also allows a single-pair interpretation and not a pair-list interpretation, when an operator intervenes between the two *wh*-phrases.

14. Boeckx (2001, sec. 4.4.2) proposes that cases involving islands that exhibit superiority effects can still be subsumed under an AC approach because movement can cross island boundaries in his approach. Allowing movement across islands, however, fails to capture the contrast between the availability of reconstruction in cases where an RP is not inside an island and the unavailability of reconstruction in cases where an RP *is* inside an island, as discussed in this chapter.

15. This is a serious weakening of the general grammatical theory, however. If illicit movement is allowed, it is not clear what the distinction between base-generation and movement is. The weakening concerning the relation between movement and reconstruction also undermines the fundamental property of movement.

16. Similarly, the fact that Chinese in-situ *wh*-phrases do not exhibit superiority effects at all, in contrast to (46)–(47) in LA, would not be captured either if Chinese differs from English or Bulgarian only with respect to how the pronunciation rule is formulated. See note 11; also see Legendre, Smolensky, and Wilson 1998 and Pesetsky 1998.

Chapter 2

1. *Relevant features* will first be defined narrowly in the discussion of *wh*-phrases (restricted only to [+*wh*] features) and later extended to include quantificational expressions (quantification features).

2. In the cases where a resumptive pronoun is replaced by a gap, the bound pronoun is linked to a gap.

3. The minimalist definition of movement includes Copy, Merge, and island conditions (or the Minimal Link Condition, which only permits "shortest move"). See Chomsky 1995, 267–268, which focuses on *wh*-islands, and Ouhalla 2001, which argues that adjunct islands are to be reduced to *wh*-islands. If the locality conditions were not part of the definition of movement, Move could apply from within an island and there would be no need for the demerging process.

4. McCloskey (1990, to appear) and Sells (1984) identify resumptive pronouns as syntactic variables—that is, as elements that are syntactically bound and whose most immediate binder is an element in an Ā-position.

5. We later generalize this condition when other cases are considered.

6. We mentioned that a variable must agree with its binding operator with respect to categorial features. A *wh*-operator is a *wh*-phrase in the Spec of Comp. It is an XP category. The variable bound by an XP *wh*-operator is therefore also an XP category, which can occupy an argument position (e.g., the variable bound by *who* or *what*) or an adjunct position (e.g., the variable bound by *why* or *how*). This definition will not mistakenly rule out a sentence such as *What did you wonder who bought?* because of the "cyclic" application of the MMC. See the discussion in section 2.4.

7. For brevity, we will no longer mention the term *c-commanding* (operator c-commanding the closest XP with a [+*wh*] feature).

8. Note that when the index $1 = 2$, the in-situ wh_2 cannot be interpreted as a bound pronoun because it has a [+*wh*] feature.

9. Strong Crossover violations can be subsumed under Principle C of binding theory or whatever other principle(s) of the grammar is (are) appropriate.

10. Parasitic gap constructions do not violate the Bijection Principle if the parasitic gap is bound by a nonovert operator (see, e.g., Chomsky 1982; Engdahl 1983, 1985; Taraldsen 1981; Cinque 1990).

11. In his important work, Richards (1997) notes that the pattern [wh_1 wh_2 [... [t_1] ... t_2]] is somewhat acceptable in Bulgarian, where wh_1 is overtly moved from within an island and wh_2 is overtly moved from a position not c-commanding t_1.

(i) ?Kakvo$_j$ kogo$_k$ kazva tozi služitel na [žurnalistite,   kojto razsledvat t$_j$],
    what   who   tells   this official to the-journalists who investigate
    če   komunistite   sa   zabludili t$_k$?
    that the-Communists AUX deceived
    'What does this official tell journalists who are investigating that the
    Communists have deceived who?'

This example contrasts with the unacceptable LA sentence (20a) and the unacceptable corresponding English sentence (ii).

(ii) *Who did you tell the investigator who interviewed t about what?

Richards (1997, 265–266) derives the noted contrast between English and Bulgarian from their difference with respect to overt and covert movement. In Bulgarian, both *wh*-phrases undergo overt movement. The island boundary becomes transparent when the second *wh*-phrase is also raised overtly. In contrast, English moves one *wh*-phrase overtly and the other covertly. The island boundary is not transparent when covert movement applies. However, judgments regarding the Bulgarian data seem not to be completely clear. Milena Petrova (personal communication) indicates that sentences like (i) are quite unacceptable for her. For more discussion of multiple *wh*-questions in Bulgarian and superiority effects, see, for instance, Bošković 1997 and Rudin 1988. See also Grewendorf 2001 for further discussion of the extraction of *wh*-phrases in multiple *wh*-questions.

12. A licenser and a licensee cannot share a referential index (*i*-index), as illustrated by the licensing of a negative polarity item by negation. Consider (i).

(i) John did not see anyone.

Not and *anyone* do not share an *i*-index. If they did, we would incorrectly expect a Principle C violation to arise in (ii).

(ii) John did not$_i$ say anything$_i$ to anyone$_i$.

13. As we will discuss in detail in chapter 3, a *wh*-interrogative contains three parts: the Question, Quantification, and Restriction parts. In LA, a *wh*-DP contains the Quantification part and the Restriction part. It has interrogative force when it occupies the Spec of Comp.

14. The unacceptability of the following LA sentences is still accounted for under the assumption that a *wh*-phrase does not undergo movement:

(i) *biħibb   miin
    likes.3MS who
    'Whom_i does he_i like?'

(ii) *l-mara   yalli htammit   f-ii   biħibb miin
     the-woman that took.care.3FS of-him likes.3FS who
     'Who_i does the woman that took care of him_i like?'

The coindexed pronoun must have a c-commanding antecedent in order to be interpreted as a bound pronoun. Under the assumption that 'whom' does not move to the Spec of Comp, the pronoun will not have a c-commanding antecedent.

15. This also indicates that an in-situ *wh*-phrase (at least a *wh*-element in an argument position) does not undergo covert *wh*-movement to the Spec of Comp even when no island boundary exists between the in-situ *wh* and the Spec of Comp as in (21d). Otherwise, (21d) would be as unacceptable as (20).

16. *Man haaðaa* is well formed as a sentence ('Who is this one?') but not as a DP.

17. Ouhalla (1996) characterizes the Iraqi Arabic *wh*-element corresponding to LA *miin* 'who' as an interrogative pronoun.

18. Considering the ramification of this analysis and the MMC, we can note that we do not find *miin* 'who' to be a resumptive strong pronoun. Instead, as indicated in (i), the strong pronoun *huwwe* is the resumptive strong pronoun forming a chain with a *wh*-element.

(i) ʔayya walad ziʕlo   min baʕdma huwwe raaħ
    which boy   cried.2P after   he   left.3MS
    'Which boy did you cry after he left?'

A [+*wh*] feature occurs with the strong resumptive pronoun (see section 2.1). In (i), the [+*wh*] feature is adjoined to the whole DP dominating the strong pronoun, and it is not generated in the Spec containing the strong pronoun. This is why this strong pronoun is not realized as *miin* 'who', which, as we will show in detail, occupies the Spec of DP and is merged with a [+*wh*] feature in D.

19. Strong pronouns, like all DPs, can be coordinated, something not possible with weak pronouns.

(i) *Strong pronoun coordination*
    huwwe wə hiyye seefaro
    he   and she   traveled.3P

(ii) *Weak pronoun coordination*
     *šəft   wə a
     saw.1P.him and her

20. It is reasonable to assume that [+human], not being a grammatical feature in LA, is a substantive feature residing in N.

21. Also see Reinhart 1997 and Barss 2000 for the distinction between *which* and non-*which* phrases in terms of choice functions; and see Barss 2000 for the optional occurrence of [+*wh*] on *wh*-expressions. Uriagereka (1998, 366) suggests an Attract Closest approach to the absence of superiority effects in cases involving *which* phrases. For such instances, Uriagereka suggests that the *wh*-element that undergoes movement is *which*, which is contained in the DP [*which* NP] and does not c-command outside the DP. Therefore, in an example like (i), *which* does not c-command *who* and does not violate Superiority.

(i) Who$_i$ did [which boy] bring x_i?

This approach would not distinguish the difference in superiority effects between *which* and non-*which* phrases in cases where neither the *wh*-phrase nor the RP c-commands the other, such as the examples in (20) containing *miin* 'who' and those in (37) containing *ʔayya* 'which'.

22. According to Aoun and Choueiri (1999), this is why certain *wh*-words cannot stay in situ. For instance, *šu* 'what' in LA cannot be D-linked and so it must undergo overt movement.

23. For English, the great majority of the examples cited to support the notion that D-linking does not exhibit Superiority contain *which* NPs. The very few cases with non-*which* phrases do not seem to have the stress and intonation pattern of standard *wh*-questions. For instance, in her discussion of Bolinger's (1978) and Pesetsky's (1987) contextual D-linked non-*which* N, Comorovski (1996, 84–85) quotes the following examples:

(i) a. I know that among all the disasters in the kitchen, Jane scorched the bean[s] and Lydia put salt in the tea: but WHAT did WHO break? I know that somebody broke something, so stop evading my question.

    b. I know that we need to install transistor A, transistor B, and transistor C, and I know that these three holes are for transistors, but I'll be damned if I can figure out from the instructions WHERE WHAT goes!

Note that the *wh*-phrases in these instances are stressed and read with an intonation break after the first *wh*-phrase. They contrast with standard multiple non-*which* or *which* questions such as *Who is going where?* or *Which review did which writer write?* that do not require such extra features.

Comorovski goes on to say, quoting Pesetsky, that judgments on these sentences are delicate. There is considerable variation in acceptability judgments of sentences involving Superiority violations when the *wh*-phrases are not *which* phrases.

In an interesting discussion on The LINGUIST List (subject line "Multiple *Wh*-XP Interrogatives," summarized by Carsten Breul on 3 December 1999), typical English sentences that violate Superiority such as (ii)–(iii) were judged as unacceptable by an overwhelming majority of participants even in clearly D-linked contexts.

(ii) What did who bring?

(iii) Which present did who bring?

24. The notion of Match in our analysis differs from the one proposed by Boeckx (2001). We claim that Match is a top-down process and is not an instance of movement. As a result, reconstruction, a property of movement, does not occur under Match in our analysis. Boeckx views both Match and Agree as instances of movement. To rule out (41), he needs to assume that when Match and Agree compete, Match has to apply. Then, to account for the well-formedness of LA sentences equivalent to 'Who did you talk to before Peter saw whom?', he needs to assume that Match and Agree do not compete when one *wh*-element c-commands the other.

25. The underlying assumption is that an element cannot form a chain with two or more different operators (i.e., be superscripted more than once).

26. The contrast between (43) and (45) distinguishes Boeckx's proposal and ours. Since his approach views Agree (Move) and Match as instances of botom-up extraction, (43) and (45) should have the same status: they should both violate Minimality.

27. Richards (1997) indicates that in languages like Bulgarian that allow multiple overt *wh*-fronting, the fronted *wh*-elements are "tucked in." If more than one XP moves to check the feature of a single head, then later XP movement takes place to an inner Spec, resulting in the order illustrated in (i).

(i) XP_1 XP_2 $[\ldots x_1 \ldots x_2 \ldots]$

Assuming that the fronted *wh*-elements are within the same cycle and that the MMC is checked in a top-down manner within the cycle, the MMC is satisfied: XP_1 binds the first available XP with a $[+wh]$ feature, which is x_1. XP_2 binds the next available $[+wh]$ XP since x_1 has already been identified as the variable bound by XP_1 and is no longer available.

What is not expected under our approach, however, is the freedom of XP_2 and XP_3 when three phrases are fronted, as in the case of Bulgarian multiple *wh*-fronting (see, e.g., Rudin 1988; Comorovski 1996; Richards 1997; Pesetsky 2000). For a question like (ii) that contains three *wh*-phrases, for instance, the order can be either (iiia) or (iiib) (for simplicity, we give only the English glosses).

(ii) John misli koj kogo s   kogo zapozna?
     John thinks who whom with whom introduced
     'John thinks who introduced whom to whom?'

(iii) a. [who$_1$ whom$_2$ to whom$_3$ [John thinks [x_1 introduced x_2 x_3]]]
      b. [who$_1$ to whom$_3$ whom$_2$ [John thinks [x_1 introduced x_2 x_3]]]

Richards proposes the Principle of Minimal Compliance (PMC) to accommodate such facts.

To account for the generalization captured by the PMC, one may speculate that a *wh*-phrase can be merged with a c-commanding *wh*-phrase before undergoing *wh*-movement (in the spirit of Saito 1994). In a structure containing $[\ldots wh_1 \ldots wh_2 \ldots wh_3]$ in the argument position, wh_2 or wh_3 can be merged with the c-commanding wh_1 in its argument position, and wh_3 can be merged with the c-commanding wh_2 in its argument position. (This merger is not an operator movement process and therefore is not subject to the MMC.) If wh_2 is merged with wh_1, the ordering after wh-movement is $[wh_1\ wh_2\ wh_3]$; if wh_3 is merged with wh_1, the ordering after wh-movement is $[wh_1\ wh_3\ wh_2]$. Note that the merger cannot be left-adjunction: it preserves the initial ordering of the merged elements.

28. Although the formulation of the MMC in (47) builds on the theory that a variable is a copy of the operator, we are not concerned with exact copies. That is, *who* is not necessarily searching for *who*. It is searching for an XP with a $[+wh]$ feature. This is because, when the operator-variable well-formedness condition is checked by the MMC on the relevant representations, it is only the relevant features of the operator and the potential variable that are taken into consideration. A wh-operator is an operator that contains a $[+wh]$ feature, and it needs to form a chain with an element with a $[+wh]$ feature. Moreover, as we show immediately in the text, a quantificational operator has a [+quantification] feature, and it needs to form a chain with an element that also has a [+quantification] feature.

29. This account rests on the assumption that the trace of a QP also has the feature [+quantification]. Again, this is in line with the notion that an operator and a trace share the same features (copies). Clearly, however, where the [+quantification] feature appears does not always mark the quantificational scope. If it did, the positions marking the quantificational scope would be all the positions in the chain containing the QP and the trace, and a QP would be interpreted as simultaneously having various scope properties. This is not surprising. Like spell-out rules taking into account only one copy in a chain for overt morphological realization, the interpretive rules also take into account only one copy for scope. See Nunes 1995 and Hornstein 1995 for relevant discussion.

Note also that the entire set of features of a wh-copy differs from the entire set of features of a QP-copy: the former has a $[+wh]$ feature and the latter does not. The MMC is only concerned with the features relevant to establishing an operator-variable relation. A wh-operator contains a $[+wh]$ feature and a [+quantification] feature; therefore, it must search for an XP that contains the same features, $[+wh]$ and [+quantification]. A quantificational operator contains a [+quantification] feature only; it searches for an XP that contains a [+quantification] feature.

30. The discussion assumes that QR does not raise a QP higher than the Spec of Comp that hosts the wh-operator (QR does not adjoin a QP to a CP). However, even if the QP can be adjoined to a position higher than the wh-operator in the Spec of Comp, as in (i)–(ii), (i) would still behave like (48b) and (ii) like (48c).

(i) *$[QP_2 \ldots wh_1 \ldots t_1 \ldots t_2]$

(ii) $[QP_1 \ldots wh_2 \ldots t_1 \ldots t_2]$

Chapter 3

1. These readings will be elaborated when they are discussed in more detail later in the text.

2. Hornstein accepts the claim that a pair-list reading is a subcase of a functional interpretation (see Chierchia 1991, 1993; Hornstein 1995; Hagstrom 1998, and the

references cited therein for extensive discussion of functional and pair-list interpretations). That is, a multiple *wh*-interrogative is answered with a list of pairs,
and the interpretation of such a multiple *wh*-interrogative is termed a pair-list
interpretation or a functional interpretation. We will neglect the distinction
between functional and pair-list interpretations for the moment. See further discussion of the need to distinguish these interpretations and their definitions in
sections 3.2 and 3.3.

3. The following quotation illustrates the notion of a generator providing a
domain:

Consider, for example, universal quantifiers which easily support pair-list readings. Universal quantifiers denote all the supersets of a given set. For example,
every man is the set of sets that have the set of men as a subpart. The set of men
"generates" the set of supersets. Universal quantifiers allow one to "retrieve a
domain" immediately. (Hornstein 1995, 114)

4. Hornstein suggests that a structural notion such as "almost c-command" can
be adopted in lieu of linking. He notes the contrast between sentences like (i) and
(ii) and argues that (iii) is the correct formulation of WCO.

(i) Someone from every small town$_i$ hates it$_i$.

(ii) *At least one picture of every senator$_i$ graced his$_i$ desk.

(iii) *Weak Crossover (Hornstein 1995, 108–110)*
     A pronoun P may be linked to a variable V iff V almost c-commands P. A
     almost c-commands B $=_{def}$ A c-commands B or the projection C that
     dominates A c-commands B. "Domination" is defined in terms of exclusion:
     A dominates B iff every segment of A dominates B.

In (i), the PP *from every small town* is adjoined to the nominal expression; in (ii),
of every senator is a complement of the head noun *picture*. The variable in (i) is
shallowly enough embedded that it meets the definition of "almost c-command"
and therefore can legitimately be linked to the pronoun in the example. In contrast, the variable in (ii) is too deeply embedded and therefore fails to "almost c-
command" the pronoun in question; thus, the pronoun cannot be linked to that
variable.

5. Although Hornstein (1995) does not discuss sentences like the following, his
analysis predicts that such sentences are unacceptable:

(i) Which song did who sing?

(i) has the representation in (ii) before deletion.

(ii) [$_{CP}$ which song$_i$ [$_{IP}$ who sing which song$_i$]]

Unlike *which man* in (5) in the text, *who* cannot be a generator because it does not
occupy the Spec of CP. Therefore, this sentence has the same status as *What did
who sing?*

6. Multiple *wh*-interrogatives have either a pair-list interpretation or a single-pair
interpretation. The latter is not a functional interpretation. It is not clear how the
existence of a single-pair interpretation should be analyzed in an approach that

requires multiple *wh*-interrogatives to always be functionally interpreted—that is, to have a pair-list interpretation.

7. The locality condition proposed by Aoun and Choueiri (1999) includes islands; however, this formulation cannot be maintained in light of examples such as (19), whose infinitival purposive clause creates an island boundary.

8. A locality condition on the availability of a pair-list interpretation for multiple *wh*-questions has been noted by, for instance, Brody (1995), Hornstein (1995), Arnaiz (1996), and Garrett (1996).

9. Beck (1996) and Beck and Kim (1997) argue that negation and other quantificational elements can block the application of LF movement. Pesetsky (2000) argues that feature movement, but not phrasal movement, is blocked by negation or other quantificational elements.

Concerning interpretations, Beck (1996) claims that the blocking effect makes an individual reading unavailable. Only a pair-list reading is possible. This claim is difficult to evaluate because a subcase of a pair-list reading is an individual reading. By contrast, an individual reading does not entail a pair-list reading. The facts in LA show that the blocking effect makes a pair-list interpretation unavailable.

10. In LA, negation alone does not block a pair-list interpretation. It is only when a negative polarity item also occurs that the intervention effect is manifested. In LA, negation can cliticize onto the verb; in this case, its c-command domain is restricted to the element it is cliticized to, and hence negation cannot act as an intervening element under these circumstances. Since a negative polarity item needs to be licensed/c-commanded by the negative element, the negation is not cliticized onto the verb, and its c-command domain is therefore not restricted to the verb in the presence of a polarity item. Therefore, negation functions as an intervening element whenever a polarity item co-occurs with it.

11. Arnaiz (1996) argues for the relevance of indicative mood and negation in determining the acceptability of multiple *wh*-questions in Spanish.

12. The condition on generating a pair-list interpretation in English, however, is difficult to define because there is no agreement on what the facts are. Hornstein (1995) seems to assume that a pair-list interpretation is subject to an island condition. Nishigauchi (1998) mentions in passing that there seems to be a clausemate condition on pairing *wh*-phrases, but that the facts are not clear. Garrett (1996) argues that pairing a matrix *wh* and another *wh*-phrase across an island depends on the relative positions of the embedded *wh* and some operator within the island (such as the relativized element in a relative clause or a *because* or *when* operator in an adjunct clause). Brody (1995) claims that two *wh*-phrases can be paired if they are separated by one island but not two islands.

13. It is not clear why something like the Island Condition should exist in this account. A pro is postulated in order to obtain a functional interpretation. Islands block the functional binding of a pronoun. In general, however, the binding of a pronoun by its antecedent is not sensitive to island conditions. This is illustrated

in (i), where different kinds of islands and more than one island separate the pronoun and its antecedent.

(i) a. Every student$_i$ thinks that the teacher will get angry if he$_i$ fails the exam.
   b. Who$_i$ wants to know whether John likes him$_i$?
   c. Who$_i$ threw away a prize that was given to him$_i$?
   d. Who$_i$ is worried that the guests will leave if they do not meet with speakers he$_i$ brought in?

14. The cases discussed by Beck and Kim involve the licensing of in-situ *wh*-phrases, not the conditions on pair-list interpretations. See, among others, Hoji 1985 and Lee 2001 for the intervention effects governing the distribution of in-situ *wh*-phrases.

15. Moltmann and Szabolcsi (1994) note that a quantifier inside an embedded interrogative (*wh*-island) can have scope over a matrix quantifier despite the intervening clause boundary (also see Sharvit 1996; Nishigauchi 1998). In other words, QR can cross a clause boundary in special contexts, such as when the clause is an embedded question. If this were the case in LA, one might claim that the putative merger is indeed due to QR. However, the relevant LA data are not limited to contexts of embedded questions. In addition, a *wh*-element inside a *wh*-island in LA cannot take scope outside the island.

16. Garrett (1996) accounts for the pair-list interpretation of two English *wh*-phrases separated by an island by a pied-piping process: moving the island containing a *wh*-phrase to a shared phrase of the higher clause containing another *wh*-phrase that occurs in the distributive phrase (Beghelli 1995, 1997; Beghelli and Stowell 1997). The English data in Garrett's work also show a subject-object asymmetry: the subject of an adjunct island can be paired with another *wh*-phrase in the higher clause, but an object cannot. However, the subject-object asymmetry extends to complex NP islands as well, in contrast to LA. Moreover, in Garrett's account, what matters is the relative position between an operator defining the island (such as a *because* or *when* operator in an adjunct clause or a relative operator in a relative clause) and the *wh*-phrase inside the island. It is not quite a subject-object asymmetry. The intervention effect is not present either, as according to Garrett the subject of a relative clause can be paired with another *wh*-phrase in the higher clause, in contrast to what happens in LA.

17. Bošković (1998) points out an interesting correlation between the application of overt *wh*-movement and the obligatoriness of a pair-list interpretation: a multiple *wh*-interrogative requires a pair-list interpretation if overt *wh*-movement applies; a single-pair reading is available when overt *wh*-movement does not apply. LA does not seem to show this correlation. There are no differences between sentences with or without overt *wh*-movement with respect to the availability of a pair-list interpretation.

18. See May 1990, 125, on using Absorption to derive pair-list interpretations.

19. Norbert Hornstein (personal communication) suggests that the domain requirement is relevant to a pair-list interpretation because of the application of head movement. He notes that a pair-list interpretation may require the absorp-

tion of two quantifiers (combining two quantifiers; see section 3.2.2), which is made possible by moving the quantificational head. Such a quantificational head movement may be blocked by Tense—the domain requirement.

20. Note that an A-relation can always be present in the three interpretations. Therefore, this observation may be interpreted as follows: A functional relation (A-relation) is present in both distributive and pair-list interpretations. A distributive interpretation adds a quantifier relation to the existing A-relation. A pair-list interpretation adds an Agree relation to the quantifier relation and the A-relation. The distinction among these interpretations thus involves addition of requirements, as summarized in (i).

(i)	Pronoun binding (A-dependency)	Quantifier intervention (quantifier interaction)	Agree (*wh*/*wh* interaction)
Functional reading	√		
Distributive reading	√	√	
Pair-list reading	√	√	√

21. This confirms the claim we made regarding Superiority in chapter 2 that in-situ *wh*-phrases do not undergo raising covertly.

22. On the tripartite structure of *wh*-expressions, see Karttunen 1977 and Tsai 1994, among others.

23. The Quantification may undergo QR, but it should stay in the same clause as the *wh*-phrase because of the clausemate constraint on QR (see, e.g., May 1977; Hornstein 1984). However, it is not empirically significant in these cases whether QR applies or not.

24. Jamal Ouhalla (personal communication) suggests the alternative of analyzing *wh*-words in these languages as not containing Question but only Quantification and Restriction. Question is generated apart from *wh*-words in both of these languages. In principle, this seems a likely alternative; the only cost, as Ouhalla notes, is that it would not capture the fact that *wh*-words in LA, for instance, are restricted to questions.

25. See the appendix for more comparison of different approaches to superiority effects.

Chapter 4

1. We will concentrate here on restrictive relative constructions and briefly discuss amount relatives, leaving other types of relatives, such as appositives, aside. For detailed studies of appositives, see Ross 1967, Emonds 1979, Demirdache 1991, and Del Gobbo 2001, among others. In these works, an appositive is not part of the clause containing the Head of the appositive (e.g., a coordination structure is involved). Also compare the "discontinuous constituent" approach proposed by McCawley (1982).

2. We will return to the issue of whether NP or DP should be adopted.

3. Schachter (1973) provides examples indicating reconstruction with respect to Principle C of binding theory.

(i) a. *The opinion of John$_i$ that he$_i$ thinks Mary has is unfavorable.
   b. *The portrait of John$_i$ that he$_i$ painted is extremely unflattering.

However, Munn (1994) and Safir (1999) do not find (ia), for instance, to be ungrammatical. Bhatt (2000) notes that the obligatory relative-clause-internal interpretation of the Head seen in (ia–b) is not a general property of relative clauses. The following example from Munn 1994 shows that the name *Al* cannot be interpreted inside the relative clause; if it were, the coindexing would be unacceptable:

(ii) In [[the picture of Al$_i$] which he$_i$ lent to us], he is shaking hands with the president.

   For discussion of these tests, see Bhatt 2000, sec. 1.3, Bhatt also demonstrates the availability of reconstruction using examples involving the scope of adjectives and pronoun binding. Also see Huang 1993, 106, n. 4 (citing Reinhart 1981), regarding the depth of embedding of the antecedent contained in an Ā-phrase.

   The above paragraphs do not seem to go along with Lebeaux's (1992) [generalization and] account for the argument-adjunct asymmetry in triggering Principle C effects under reconstruction. Also see Nunes 2001, where a "minimalist" analysis of Lebeaux's generalization is proposed that is compatible with a head-raising analysis of relative clauses.

4. As discussed further in section 4.4 and note 24, the purpose of the matching/ agreement relation between the Head and the *wh*-operator is to license the *wh*-operator. This, however, does not mean that the Head and the *wh*-operator must bear the same Case (Bianchi 2000b). This is very much like the fact that a pro is identified and licensed by a higher nominal (its binder/licenser) (see, e.g., Huang's (1982) generalized control rule), but the two do not bear the same Case feature. Where the two do agree, however, is in their interpretive features, including "substantive" features. See note 5.

5. The first use of the term *matching analysis* by Schachter (1973) referred to the fact that the derivation of a relative clause involves deletion of a nominal expression in the relative clause under identity with the base-generated Head (see Lees 1960, 1961; Chomsky 1965; Kuroda 1968). We use the term to refer to the fact that the Head and the *wh*-operator must agree in all interpretive features, including "substantive" features, capturing the fact that, for example, when the Head is [+human], the *wh*-operator must be *who* and cannot be *which*, *where*, *why*, and so on. *"Substantive" features* is a convenient label for features that normally occur in N such as [+human], [+thing], [+place], in contrast to grammatical/functional features such as [+singular] and [+definite]. The term does not include categorial features such as [+N], either. An adverb such as *why* also has a "substantive" feature [+reason], even though a *why* phrase is not a nominal phrase.

6. Smith (1964) argues that a relative clause is part of the determiner. Larson (1991) develops this idea further: he proposes that the determiner and the relative clause are subsumed under one bigger node [NP [Det + Relative Clause]] and that the determiner undergoes movement, deriving the word order [Det + NP + Relative Clause].

7. More examples are:

(i) *He is a brilliant actor that everyone wants to be and stupid producer that nobody wants to be.

(ii) *He is the brilliant doctor that everyone said he would be and miserable husband that his wife predicted.

8. More generally, demonstratives and *wrong*-type adjectives behave like relative clauses in these contexts: they make the relevant expressions acceptable.

(i) a. *John bought the type of house.
 b. John bought the wrong type of house.

(ii) a. *John bought the type of house.
 b. John bought that type of house.

See Schmitt's (2000) extension of her complement analysis (which adopts the insight of Kayne 1994) to these structures.

9. Carlson (1977) suggests that the patterns illustrated by the sentences in (i) all display a selection relation between the determiner and the complementizer of the embedded clause and that therefore, such an embedded clause has a determiner source; that is, it is generated under the determiner node and is subsequently extraposed.

(i) a. Max is tallER [THAN Marie is].
 b. Max is SO tall [THAT he has to crawl through doors].
 c. Max is AS short [AS I thought he was].
 d. Max is TOO tall [FOR us to hire (him) as our resident dwarf].

10. A fourth argument discussed by Bianchi (1999, 46–48), which we will not repeat here, concerns floating quantifiers in Italian.

11. In addition to providing synchronic support, Bianchi (2000a) argues from a historical perspective that the complementation structure, where CP is a complement of D, bears great similarity to the correlative construction. Citing data from Latin, Ancient Greek, Old English, and Old High German, she shows that these Indo-European languages have both correlative clauses and headed relative clauses and that the two constructions exploit exactly the same relative morpheme (p. 55). She argues with Haudry (1973) that the headed relative developed from an earlier correlative structure (p. 56). The important step in the transition from a correlative structure to a headed relative clause is the addition of a D to the correlative CP: [D CP]. The historical development from correlatives to relative clauses is therefore taken to be an argument for the [D CP] relative clause structure. This argument may hold for the languages discussed by Bianchi. However, Arabic does not seem to behave the same way. As we will show, LA has the same

relative clause structure as English. Nevertheless, LA does not and did not have a correlative construction.

12. In discussing derivations, we will show that failure to license an empty internal D renders Head raising unavailable to derive a relative construction.

13. In a promotion analysis such as Kayne's (1994), what is moved can be a *wh*-NP with the NP raised to the Spec of the *wh*-phrase. That is, the Head is still moved to its surface position. What is important in our discussion is that the Head is base-generated and bears an indirect interpretation relation, rather than a direct movement relation, to the *wh*-operator.

14. The discussion regarding English in this section would have been impossible without the generous help and arduous work on the data by Patricia Schneider-Zioga.

15. Some speakers do not find a contrast between *wh*-relatives and non-*wh*-relatives with respect to reconstruction. They regard the two types merely as stylistic variations: the use of a *wh*-pronoun is more formal or more polite than the use of *that* or Ø. Andrew Simpson (personal communication) suggests that, for such speakers, the *wh*-relative pronouns are reanalyzed as an X^0 in the complementizer position, rather than an XP in the Spec position. That is, for these speakers, the *wh*-pronouns function more or less like *that* syntactically (differing only stylistically). If such *wh*-pronouns are clearly XPs, reconstruction is difficult even for these speakers. For instance, the pronoun in the Head of (i) cannot be bound by the QP in the relative clause and the QP in the relative clause in (ii) cannot take scope over the Head QP.

(i) *I saw the girl of his$_i$ dreams whose pictures (John said) every boy$_i$ was showing off.

(ii) I saw the two students whose friends (John thought) every teacher visited.   (no narrow scope for *two students*)

16. There should be a third type involving base-generation of both Head and operator—that is, a variant according to which the Head is base-generated, not raised, and the operator is base-generated, not moved—in order to account for cases involving resumptive pronouns in English and the lack of reconstruction in such cases (for the role of an operator in base-generated structures, see sections 4.3 and 7.2).

Prince (1990) shows that even though relative clauses with resumptive pronouns are officially ungrammatical in English, they are in fact not uncommon in speech. Resumptive pronouns are found not only in contexts inaccessible to movement but also in positions where a gap is possible. Prince gives the following examples:

(i) a. ... the man who this made him feel sad ...
   b. Some of the same judges who we told them that if you mess with John Africa, you're going to ...

(ii) a. They were just towed across the Midway onto the bridle path, where they were just sitting there peacefully.

   b. That's a suggestion of yours which I followed, which I didn't even want to do that.

   c. I have a friend who she does all the platters.

However, the use of resumptive pronouns makes reconstruction impossible; compare (iiia) and (iiib).

(iii) a. *I am resolved to meet the girl of his$_i$ dreams that every man$_i$ is convinced she will love him passionately.

    b. I am resolved to meet the girl of his$_i$ dreams that every man$_i$ is convinced Ø will love him passionately.

Resumption in relative constructions is correlated with lack of reconstruction in English; that is, resumption is correlated with lack of movement.

17. To be noted, however, is that even though the presence of an overt *wh*-phrase in a relative clause (the *wh*-relative) indicates that the relative is derived by operator movement, the absence of an overt *wh*-phrase, as in a *that* relative or a relative without *that* or *wh*, does not indicate how the relative must be derived. Either Head raising or operator movement could be at work.

18. Philippe Schlenker (personal communication) points out that the *wh*-operator movement analysis can also account for nonrestrictive relative clauses (appositives) in English, which also fail to exhibit reconstruction effects.

19. Andrew Simpson (personal communication) notes that stacking *is* possible with *headway*, in contrast to Carlson's example in (62b).

(i) Jack noticed the headway that WE made ____ that the other team miserably FAILED to make ____.

This may suggest that a relative formed on *headway* is not an amount relative, if Carlson's generalization is correct that stacking is impossible with amount relatives.

20. The lack of a reconstructed scope reading for structures like this is observed by Bianchi (1999), who claims that *some* is obligatorily raised to the external D position, which is not part of the Head, and is not reconstructed. However, one might plausibly argue that the empty internal D is licensed/identified by *some*. Such an empty D may assume the properties of *some* after the licensing. On the other hand, if there is simply no DP raising in such cases (e.g., because the empty D fails to be licensed), we need not be concerned with whether or not it is appropriate that the licensing allows the internal D to assume the properties of the external D.

21. Structures involving anaphors are the least clear. In some cases, the "reconstructed" interpretation is perfectly acceptable. We have no account for this fact. This also reminds us of the complexity of defining which anaphors are true anaphors subject to binding, as discussed extensively in the literature (see, e.g., Reinhart and Reuland 1993; Ueyama 1998; Hoji, to appear).

22. For some speakers, using the quantifier *every* for the QP in the relative clause seems to allow the reconstructed interpretation more easily. This may be related to the possibility of "quirky binding" as discussed by Ueyama (1998).

23. The unacceptability of coordination in (i) also supports the claim that the occurrence of a relative clause requires the presence of a D.

(i) *He is an [[actor who wants to do everything] and [producer who wants to please everyone]].

The unacceptability of (16a) can be analyzed as a failure to license the internal D in the second conjunct, because it is too far away from the external D. ((iia–b) represent two possible coordination structures—see, e.g., Ross 1967; Grimshaw 1990; Munn 1992; Kayne 1994, 59; Bianchi 1999, 263).

(ii) a. *He is an [$_{ConjP}$[$_{CP}$[Ø actor] [that wants to do everything]] [$_{Conj'}$ and [$_{CP}$[Ø producer] [that wants to please everyone]]]].
   b. *He is an [$_{CP}$[$_{CP}$[Ø actor] [that wants to do everything]] and [$_{CP}$[Ø producer] [that wants to please everyone]]]].

The question is why (iiia–b), which do not contain two empty internal determiners, are also unacceptable.

(iii) a. *He is an [$_{ConjP}$[$_{CP}$[actor] [who wants to do everything]] [$_{Conj'}$ and [$_{CP}$[producer] [who wants to please everyone]]]].
   b. *He is an [$_{CP}$[$_{CP}$[actor] [who wants to do everything]] and [$_{CP}$[producer] [who wants to please everyone]]]].

The unacceptability of (iiia–b) is to be contrasted with the acceptability of (iv).

(iv) He is an [$_{ConjP}$[$_{NP}$ actor] [$_{Conj'}$ and [$_{NP}$ producer]]].

Possibly this contrast is due to a requirement that a determiner be associated with an NP semantically. The elements conjoined in (iv) are NPs, and the entire conjunct is also an NP (the ConjP being an extended functional projection—regarding extended functional projections, see, e.g., Fukui and Speas 1986; Abney 1987; Grimshaw 1990). In (iv), the D is associated with the entire conjunct, which is essentially an NP; in (iii), by contrast, it is a CP.

24. In our analysis, the matching relation between the Head nominal and the operator is encoded in a predication or agreement relation between the Head and the operator, which is derived from the need to license the operator in a relative clause.

25. Indeed, it is an important question whether English does generate a ForceP and a TopP and whether the Head and *wh*-operator of relative constructions occupy the positions indicated in these structures (Elabbas Benmamoun and Andrew Simpson, personal communications). Here, we only attempt to build on the structure proposed by Bianchi, without further justifications. Other structures could plausibly be entertained, such as those making use of multiple Spec of CP positions or Spec of Spec of CP positions. Regardless of labeling variations, the essence of the analysis proposed here can still be maintained, namely, that (1) two derivations are possible, as indicated by the (un)availability of reconstructing the Head and (2) a complementation structure can be adopted (to capture the fact that a relative construction requires a DP projection).

26. See Bianchi 2000a for possible solutions to questions regarding coordination and extraposition that seem to pose problems for a complementation structure.

27. The complementation structure can also capture the facts regarding LA relative constructions, which are also Head-initial and which are also derived by either Head raising or operator movement. The only difference between English and LA lies in the fact that relative operators in LA are not *wh*-expressions.

28. Judgments vary in cases containing *when* and *where*—not surprisingly, since these are more argument-like phrases.

29. Larson (1985) observes that, when a relative clause contains a trace in an adjunct position, the Head is a bare NP–adverb.

(i) a. the way$_i$ [that you talk t$_i$]
    b. *the manner/fashion [that you talk t$_i$]
    c. You talked that way.
    d. *You talked that manner/fashion.

This is peculiar to *how* expressions. A logical possibility might be that reconstruction of the Head (Head raising) is available in these bare NP–adverb cases. The facts, unfortunately, are not quite clear.

30. Still, the sentences involving relative clauses (86) are worse than those involving a simple *wh*-island (87). This is expected, because a relative construction involves more barriers than a *wh*-island (Chomsky 1986a), however the notion of barrierhood is to be captured in the Minimalist Program.

31. Åfarli's (1994) analysis of Norwegian relative constructions includes two classes: one involves a (Head-)raising analysis as in Kayne 1994, and the other involves an operator analysis as in Chomsky 1977b. A relative clause that involves an overt relative pronoun (a *der* relative) is not derived by raising, while a relative clause that does not involve an overt relative pronoun (a *som* relative) is derived by raising. Åfarli also mentions the possible existence of two derivations for English relative constructions. Also see Munn 1994 regarding reconstruction effects in English relatives. Bhatt (2000) notes as well that some English relative clauses cannot be derived by Head raising, especially those that involve complex pied-piping, such as (i). Also see Sauerland 1998 for two relative structures.

(i) the first movie *whose score* John ever said that Shostakovich composed

See note 15 regarding speaker variations.

32. Comparing relatives in English and LA, we note that Choueiri (2002) does not propose that the operator movement (matching) analysis derives relatives in LA, even though she argues that it is available in English. Alternatively, it is possible to suggest that operator movement still applies in the cases where movement is allowed, but that its effects are obscured because base-generation structures do not show reconstruction effects, either.

Chapter 5

1. Our work reported in Aoun and Li 1993a was carried out in the principles-and-parameters framework (Chomsky 1981), which embodies a central notion of government. In the Minimalist Program (Chomsky 1995), the notion of government is abandoned. It should still be recognized, however, that there is a domain

requirement between 'all' and the nominal phrase it is associated with. For ease of presentation, we will continue using the term *government*, with the understanding that the government domain requirement might best be captured in some other manner.

2. Not surprisingly, the idiom chunk can be related to the relative clause and the matrix clause simultaneously. (Regarding the structure of the idioms in (i), see notes 3 and 4.)

(i) a. ta *chi*-le [[ta bu yinggai *chi* e_i de] cu_i]
        he *eat*-LE he not should *eat*   DE *vinegar*
        'Lit. He eats vinegar that he should not eat.'
        'He was unnecessarily jealous.'

    b. ta *you*-le [[ta bu yinggai *you* e_i de] mo_i]
        he *hu*-LE he not should *hu*- DE *-mor*
        'Lit. He hu-ed the -mor that he should not hu-.'
        'He said a humorous thing that he should not have said.'

3. The idiom *chi-cu* 'eat vinegar', meaning 'be jealous,' has a [V + O] structure.

4. *You-mo* is a transliteration of the English expression *humor*. It takes a [V + O] structure, the first syllable being analyzed as a verb and the second as an object of the verb.

(i) ta hen xihuan *you* ni-de   *mo*
     he very like   *hu*- you-DE *-mor*
     'He likes to *humor* you.'

5. In English, the external D is not part of the Head that is raised to its surface position and therefore is not reconstructed with the Head. The Head contains a null determiner if it is not a *wh*-element. One might wonder whether English actually raises an NP in the non-*wh* relatives, instead of a DP, just as Chinese does (see Kayne 1994; Bhatt 2000). However, this option faces the problems raised by Borsley (1997). (We will return in chapters 6 and 7 to an account for why Chinese allows NP movement but not DP movement.) Moreover, it does not explain why Chinese does not allow reconstruction with respect to scope but English does.

6. Two VPs connected by *jian* express dual activities performed by one person or simultaneous activities. Otherwise, the connector is *erqie*, which can be used to connect any nonnominal expressions. The conjuncts connected by *jian* cannot contain aspect markers (or negation or any other functional categories above VP).

(i) *ta nian-zhe/le/guo shu, jian zuo-zhe/le/guo shi
     he read-ASP   book and do-ASP   jobs

7. Does *erqie* connect CPs, or IPs, or both? (27a–b) demonstrate that *erqie* connects full clauses. If clauses are CPs, then *erqie* connects two CPs. There are other clearer examples, such as those containing a 'because' clause, which may provide clues to whether C is included or excluded (CP or IP) in cases of *erqie* conjunction. (i) shows that *erqie* can connect two conjuncts without repeating *yinwei* 'because'. If *yinwei* heading a 'because' clause is analyzed as C, then *erqie* can connect two IPs.

(i) yinwei ta dedao zuida de jiang erqie ta you you xi   shi
    because he get   biggest DE prize and he also have good thing
    jiang-lin,   women dou wei ta   gaoxing
    forth-coming we   all for him happy
    'We are all happy for him because he got the biggest prize and he is having a
    happy event.'

(ii) shows that *erqie* can also connect two conjuncts each of which begins with
'because'. That is, *erqie* can connect two CPs as well.

(ii) women dou wei ta   gaoxing, yinwei ta dedao zuida de jiang erqie
     we   all for him happy   because he got   biggest DE prize and
     yinwei ta you xi   shi   jiang-lin
     because he have good thing forth-coming
     'We are all happy for him because he got the biggest prize and because he is
     having a happy event.'

8. This requirement on *jian* may have to do with the fact that *jian* can be a verb
meaning 'do one thing simultaneously with another', as indicated by the [V + O]
compound *jian-chai* 'jian − job = do part-time work, do jobs simultaneously'.

9. Note 7 gives examples of *erqie* conjoining CPs and IPs. (i) and (ii) illustrate
erqie conjoining AdjPs and VPs.

(i) ta hen congming erqie hen piaoling
    she very bright   and very pretty
    'She is bright and pretty.'

(ii) ta changchang jiao   wo shuxue erqie jie   wo qian
     he often   teach me math and lend me money
     'He often teaches me math and lends me money.'

10. Some speakers accept such sentences, especially if they are made more complicated. One such speaker notes that such sentences sound "interpretable but not
logical" (Bingfu Lu, personal communication).

11. Only one-syllable adjectives describing size can occur between a number and
a classifier.

(i) a. san   da zhang zhi
       three big piece paper
       'three big pieces of paper'
    b. yi   xiao bei shui
       one small cup water
       'one small cup of water'
    c. yi da tou niu
       one big head cow
       'a big cow'

It is no surprise from a semantic point of view that adjectives preceding classifiers
are restricted to size if we assume that an adjective modifies what immediately
follows: the modification of classifiers (unit expressions) is inherently restricted.
What needs to be stipulated is the morphosyntactic fact that the number and

classifier and the intervening size adjective form a compound. This reflects a general pattern within nominal phrases that, if *de* disappears in a nominal expression containing a prenominal element XP [XP *de* ____], the XP must be compounded with the following element (the exception being [XP *de* Demonstrative ...], where *de* can disappear without XP and Demonstrative forming a compound; see note 12).

12. The "modifiers" always end with the marker *de*, which indicates that a noun must follow. The status of *de* is a matter of debate. *De* occurs in the pattern [XP *de* NP], where NP can be replaced by ClP or DP, and where XP can be nominal, adjectival, or clausal. It seems to be a genitive marker when XP is a nominal and the nominal is interpreted as a possessor. However, it is more than a genitive marker, as its wider distribution indicates. Two issues have been widely debated: (1) Is there one *de* or more than one? Should all occurrences of *de* be analyzed as one and the same? (2) Does *de*, which can be phonologically dependent on the preceding syllable, syntactically form a constituent with the preceding XP or actually head a projection? The coordination facts we will present shortly indicate that *de* can form a constituent with the preceding XP. If it indeed does so, then it does not itself head a projection. The answer to the first question, however, seems to be more theory internal.

The question, of course, is what *de* is if it does not head a projection itself. One speculation is that *de* is simply "a marker of nonlexical phrases" (Chao 1968, 287). To put it in other terms, it indicates a noncompounding structure. A form without *de* [XP N(P)] is always a compound; a form with *de* [XP de N(P)] is a phrasal category, not a compound. Expressions like those in (i) are compounds, but those in (ii) are phrasal categories "associated" with the head N (Li and Thompson 1981, 113–116). In Li and Thompson's terms, *de* is an associative marker, indicating that the XP in [XP *de* N] bears some relation to (is associated with) the head N.

(i) a. zhongguo yinhang
       China   bank
       'China Bank' (name of a bank)
    b. xiao haizi
       small child
       'children'
    c. hei   ban
       black board
       'blackboard'

(ii) a. zhongguo de yinhang
        China   DE bank
        'Chinese bank; bank of China' (not the name of a bank)
     b. xiao de haizi
        small DE child
        'small kid'
     c. hei   de ban
        black DE board
        'board that is black'

13. Zhang (2001, 2–3) notes that *yi* 'one, a' is compatible with a preceding adjective, pronoun, or proper noun, but is not compatible with a relative clause containing a subject gap, suggesting that the distribution of relative clauses differs from that of adjectives. This observation, however, is not quite true. The following minimal pairs, for instance, show no contrast at all, according to the native speakers consulted.

(i) a. wo kanjianle hen fei de yi-tou zhu   (Zhang's (5a))
     I   saw   very fat DE one-CL pig
     'I saw a very fat pig.'
  b. wo kanjianle zhang-de hen fei de yi-tou zhu
     I   saw   grow-DE very fat DE one-CL pig
     'I saw a pig that is very fat.'

(ii) a. ta toule ni-de   yi-feng xin   (Zhang's (6a))
     he stole you-DE one-CL letter
     'He stole a letter of yours.'
  b. ta toule ni gei ta   de yi-feng xin
     he stole you give him DE one-CL letter
     'He stole a letter you gave to him.'

14. Because *hen*, generally translated as 'very', occurring with an adjectival predicate does not carry much meaning, it has been claimed and widely accepted that the interpretation of *hen* can be used as a test to distinguish adjectives from verbs (see, e.g., Li and Thompson 1981). If a predicate phrase needs *hen* without the intensifier meaning, it is an adjective. However, this claim needs to be viewed with caution because semantically bleached *hen* often occurs with gradable verbs as well.

(i) ta hen xihuan ni
    he very like   you
    'He likes you.'

15. Sproat and Shih (1991) suggest that in Chinese, all adjectives followed by *de* are reduced relative clauses and that true adjectives modifying nouns (those that cannot be reduced relative clauses) do not occur with *de*. They give the two pairs of examples in (ia–d) (their (22a–d), p. 574). (Their examples (22a–b) (= (ia–b)) were taken from Huang 1987. However, Huang used these examples to make a point very different from Sproat and Shih's; see Huang 1987, 93–95.) According to Sproat and Shih, these examples show that *qian* 'former' and *wei* 'fake' cannot be predicates (ic–d) and that they occur with nouns without *de* (ia–b).

(i) a. *qian-de   zongtong   vs. qian   zongtong
     former-DE president   former president
  b. *wei-de yao   vs. wei yao
     fake-DE medicine   fake medicine
  c. *zhege zongtong qian
     this   president former
  d. *neifu yao   wei
     that   medicine fake

It is not clear that the correlation between nonoccurrence with *de* and failure to be a predicate holds, however. Note that 'former' and 'fake' in these instances are prefixes in modern Mandarin. If one uses these words the way they were used in earlier Chinese, instead of as prefixes, they can function as predicates.

(ii) a. ci   zhen bi   wei
        this true that fake
        'This is true and that is fake.'
     b. ci   qian   bi   hou
        this former that latter
        'This is the previous one and that is the following one.'

When 'former' and 'fake' are prefixes, they do not occur independently and do not function as predicates. Further, note that when an adjective occurs without *de*, it is always combined with the noun (as a prefix or a component of compounding); see note 12. This captures the fact that such adjectives must be bare and cannot be further modified as in (iii) (unless this further modification is also compounded as in (iv)).

(iii) *hen/ji/bu/shifen   wei yao
       very/very/not/absolutely fake medicine

(iv) fen-hong-lian-se
     powder-red-face-color
     'pink face (color)'

16. The following sentence is acceptable because the adjective is still used as a prenominal modifier, rather than a predicate:

(i) zhe-tiao daolu shi zhuyao de (daolu)
    this-CL road be main   DE road
    'This road is the main one.'

17. Inside a separate projection, an adjective can be a head (head analysis—e.g., Abney 1987; Kester 1993; Bernstein 1993) or a specifier (specifier analysis—e.g., Cinque 1994; see also Jackendoff 1977; Giorgi and Longobardi 1991; Longobardi 1994). See Bhattacharya 1999, sec. 2.4, for discussion of these analyses.

The distinction between a specifier analysis and an adjunction analysis is not clear when multiple specifiers are allowed in a projection and an adjective is the specifier of an NP (see, e.g., Bhattacharya 1999). What is important here is to determine whether an adjective occupies a separate functional projection, different from the projections within a nominal expression we have discussed so far (DP, NumP, ClP, NP).

18. Compounding in Chinese generally obeys rigid restrictions on the number of syllables in each component. For instance, (44f) is better if the first adjective has two syllables (see Feng 1995 on the effect of prosody on word order).

(i) fenhong xiao che
    pink   small car

19. The expressions in (44c) and (44d) are ambiguous. Both can have a conjoined reading: (44c) is 'small and red' and (44d) is 'red and small'. Alternatively, they

can have a hierarchical interpretation: (44c) means 'the small one(s) among the red ones' and (44d) means 'the red one(s) among the small ones'. See Huang 1982 regarding the scope relations of stacked modifiers: the one on the left has scope over the one on the right.

20. If *he/gen* replaces *erqie*, the conjuncts are DPs.

(i) gongtong de he/gen meiren keyi dai hui-qu   de dongxi
    common DE and   nobody can take back-go DE thing
    'things that are shared and (things that) nobody can take back'

The distinction between (i) and (48) can be mechanically expressed by saying that an empty category exists in the conjuncts in (i) but not in the conjuncts in (48).

21. As noted earlier in this section, a relative clause can not only immediately precede an NP but also occupy a higher position such as the one preceding a demonstrative.

(i) zhe jiu   shi [[zhangsan xie   t de] na-fen baodao]
    this exactly is   Zhangsan wrote DE that-CL report
    'This is the report that Zhangsan wrote.'

If relative clauses are adjoined to NPs, creating NP structures, a relative clause like that in (i) must be derived by a raising process. When multiple relative clauses are involved, the one on the left always has scope over the one on the right.

(ii) zhe jiu   shi [[zhangsan$_i$ yiwei women yijing   kan-guo de] [you guan
     this exactly is   Zhangsan think we   already seen   DE have relation
     ta$_i$ fuqin de] na-fen baodao]
     he father DE that-CL report
     'This is the report about his father that Zhangsan thinks that we have
     already seen.'

This indicates that the raising of relative clauses to higher positions does not change the original order (RC_1 and RC_2 indicate relative clauses 1 and 2).

(iii) [RC$_1$ [RC$_2$ ... [t$_1$ [t$_2$ [NP]]]]]

This is reminiscent of the "tucking-in" phenomenon discussed by Richards (1997) and noted in chapter 2. What is important, however, is that the "scope of modification" of relative clauses should be read off their overt positions, like that of adjectives and adverbs. Note further that the fact that relative clauses in Chinese are adjoined to different nodes is reminiscent of an interesting distinction between types of relative clauses noted by Larson and Takahashi (2002), who claim that relative clauses (and adjectives) can be either i-level (individual-level) or s-level (stage-level) modifiers. The former modify NP and the latter, DP.

22. According to Kayne (1994, chap. 8), a relative clause is nonrestrictive as long as it is outside the c-command domain of D, even though it is still inside the complex DP, as illustrated in (50). This view differs from the views of the appositive or nonrestrictive relative clause put forward by Ross (1967), Emonds (1979), Demirdache (1991), and others, according to whom, an appositive is not part of the clause containing the Head of the appositive (e.g., a coordination structure is

involved; also see McCawley's (1982) "discontinuous constituent" approach). When an appositive is not part of the clause containing the Head of the appositive, no constituents of the clause can c-command the appositive. For instance, the subject of the clause cannot c-command the appositive, and it therefore also cannot bind a pronoun inside the appositive.

(i) *Everyone$_i$ likes Mary, who will bring his$_i$ favorite picture.

In Kayne's analysis of nonrestrictive relatives, the relative clause is simply outside the scope of D but is not outside the containing complex DP. Accordingly, the subject of the main clause should be able to bind a pronoun within such a "nonrestrictive relative clause." The binding relation in (i) should be acceptable if (i) contains a "nonrestrictive relative clause." Kayne (1994, 164, n. 72) suggests that (i) is unacceptable because the complex nominal is a definite expression, which is opaque for binding. Bianchi (1999, 152) suggests a further movement process that raises the IP of the appositive to a topic position of the matrix clause. See Bianchi 1999, chap. 5, for an extensive review of various approaches and arguments supporting Kayne's approach to appositives.

23. In Chinese, relative clauses and adjectives occurring in different positions are interpreted differently: they modify what immediately follows. When they precede and therefore modify a demonstrative, they modify/restrict the reference of the demonstrative. When they precede and modify a noun, they further describe the property denoted by the noun. Relative clauses preceding a demonstrative have been termed restrictive and those following a demonstrative and preceding a noun have been termed nonrestrictive, or descriptive (Chao 1968; Huang 1982). For instance, as Huang (1982) observes, to further describe New York City, a Chinese speaker would use the order [Demonstrative + Relative Clause], shown in (i).

(i) niu yue, zhe-ge conglai bu mie   deng de chengshi
    New York this-CL ever   not extinguish light DE city
    'New York, the city that never goes dark'

The relative clause only further describes the city of New York. It does not restrict the reference of *chengshi* 'the city'. Note that the choice of relative clause is important. The acceptability of an expression like (ii) increases as the relative clause becomes more likely to help identify which city the speaker is referring to.

(ii) ??niu yue, conglai bu mie   deng de zhe-ge chengshi
     New York ever   not extinguish light DE this-CL city
     'New York, the city that never goes dark'

It is not always the case that mentioning a specific city prevents the speaker from using the form [Relative + Demonstrative]. The speaker may choose to help the hearer identify which city he is talking about by using a relative clause restricting the reference of the city: for example, *niu yue, zai meiguo dongbu de na-ge zui zhuyao de chengshi* 'New York, the important city that is on the East Coast of the United States'. If the proper name clearly needs no reminding description, the contrast is sharper.

(iii) a. ta dui zhongguo, zhe-ge lishi   youjiu de guojia, hen you xingqu
          he to China   this-CL history long   DE country very have interest
          'He is quite interested in China, a country with a long history.'
      b. ??ta dui zhongguo, lishi   youjiu de zhe-ge guojia, hen you xingqu
          he to China   history long   DE this-CL country very have interest
          'He is quite interested in China, a country with a long history.'

The following sentences give contexts facilitating the interpretation that the relative clause serves to identify the referent. In such contexts, the relative clause precedes the demonstrative; compare (iv) with (v).

(iv) ta nar   you wangwu xie   de shu, lisi xie   de shu, zhangsan xie
     he there have Wangwu write DE book Lisi write DE book Zhangsan write
     de shu; keshi wo zhidao *wangwu xie   de naxie* shu   quanbu bei
     DE book but I   know   Wangwu write DE those book all   by
     jie-zou   le
     borrow-away LE
     'He has books written by Wangwu, books written by Lisi, books written by Zhangsan; but I know that all the books written by Wangwu have been borrowed.'

(v) ??ta nar   you wangwu xie   de shu, lisi xie   de shu, zhangsan xie
    he there have Wangwu write DE book Lisi write DE book Zhangsan write
    de shu; keshi wo zhidao *naxie wangwu xie   de* shu   quanbu bei
    DE book but I   know   those Wangwu write DE book all   by
    jie-zou   le
    borrow-away LE

Note that the use of *nonrestrictive* here should be compared with its use in the previous note. Structurally, such descriptive or nonrestrictive relative clauses are still inside the complex nominal and therefore can be c-commanded by any higher phrase within the complex nominal or the clause containing the complex nominal. The acceptability of binding a reflexive in (vi) illustrates the hierarchical relation.

(vi) zhangsan$_i$ hen xihuan na-pian miaoshu ziji$_i$ de wenzhang
     Zhangsan very like   that-CL describe self DE article
     'Zhangsan likes the article that describes himself.'

Such "nonrestrictive" relative clauses are not the same as the appositive relative clause found in English. Indeed, Del Gobbo (2001) argues that a relative clause with the order [Relative Clause + Demonstrative + Classifier + Noun] or [Demonstrative + Classifier + Relative Clause + Noun] is uniformly a restrictive relative clause, not an appositive. Her arguments are based on the following generalizations:

(vii) a. Appositives are used to qualify unmodified proper nouns; restrictives usually are not.
      b. Appositives allow pied-piping; restrictives do not. (Emonds 1979)
      c. The antecedent of an appositive can be any maximal projection. (e.g., Sells 1985)
      d. Appositives follow the modifiers of a noun.

e. Restrictives allow stacking; appositives do not.

f. A quantifier cannot be the antecedent of an appositive. (Ross 1967)

g. No quantifier in the matrix clause can have scope over a pronoun in the appositive clause. (Safir 1986)

h. Appositives are affected by the presence of negation in the main clause. (Sells 1985)

The terms *nonrestrictive*, *descriptive*, *appositive*, and so on, are used differently in different works. What matters is that Chinese does not have the counterpart of the English appositive (with the properties listed above) as a subtype of relative clauses.

24. (52c) and (52d) are acceptable under the nonidiomatic interpretation.

25. To provide more support for a [D CP] structure for relative clauses in general, Bianchi (2000b) draws on the similarity between correlatives and relatives. This type of support is not applicable in Chinese. The best candidate for a correlative in Chinese contains a *wh*-phrase in the conditional clause and a coindexed expression in the main clause (Cheng and Huang 1996). The *wh*-phrase stays in situ; that is, it is not moved to the peripheral position. There is no prominent NP at the edge of the sentence (foregrounded, as in Schachter 1973) that "induces" the addition of a D on top of the clause to create an externally headed relative clause.

(i) ruguo ni   xihuan shei$_i$, wo jiu   qing   ta/na-ge ren$_i$ lai
    if   you like   who   I   then invite   him/that person come
    'If you like anyone, I will invite him/that person.'

26. One might suggest that the equivalent of a DP in English is a Classifier Phrase in Chinese (Cheng and Sybesma 1999), hence that Chinese relative constructions have ClP raising (in place of DP raising) and that the relative CP is complement to Cl (in place of D). This alternative cannot be adopted, however, because (1) it is not quite appropriate to claim that a Chinese ClP is the equivalent of an English DP and (2) the ClP account is not adequate for the facts regarding Chinese relative constructions.

First of all, it is not appropriate to equate a Chinese ClP with an English DP. Cheng and Sybesma (1999, 535–536) adopt the claim that a classifier in Chinese is involved in grammatical number. This makes a Cl + N expression in Chinese the equivalent of N-*s* in English (NP), not DP. Indeed, if a ClP in Chinese is like a DP in English, it is not expected that a number projection must precede the ClP in Chinese (the putative equivalent of DP) but must follow D in English.

Specific to relative constructions, if the analysis used for English relative constructions were adopted for Chinese, with D replaced by Cl, most of the facts discussed in this chapter would not be accounted for. For instance, it is not clear how the word order [Classifier + Relative Clause + Noun] can be derived. In order to derive Head-final word order, a relative clause minus the Head needs to move to the Spec of Cl/D, according to this revised Kayne-style approach. It is not clear how a relative clause can follow a classifier. It also is not clear how the NP conjunction facts in Chinese, in contrast to the obligatory DP conjunction found in English relative constructions, can be accounted for. Nor is it obvious how the reconstruction facts follow from such an alternative.

Chapter 6

1. The failure of the Head to c-command the relative clause is a welcome result with respect to Kayne's (1994, chaps. 1–2) Linear Correspondence Axiom: the one on the right should be c-commanded by, not c-command, the one on the left.

2. The distinction between adjunction and substitution lies in the projections and labeling of α: is it a projection of a maximal projection or of a nonmaximal projection?

3. Andrew Simpson (personal communication) questions why such a movement structure is not more generally available. For instance, why doesn't this process raise the subject of an adjunct clause in English as in [[*because people criticized t_i severely*] *Mary$_i$*]? It is possible that movement does not apply randomly (movement being a last resort operation; see Chomsky 1995, 28, 256–257). In the cases discussed in the text, a relative clause needs to be merged with a nominal Head in order to generate a relative construction.

4. Examples of this type are not easy to construct because, as mentioned in chapter 5, *jian* expresses two properties of one individual.

5. According to Kayne (1994, sec. 8.2), relative *wh*-pronouns occupy D. D is empty when there is no relative *wh*-pronoun.

6. Jamal Ouhalla and Andrew Simpson (personal communications) have independently suggested the possibility of analyzing the determiner occurring in a relative construction (***the** person that came*) as an internal D, not an external D (also see Ouhalla 1999, especially the discussion of Amharic). The cost of such an alternative would be the failure to account for the facts in support of the external D hypothesis. Moreover, the reconstruction facts in Chinese would not be captured straightforwardly.

7. We set aside any possible intervening functional projections here, such as a Number projection. What matters is the position of D.

8. We claim that bare *wh*-words are generated as NPs, not as DPs. The quantification force is obtained from a quantifier at the clausal level. This raises the question of what the structure should be for expressions like *na-ge-ren* 'which-CL-person = which person'.

(i) ni xihuan na-ge   ren,   wo jiu   qing ta   lai
    you like   which-CL person I   then invite him come
    'If you like someone, I will invite him over.'

The occurrence of classifiers indicates that such expressions have a projection larger than an NP. Crucially, however, the quantification is not generated together with the nominal expression. It is possible that *na* in D of *na-ge-ren* 'which person' is anaphoric in nature or is a variable that needs to be bound by a quantifier outside the nominal expression. The existence of such expressions, however, does not argue against labeling bare *wh*-words as NPs, which do not contain number and classifier expressions. See note 12.

9. Note that, although N-to-D raising takes place in Chinese to derive definite nominals, modifiers (adjectives, possessors, etc.) never occur postnominally, in contrast to, for instance, what Longobardi (1994) reports about Italian. Longobardi suggests that an adjective or a possessor, which is in the Spec of a projection between N and D (or the Spec of N), can occur postnominally. Thus, word order facts of this type are used to support the existence of N-to-D raising in Italian. In Chinese, the equivalent expressions are the so-called *de* expressions, which are quite free in ordering except that they must occur prenominally. We have argued in section 5.3 that they are adjoined structures, not occupying the Spec of certain functional projections. If we adopt Sportiche's (1988) proposal that modifiers (adjuncts) must be in a close structural relation with their modifiee overtly, we can account for the word order. The difference between a Chinese-type language and an Italian-type language vis-à-vis the distribution of modifiers lies in whether functional projections for the various modifiers are projected (Italian-type language) or whether modification is accomplished via adjunction alone (Chinese-type language). If modifiers occupy (the Spec of) functional projections, they are more fixed in their positions and movement of NPs can create pre- and postnominal modifiers. If modifiers are not located in separate functional projections, they are adjoined to the element that they modify and consistently occur before the modifiee as in Chinese.

10. Andrew Simpson (personal communication) raises the question of why an N cannot raise to a Cl occupied by a lexical classifier and combine with the classifier before moving further up. The answer may lie in the morphological properties of classifiers and nouns. Although a noun can be suffixed with a plural morpheme -*men*, it cannot be compounded with a classifier. A classifier is not an affix to an N, either.

11. Interestingly, Romanian and the Scandinavian languages exhibit a common alternation whereby an indefinite article precedes a noun and a definite article is suffixed to a noun: 'a book' versus 'book-the' (Longobardi 1994, 611—also see Grosu 1988; Dobrovie-Sorin 1987). That is, N can be raised to D in definite expressions, whereas raising does not take place in indefinite expressions. This would follow from the suggestion in the text that N-to-D raising has taken place in cases with a [+definite] D. However, the picture might be much more complicated. We will return to this issue in section 7.2, where we discuss options for deriving relative constructions in different languages and propose that the composition of *wh*-words is indicative of the nominal structures.

12. The assumption here is that a category is projected only if it is needed. A D needs to be projected when a lexical determiner appears or a [+definite] feature is present. In the case of English indefinite expressions, a D is also projected when a default existential operator occurs within the nominal expression (in contrast to Chinese, which generates the existential quantifier outside the nominal expression). When a D is projected, Num and Cl can be projected. If a D is not projected and there is no overt classifier, what is projected is only an NP.

13. This does not mean that English relativization also moves an NP, rather than an NP with an empty D. Languages may differ in whether D is obligatorily generated with the NP. As noted, English does not allow an NP to be generated separately from D; thus, an empty D needs to be postulated. For more details, see section 7.2.

14. In Li's (1992) terms, the licensing of a *wh*-phrase in Chinese obeys a minimality condition. When a relative operator (Rel Op) occurs in a relative clause, it intervenes between the *wh*-phrase inside the relative clause and the question licenser (Q) outside the relative clause: [Q ... Rel Op ... *wh* ...]. The lack of *wh*-island effects in *wh*-questions as discussed by Huang (1982) may be understood like this: a *wh*-word is licensed by an embedded interrogative operator in the embedded clause and interpreted with an interrogative operator in the matrix clause.

15. Ning (1993, 53) states that *the way how* is acceptable only in certain dialects.

16. Although time and place expressions often occur with the marker *zai* 'at', it is not clear that time and place expressions are true PPs and behave like adjuncts. Native speakers' judgments are uncertain. We will therefore only use the canonical adjunct expressions 'how' and 'why' to distinguish adjunct from argument NPs.

17. Jiang (1991, 162) claims that "when a topic-comment sentence is ungrammatical its corresponding relative clause is also ungrammatical." A relative construction is derived from a topic-comment structure via deletion (or relativization) of the topic. Kuno (1973, chap. 5) notes that Japanese relativization is theme deletion ("theme" seeming to correspond to "topic"). The facts pointed out by Ning (1993), however, show that relativization *can* be grammatical even though the corresponding topic-comment sentences are not.

In his revision of his 1982 dissertation, Huang extensively discusses the contrasts between relativization and topicalization. To summarize briefly: Huang states that it is now common knowledge that Chinese topic structures need not involve coindexed chains (see Shi 1992 for another view, namely, that all topic structures are formed by movement). The following examples are familiar from the literature (see, e.g., Tsao 1979; Tang 1979; Li and Thompson 1981; and cf. Chao 1968, Teng 1974):

(i) nei-chang huo, xingkui   xiaofangdui lai-de   kuai
    that-CL   fire fortunately fire-brigade come-DE fast
    '(As for) that fire, fortunately the fire brigade came fast.'

(ii) shuiguo, wo zui   xihuan xiangjiao
     fruit   I   most like   banana
     '(As for) fruits, I like bananas most.'

A topic structure without a chain may be acceptable as long as the comment can be understood as saying something about the topic—as long as an "aboutness relation" holds. This relation is not sufficient, however, to license a relativized construction.

(iii) *[$_{NP}$[$_{S'}$ xingkui   xiaofangdui lai-de   kuai de] nei-chang huo]
              fortunately fire-brigade come-DE fast DE that-CL   fire
         '*the fire such that fortunately the fire brigade came fast'

(iv) *[$_{NP}$[$_{S'}$ wo zui   xihuan xiangjiao de] shuiguo]
              I   most like   banana DE fruit
         '*the fruit such that I like bananas most'

The contrast between topic and relative structures is further illustrated by (va–b),
according to Huang.

(v) a.   tamen, yiwai   fasheng-le
          they   accident happen-LE
          '(As for) them, an accident happened.'
     b. *[$_{NP}$[$_{S'}$ yiwai   fasheng   de] neixie ren]
              accident happened DE those person
          '*the people such that an accident happened'

In other contexts, a relativized construction may be well formed where a corresponding topic structure is not. For example, an adjunct can be relativized, but
often cannot be used as a topic.

(vi) a.   [ta chang ge   de shengyin] hen hao   ting
           he sing   song DE voice   very good hear
           'The voice with which he sings is nice to listen to.'
      b. *nei-ge   shengyin, ta chang ge
           that-CL voice   he sing   song

(vii) a.   [ta duidai lisi de fangshi] hen bu hao
           he treat Lisi DE style   very not good
           'The manner in which he treated Lisi is very bad.'
      b. *zhei-ge fangshi, ta duidai lisi
           this-CL manner he treat   Lisi

Interestingly, differences between topicalization and relativization have also
been claimed to exist in Japanese. McCawley (1972, 209) quotes Muraki (1970)
on such a difference: "Specifically, the particle *de* and the dative (as opposed to
locative) occurrences of *ni* cannot be deleted before *wa*; nevertheless, corresponding relative clauses are possible." See McCawley 1972 for the relation between
topicalization and relativization in Japanese.

18. However, a null operator cannot be the equivalent of an English expression
such as (i), containing a "nonrecoverable" P and an NP.

(i) This is the girl *with whom* I danced yesterday.

(ii) *zhe shi wo zuotian   tiaowu de guniang
      this is I   yesterday dance DE girl
      'This is the girl with whom I danced yesterday.'

Ning argues that a null operator cannot be the equivalent of *with whom* because
the P in this case cannot be deleted: if it were, it would violate the recoverability
condition on deletion.

19. In principle, the gap can also be bound by an operator, rather than the Head NP. Empirically, however, the effects of this option cannot be demonstrated because of the availability of NP movement.

20. To account for relative constructions with an empty Head, it has occasionally been claimed that the Head NP can be moved away from the relative clause. It has also been proposed that the Head can simply be deleted. The unacceptability of an empty Head in cases of PP relativization and resumption argues against such analyses.

21. These facts regarding when the Head can be empty also argue against analyzing all prenominal modifiers, including adjectives and nominals, as being derived from relative clauses.

22. Judgments concerning 'how' fluctuate more from speaker to speaker than do those concerning 'why', much the way the acceptability of 'how' in various non-interrogative uses fluctuates.

23. This may be able to be reduced to the question of whether a certain *wh*-word belongs to the category NP. See Tsai 1994.

24. Probably the bare conditional contexts (see Cheng and Huang 1996) illustrated in (58e) are the most acceptable.

(i) a. ta weishenme shengbing, wo jiu   weishenme shengbing
       he why   get-sick   I   then why   get-sick
       'I got sick for the same reason he got sick.'
    b. ta zenme xiu che, ni   jiu   yinggai zenme xiu che
       he how   fix car you then should how   fix car
       'You should fix cars in the same way he fixes cars.'

In a way, then, an adjunct of this type can still be a variable-like element, though it is more restricted. It is not clear, however, why the "variable" status is so restricted.

25. This, of course, raises the question of why the movement must take place at LF, because Chinese does not allow 'how'/'why' to occur in the peripheral operator position of a relative clause. One option might be to explore the notion of feature movement (Pesetsky 2000). Another option is to examine the "resumptive" nature of *wh*-adjuncts. We leave this issue for further research.

26. It is not surprising that the Chinese counterpart of the English [NP [P XP]] is [XP *de* NP]. The prepositions in question are generally quite empty: *the result of his exam, the consequence of his evildoing*, and so on. Chinese rarely uses such empty prepositions within nominal expressions (except for *dui*, which occurs with some complements; see Fu 1994). In Chinese, modifiers always appear to the left of N, in contrast to English, where modifiers may appear to the right of N. *De* appears after a phrasal category within a Chinese nominal expression. A question, of course, is whether the prenominal modifier is a tensed clause or a gerundive expression. The distinction is not easily made in such cases. See Fu 1994 for relevant discussion.

27. Murasugi (1991) notes a locality condition on "gapless" relative clauses in Japanese, which is similar to the one for Chinese. She and other Japanese linguists have taken such relative clauses as the basic construction and tried to derive the other relative clauses by resorting to the same mechanism of nonmovement and aboutness licensing (see chapter 7 for details). Murasugi (2000a) in fact claims that Japanese does not have relative clauses. It only has "pure complex NPs." In contrast, we claim that the so-called gapless relative clauses are different from the other relative clauses and should be analyzed separately.

Chapter 7

1. Fukui and Takano (2000) label the Head *N* and the relative clause *CP*. Thus, left-adjunction of the relative clause to the Head NP is notated [CP N]. Such an account does not distinguish complementation structures from adjunction structures, as a complement XP is a sister of N and a complementation structure is also [XP N].

2. Fukui and Takano (2000) assume as in previous work (Takano 1996; Fukui and Takano 1998) that a complement is generated to the left of a head.

3. Fukui and Takano's proposal requires N-to-D raising to apply in all cases in English. This contrasts with, for instance, Chierchia's (1998) and Longobardi's (1994) analyses, where N does not raise to D when an article occurs (at least overtly). In these analyses, an article occupies the D position and N stays in the N position, N being a property-denoting, predicate type of expression. Fukui and Takano place the definite article *the* in a position higher than the Spec of D that hosts the raised N, N-to-D raising being a substitution process. See section 7.1.2 for further discussion.

4. The definition adopted by Fukui and Takano (2000, 232) is this:

(i) X c-commands Y iff X excludes Y and every element that dominates X dominates Y.

(ii) X excludes Y iff no segment of X dominates Y.

The two-segment category $[N_1, N_1]$ is the relative Head. The Head does not exclude CP. The upper N_1, a segment of $[N_1, N_1]$, dominates the CP.

5. Fukui and Takano's argument is not easy to follow here. The fact that an operator in the Spec of a CP is not needed does not mean that the head is not needed, and therefore it does not mean that a CP projection is not needed. Consider the English example (i).

(i) That he is here is important.

In this sentence, there is no requirement that an operator be present in the Spec of CP. Nonetheless, the complementizer *that* must be present. The fact that a Spec of CP is not needed does not mean that the head C is also not needed.

6. On the basis of expressions containing *kare-zisin* 'he-self', Ishii (1991, sec. 2.2.2) suggests that Japanese relativization shows reconstruction effects, although reconstruction is not available in cases containing *zibun* 'self'.

(i) mary-wa [[john$_i$-ga e taipu-sita] kare-zisin$_i$-no ronbu]-o   mottekita
Mary-TOP John-NOM typed   himself-GEN paper-ACC brought
'Mary brought himself$_i$'s paper that John$_i$ typed.'

It is plausible that (i) involves an intensifier, not a true anaphor subject to binding principles.

7. Because Japanese also has a pro option, the irrelevance of island conditions does not argue against the existence of operator movement. It is the lack of long-distance relativization and reconstruction effects that argues against the application of movement in this language.

8. In fact, there is some debate about whether this construction exists in Japanese. Kuroda (1992) claims that Japanese has head-internal relative clauses. However, Murasugi (2000a,b) argues that what has been called a head-internal relative clause in Japanese is not a relative clause at all, but a circumstantial adverbial phrase. Kuroda (1999) again argues for the existence of head-internal relative clauses, which cannot be derived by movement.

9. We have not discussed the correlation concerning the complementizer. In Chinese, it is not clear whether a complementizer does or does not exist in relative clauses. The difficulty lies in identifying a complementizer in Chinese in general. We leave this issue for further research.

10. Fukui and Takano (2000) assume that the landing site of N, after N-to-D raising, is the Spec of D. The article *the* needs to occur in a higher Spec to derive the order *the N*. Prenominal adjectives probably also occur in a Spec position between the raised N and the D. It is not clear what the full nominal structure is for English in this analysis.

11. One main difference between English and LA relative constructions lies in the fact that a relative clause is a clause in English but a nominal expression in LA, as Choueiri (2002, chap. 4) discusses.

12. This raises the question of why Swedish has an N-CP complementation structure as proposed by Platzack (2000). A relative construction is also required to project to a DP in Swedish, according to Platzack. What led Platzack to an N-complementation proposal was that Swedish relative constructions do not exhibit reconstruction effects. We may reinterpret such facts as indicating that Swedish relative constructions only use the strategy of operator movement. Head raising does not apply. It is possible that Head raising, which raises a DP with an empty D to Head position, is not available because of the failure of the empty D to be licensed (see the discussion of English and LA indefinite relative constructions). The need to check the features of the complementizer *som* by the external D may play an important role, a fact that Platzack discusses. However, because we do not understand the finer details of Swedish, we will not speculate on a solution here. Demeke (2001) has proposed a similar analysis for Amharic, which has a Head-final relative construction (see note 15).

13. Of course, it does not matter whether N-to-D raising applies, as discussed earlier.

14. The D can be a Demonstrative node in Hindi. In such languages, there does not seem to be much empirical significance in distinguishing a Determiner node from a Demonstrative node.

15. A relative clause in Hindi can be either postposed or preposed to a clause-peripheral position, creating more variations (though it is controversial whether the postposed and preposed ones are true relatives). Moreover, under quite limited circumstances, a relative clause may occur prenominally in Hindi. For one thing, such a relative clause must be in participial form, which is exactly what a complementation structure predicts, according to Kayne (1994, chap. 8). Indeed, it seems to be the case that, when a language essentially has Head-initial relative constructions, the Head-final variation is often restricted to participials. On the other hand, a language like Chinese, which allows only Head-final relative constructions, does not show such limitations on prenominal relatives.

Amharic relative clauses precede the determiner and are N-final (see Kayne 1994, sec. 8.3, also quoting Gragg 1972). Kayne suggests that such relative clauses are not CPs. For lack of detailed data regarding reconstruction, long-distance relativization, adjunct relativization, and so on, we will not try to provide an analysis of relative constructions in Amharic (but see Ouhalla 1999 and Demeke 2001, for instance, for analyses of Amharic relative constructions).

16. An operator can also be a DP, as *who* is in English. The terms *DP movement* and *operator movement* are convenient labels for distinguishing between movement of a DP with an empty D and movement of a DP with a quantificational D, such as *who*.

17. According to Hagstrom (1998) and Miyagawa (2001), the Q-particle expresses existential quantification. This is supported by the fact that the Q-particle is required for the relevant *wh*-phrases to be quantificational. See the discussion regarding (43)–(46).

18. In LA, if operator movement is not adopted, a relative clause can be licensed by an agreement relation between the Head and the complementizer. In LA, a complementizer such as *yalli* in a definite relative construction must agree with the Head in φ-features. An indefinite relative would have a null complementizer agreeing with the Head. See Choueiri 2002, chap. 4.

19. Note that even in English (as well as LA and Japanese), it is possible for an indefinite nominal interpreted with a quantifier to be generated in a position separate from the quantifier (Lewis 1975; Kamp 1981; Heim 1982). For instance, the indefinites in the following sentences (from Diesing 1992, 5) can vary in quantificational force depending on the context in which they appear:

(i) a. A contrabassoonist usually plays too loudly.
    b. Most contrabassoonists play too loudly.

(ii) a. Cellists seldom play out of tune.
     b. Few cellists play out of tune.

To be noted, however, is that the indefinite noun phrases in such cases are still structurally headed by a determiner. In other words, even though semantically such indefinite noun phrases are interpreted as variables, their D position is occupied syntactically. (The indefinite article might not have originated in D. However, the indefinite article is in complementary distribution with other elements in D such as *the*, *this*, or *that*.) It is possible that the indefinite determiner is also generated in D directly, or is generated in a Q or Number projection and is then raised to D (Diesing 1992). Alternatively, it may be generated in, and stay in, a Q or Number position; but in this case, D is occupied by a variable, to be bound by a quantifier from outside (see Borer, to appear). No matter which option is taken, D is projected in such cases. This contrasts with indefinite noun phrases in Chinese, which can be projected as NPs. The clue to such a structural distinction is the behavior of *wh*-phrases and, in the case of Chinese, the distribution of the plural marker.

Note that such an analysis of Chinese NPs still keeps the spirit that a Restriction needs to be related to a quantifier (operator). That is, even though an NP can be generated in an argument position, it is not sufficient by itself for interpretation. In this sense, a type-shifting rule to change the type of a Chinese NP from a predicate to an argument is not necessary (Chierchia 1998).

20. Bhatt (2000) proposes an NP-raising process to derive English relative constructions, instead of a DP-raising process. Such a proposal fails to explain why English and Chinese differ as they do and why English does not generate NPs in argument positions in constructions other than relatives.

21. As noted earlier, many languages (e.g., Hindi) use different lexical items to form *wh*-questions and relative constructions. What matters here is not the exact form of such words but their morphological structure: whether a word expresses only Restriction or Quantification plus Restriction.

22. Recall that such in-situ *wh*-phrases are not raised covertly, as shown in chapter 2.

23. The in-situ 'how' and 'why' generally need not occur.

24. It is not the case that an adjunct is always an operator and therefore always undergoes movement. Recall that an adjunct can behave like a variable in some contexts such as *donkey*-type sentences (containing a conditional clause).

25. In the case of non-DP adjuncts, it is the maximal projection of an adverbial category that contains Quantification and *wh*.

Appendix

1. If the third *wh*-phrase is not in the correct configuration, the sentence cannot be rescued. For details, see Kayne 1983.

2. See Hoji 1985, chap. 2, and 1986 regarding the application of the linking mechanism to various binding relations, including WCO.

3. Hornstein's and Pesetsky's approaches differ with respect to the structure in (i), illustrated by (ii), where the fronted *wh*-phrase is the lowest *wh*-phrase.

(i) wh_3 [wh_1 ... wh_2 ... x_3]

(ii) Who did who persuade whom to dance with?

Pesetsky's account predicts such a sentence to be acceptable. Hornstein's, however, should predict it to be unacceptable: the variable x_3 cannot avoid being linked with a pronoun on its left.

4. Interestingly, Norbert Hornstein (personal communication) notes that similar effects are found with pronoun binding. For him, the improvement of (ib) and (iib) over (ia) and (iia) is not as significant as the improvement of (5b) over (5a).

(i) a. To whom$_i$ did his$_i$ mother say that Mary would buy a car?
   b. To whom$_i$ did his$_i$ mother say that Mary would buy his$_i$ car?

(ii) a. Who$_i$ did his$_i$ mother introduce to guests that came from England?
    b. Who$_i$ did his$_i$ mother introduce to guests that came from his$_i$ school?

If the contrast is significant, linking theory might need to be revised to accommodate it.

5. There are other interesting nonmovement approaches to superiority effects. For instance, superiority effects are characterized by Lasnik and Saito (1992, 120–121) as an S-Structure condition.

(i) a. A WH-phrase X in SPEC of CP is Op-disjoint (operator-disjoint) from a WH-phrase Y if the assignment of the index of X to Y would result in the local Ā-binding of Y by X. (S-Structure)
   b. If two WH-phrases X and Y are Op-disjoint, then they cannot undergo absorption.

To this proposal, it does not matter whether an overtly in-situ *wh*-phrase undergoes covert movement at LF. Stroik (1995) argues against such an analysis (for details, see Stroik 1995, 243–245). He claims that an in-situ *wh* stays in situ at LF (see Stroik 1992; Aoun and Li 1993b; Chomsky 1995, chap. 3). His account of superiority effects is an "inner-island analysis" (Stroik 1995, 250). In a multiple *wh*-question, $[_{CP}$ *wh*$_1$ $[C$ $[_{IP} \dots$ *wh*$_2 \dots$ t$_1 \dots]]]$, where *wh*$_1$ is raised from t$_1$ to Spec of C and *wh*$_2$ is in situ, *wh*$_2$ prevents the *wh*-operator (*wh*$_1$) from antecedent-governing its trace (t$_1$). Main supporting data for this analysis are those involving D-linking *wh*-phrases and the absence of superiority effects in multiple *wh*-questions like these:

(ii) a. Who knows what who said?
    b. I know what who said to whom.

(iii) a. Who do books about what annoy most?
     b. Who were stories about whom being told to?
     c. What did the children sitting on whose lap want to read?

For D-linking *wh*-phrases, see section 2.2.3 of this book and especially example (38). Sentences (iia–b) concern the rescuing effects of an additional *wh*-phrase, which is dubious as shown here in the appendix. Questions (iiia–c) concern the absence of superiority effects resulting from an in-situ *wh*-phrase embedded within a nominal phrase. However, just like the obscure rescuing effect of an additional *wh*-phrase, the depth of embedding of a *wh*-phrase does not always made superiority effects disappear, as demonstrated by the unacceptability of the following sentences:

(iv) a. *What did books about whom cause many readers to get annoyed about?

    b. *Who would friends of whom say to Mary that stories were being told
      to?

    c. *What did the children sitting on whose lap think that you would read?

It remains a question, however, why (iiia–c) are acceptable.

6. A lower argument *wh* can also save the structure. Saito proposes an LF raising analysis to assimilate these cases to those with an additional c-commanding *wh*.

7. For a recent account based on Saito 1994 concerning the same facts in Japanese and German, see Grewendorf 2001.

References

Abney, Steven. 1987. The English noun phrase in its sentential aspect. Doctoral dissertation, MIT, Cambridge, Mass.

Åfarli, Tor A. 1994. A promotion analysis of restrictive relative clauses. *The Linguistic Review* 11, 81–100.

Alexiadou, Artemis, Paul Law, Andre Meinunger, and Chris Wilder. 2000. Introduction. In Artemis Alexiadou, Paul Law, Andre Meinunger, and Chris Wilder, eds., *The syntax of relative clauses*, 1–52. Amsterdam: John Benjamins.

Aoun, Joseph. 1985. *A grammar of anaphora*. Cambridge, Mass.: MIT Press.

Aoun, Joseph. 1986. *Generalized Binding*. Dordrecht: Foris.

Aoun, Joseph. 1999. Clitic-doubled arguments. In Kyle Johnson and Ian Roberts, eds., *Beyond principles and parameters: Essays in memory of Osvaldo Jaeggli*, 13–42. Dordrecht: Kluwer.

Aoun, Joseph, and Elabbas Benmamoun. 1998. Minimality, reconstruction, and PF movement. *Linguistic Inquiry* 29, 569–597.

Aoun, Joseph, and Lina Choueiri. 1997. Resumption and Last Resort. Ms., University of Southern California, Los Angeles.

Aoun, Joseph, and Lina Choueiri. 1999. Modes of interrogation. Ms., University of Southern California, Los Angeles.

Aoun, Joseph, and Lina Choueiri. 2000. Epithets. *Natural Language and Linguistic Theory* 18, 1–39.

Aoun, Joseph, Lina Choueiri, and Norbert Hornstein. 2001. Resumption, movement, and derivational economy. *Linguistic Inquiry* 32, 371–404.

Aoun, Joseph, and Yen-hui Audrey Li. 1989. Constituency and scope. *Linguistic Inquiry* 20, 141–172.

Aoun, Joseph, and Yen-hui Audrey Li. 1993a. *Syntax of scope*. Cambridge, Mass.: MIT Press.

Aoun, Joseph, and Yen-hui Audrey Li. 1993b. *Wh*-elements in-situ: Syntax or LF? *Linguistic Inquiry* 24, 199–238.

Arnaiz, Alfredo. 1996. *N*-words and *wh*-in-situ: Nature and interactions. Doctoral dissertation, University of Southern California, Los Angeles.

Baker, C. L. 1970. Notes on the description of English questions: The role of an abstract question morpheme. *Foundations of Language* 6, 197–219.

Barss, Andrew. 1986. Chains and anaphoric dependencies. Doctoral dissertation, MIT, Cambridge, Mass.

Barss, Andrew. 2000. Minimalism and asymmetric *wh*-interpretation. In Roger Martin, David Michaels, and Juan Uriagereka, eds., *Step by step: Essays on minimalist syntax in honor of Howard Lasnik*, 31–52. Cambridge, Mass.: MIT Press.

Beck, Sigrid. 1996. Quantified structures as barriers for LF movement. *Natural Language Semantics* 4, 1–56.

Beck, Sigrid, and Shin-Sook Kim. 1997. On *wh*- and operator scope in Korean. *Journal of East Asian Linguistics* 6, 339–384.

Beghelli, Filippo. 1995. The phrase structure of quantifier scope. Doctoral dissertation, University of California, Los Angeles.

Beghelli, Filippo. 1997. The syntax of distributivity and pair-list readings. In Anna Szabolcsi, ed., *Ways of scope taking*, 349–408. Dordrecht: Kluwer.

Beghelli, Filippo, and Tim Stowell. 1997. Distributivity and negation: The syntax of *each* and *every*. In Anna Szabolcsi, ed., *Ways of scope taking*, 71–108. Dordrecht: Kluwer.

Bernstein, Judy. 1993. Topics in the nominal structure across Romance. Doctoral dissertation, City University of New York.

Bhatt, Rajesh. 2000. Adjectival modifiers and the raising analysis of relative clauses. In Masako Hirotani, Andries Coetzee, Nancy Hall, and Ji-yung Kim, eds., *NELS 30*, 55–67. Amherst: University of Massachusetts, GLSA.

Bhattacharya, Tanmoy. 1999. The structure of Bangla DP. Doctoral dissertation, University College London, London.

Bianchi, Valentina. 1999. *Consequences of antisymmetry: Headed relative clauses*. New York: Mouton de Gruyter.

Bianchi, Valentina. 2000a. The raising analysis of relative clauses: A reply to Borsley. *Linguistic Inquiry* 31, 123–140.

Bianchi, Valentina. 2000b. Some issues in the syntax of relative determiners. In Artemis Alexiadou, Paul Law, Andre Meinunger, and Chris Wilder, eds., *The syntax of relative clauses*, 53–82. Amsterdam: John Benjamins.

Boeckx, Cedric A. 2001. Mechanisms of chain formation. Doctoral dissertation, University of Connecticut, Storrs.

Bolinger, Dwight. 1978. Asking more than one thing at a time. In Henry Hiz, ed., *Questions*, 107–150. Dordrecht: Reidel.

Borer, Hagit. To appear. Exo-skeletal vs. endo-skeletal explanations: Syntactic projections and the lexicon. In Maria Polinsky and John Moore, eds., *Explanation in linguistic theory*.

Borsley, Robert D. 1997. Relative clauses and the theory of phrase structure. *Linguistic Inquiry* 28, 629–647.

Bošković, Željko. 1997. On certain violations of the Superiority Condition, AgrO, and economy of derivation. *Journal of Linguistics* 33, 227–254.

Bošković, Željko. 1998. Multiple *wh*-fronting and economy of derivation. In Emily Curtis, James Lyle, and Gabriel Webster, eds., *The Proceedings of the Sixteenth West Coast Conference on Formal Linguistics*, 49–64. Stanford, Calif.: Stanford University, Center for the Study of Language and Information.

Bošković, Željko. 1999. On multiple feature checking: Multiple *wh*-fronting and multiple head movement. In Samuel David Epstein and Norbert Hornstein, eds., *Working minimalism*, 159–187. Cambridge, Mass.: MIT Press.

Brame, Michael. 1968. A new analysis of the relative clause: Evidence for an interpretive theory. Ms., MIT, Cambridge, Mass.

Brody, Michael. 1995. *Lexico-Logical Form: A radically minimalist theory*. Cambridge, Mass.: MIT Press.

Browning, M. A. 1987. Null operator constructions. Doctoral dissertation, MIT, Cambridge, Mass.

Carlson, Greg N. 1977. Amount relatives. *Language* 53, 520–542.

Carstens, Vicki. 1991. The morphology and syntax of determiner phrases in Kiswahili. Doctoral dissertation, University of California, Los Angeles.

Cecchetto, Carlo, and Gennaro Chierchia. 1999. Reconstruction in dislocation constructions and the syntax/semantics interface. In Kimary Shahin, Susan Blake, and Eun-Sook Kim, eds., *The Proceedings of the Seventeenth West Coast Conference on Formal Linguistics*, 132–146. Stanford, Calif.: Stanford University, Center for the Study of Language and Information.

Chao, Yuen-Ren. 1968. *A grammar of spoken Chinese*. Berkeley, Calif.: University of California Press.

Cheng, Lisa L.-S. 1991. On the typology of *wh*-questions. Doctoral dissertation, MIT, Cambridge, Mass.

Cheng, Lisa L.-S. 1995. On *dou*-quantification. *Journal of East Asian Linguistics* 4, 197–234.

Cheng, Lisa L.-S., and C.-T. James Huang. 1996. Two types of donkey sentences. *Natural Language Semantics* 4, 121–163.

Cheng, Lisa L.-S., and Rint Sybesma. 1999. Bare and not-so-bare nouns and the structure of NP. *Linguistic Inquiry* 30, 509–542.

Chierchia, Gennaro. 1991. Functional *wh* and weak crossover. In Dawn Bates, ed., *The Proceedings of the Tenth West Coast Conference on Formal Linguistics*, 75–90. Stanford, Calif.: Stanford University, Center for the Study of Language and Information.

Chierchia, Gennaro. 1993. Questions with quantifiers. *Natural Language Semantics* 1, 181–234.

Chierchia, Gennaro. 1998. Reference to kinds across languages. *Natural Language Semantics* 6, 339–405.

Chiu, Bonnie. 1998. Relative clauses in child Chinese. Ms., National Taiwan University, Taipei.

Chomsky, Noam. 1964. *Current issues in linguistic theory*. The Hague: Mouton.

Chomsky, Noam. 1965. *Aspects of the theory of syntax*. Cambridge, Mass.: MIT Press.

Chomsky, Noam. 1976. Conditions on rules of grammar. *Linguistic Analysis* 2, 303–351. (Reprinted in Chomsky 1977a, 163–210.)

Chomsky, Noam. 1977a. *Essays on form and interpretation*. New York: North-Holland.

Chomsky, Noam. 1977b. On *wh*-movement. In Peter Culicover, Thomas Wasow, and Adrian Akmajian, eds., *Formal syntax*, 71–132. New York: Academic Press.

Chomsky, Noam. 1981. *Lectures on government and binding*. Dordrecht: Foris.

Chomsky, Noam. 1982. *Some concepts and consequences of the theory of government and binding*. Cambridge, Mass.: MIT Press.

Chomsky, Noam. 1986a. *Barriers*. Cambridge, Mass.: MIT Press.

Chomsky, Noam. 1986b. *Knowledge of language*. New York: Praeger.

Chomsky, Noam. 1995. *The Minimalist Program*. Cambridge, Mass.: MIT Press.

Chomsky, Noam. 2000. Minimalist inquiries: The framework. In Roger Martin, David Michaels, and Juan Uriagereka, eds., *Step by step: Essays on minimalist syntax in honor of Howard Lasnik*, 89–156. Cambridge, Mass.: MIT Press.

Chomsky, Noam. 2001. Beyond explanatory adequacy. Ms., MIT, Cambridge, Mass.

Choueiri, Lina. 2002. Re-visiting relatives: Issues in the syntax of resumptive restrictive relatives. Doctoral dissertation, University of Southern California, Los Angeles.

Cinque, Guglielmo. 1990. *Types of Ā-dependencies*. Cambridge, Mass.: MIT Press.

Cinque, Guglielmo. 1994. On the evidence for partial N-movement in the Romance DP. In Guglielmo Cinque, Jan Koster, Jean-Yves Pollock, Luigi Rizzi, and Raffaella Zanuttini, eds., *Paths towards Universal Grammar*, 85–110. Washington, D.C.: Georgetown University Press.

Cinque, Guglielmo. 1999. *Adverbs and functional heads: A cross-linguistic perspective*. New York: Oxford University Press.

Cole, Peter. 1987. The structure of internally headed relative clauses. *Natural Language and Linguistic Theory* 5, 277–302.

Comorovski, Ileana. 1996. *Interrogative phrases and the syntax-semantics interface*. Dordrecht: Kluwer.

Dayal, Veneeta Srivistav. 1996. *Locality in WH quantification: Questions and relative clauses in Hindi*. Dordrecht: Kluwer.

Del Gobbo, Francesca. 2001. Appositives schmappositives in Chinese. In Maki Irie and Hajime Ono, eds., *UCI working papers in linguistics* 7, 1–25. Irvine: University of California.

Delsing, Lars Olof. 1988. The Scandinavian noun phrase. *Working Papers in Scandinavian Syntax* 42, 57–80.

Demeke, Girma A. 2001. N-final relative clauses: The Amharic case. *Studia Linguistica* 55, 191–215.

Demirdache, Hamida. 1991. Resumptive chains in restrictive relatives, appositives and dislocation structures. Doctoral dissertation, MIT, Cambridge, Mass.

Diesing, Molly. 1990. Verb-second in Yiddish and the nature of the subject position. *Natural Language and Linguistic Theory* 8, 41–79.

Diesing, Molly. 1992. *Indefinites*. Cambridge, Mass.: MIT Press.

Dobrovie-Sorin, Carmen. 1987. A propos de la structure du groupe nominal en roumain. *Rivista di grammatica generativa* 12, 123–152.

Emonds, Joseph. 1979. Appositive relatives have no properties. *Linguistic Inquiry* 10, 211–243.

Engdahl, Elisabet. 1983. Parasitic gaps. *Linguistics and Philosophy* 6, 5–34.

Engdahl, Elisabet. 1985. Parasitic gaps, resumptive pronouns and subject extractions. *Linguistics* 23, 3–44.

Engdahl, Elisabet. 1986. *Constituent questions*. Dordrecht: Reidel.

Fabb, Nigel. 1990. The difference between English restrictive and appositive clauses. *Journal of Linguistics* 26, 57–78.

Fassi Fehri, Abdelkader. 1989. Generalised IP structure, Case and VS order. In Itziar Laka and Anoop Mahajan, eds., *Functional heads and clause structure*, 75–113. MIT Working Papers in Linguistics 10. Cambridge, Mass.: MIT, Department of Linguistics and Philosophy.

Feng, Shengli. 1995. Prosodic structure and prosodically constrained syntax in Chinese. Doctoral dissertation, University of Pennsylvania, Philadelphia.

Fiengo, Robert, C.-T. James Huang, Howard Lasnik, and Tanya Reinhart. 1988. The syntax of *wh*-in-situ. In Hagit Borer, ed., *The Proceedings of the Seventh West Coast Conference on Formal Linguistics*, 81–98. Stanford, Calif.: Stanford University, Center for the Study of Language and Information.

Fu, Jingqi. 1994. On deriving Chinese derived nominals: Evidence for V-to-N raising. Doctoral dissertation, University of Massachusetts, Amherst.

Fukui, Naoki, and Margaret Speas. 1986. Specifiers and projection. In Naoki Fukui, Tova R. Rapoport, and Elizabeth Sagey, eds., *Papers in theoretical linguistics*, 128–172. MIT Working Papers in Linguistics 8. Cambridge, Mass.: MIT, Department of Linguistics and Philosophy.

Fukui, Naoki, and Yuji Takano. 1998. Symmetry in syntax: Merge and Demerge. *Journal of East Asian Linguistics* 7, 27–86.

Fukui, Naoki, and Yuji Takano. 2000. Nominal structure: An extension of the Symmetry Principle. In Peter Svenonius, ed., *The derivation of VO and OV*, 219–254. Amsterdam: John Benjamins.

Garrett, Edward. 1996. *Wh*-in-situ and the syntax of distributivity. In Edward Garrett and Felicia Lee, eds., *Syntax at sunset* 129–145. UCLA Working Papers in Linguistics 1. Los Angeles: University of California, Los Angeles.

Gasde, Horst-Dieter, and Waltraud Paul. 1996. Functional categories, topic prominence, and complex sentences in Mandarin Chinese. *Linguistics* 34, 263–294.

Giorgi, Alessandra, and Giuseppe Longobardi. 1991. *The syntax of noun phrases*. Cambridge: Cambridge University Press.

Gragg, Gene B. 1972. Sumerian and selected Afro-Asiatic languages. In Paul M. Peranteau, Judith N. Levi, and Gloria C. Phares, eds., *The Chicago which hunt: Papers from the Relative Clause Festival*, 153–168. Chicago: University of Chicago, Chicago Linguistic Society.

Grewendorf, Günther. 2001. Multiple *wh*-fronting. *Linguistic Inquiry* 32, 87–122.

Grimshaw, Jane. 1990. *Argument structure*. Cambridge, Mass.: MIT Press.

Groenendijk, Jeroen, and Martin Stokhof. 1984. *Studies on the semantics of questions and the pragmatics of answers*. Amsterdam: Academisch Proefschrift.

Grosu, Alexander. 1988. On the distribution of genitive phrases in Rumanian. *Linguistics* 26, 931–949.

Grosu, Alexander, and Fred Landman. 1998. Strange relatives of the third kind. *Natural Language Semantics* 6, 125–170.

Hagstrom, Paul Alan. 1998. Decomposing questions. Doctoral dissertation, MIT, Cambridge, Mass.

Hamblin, Charles L. 1973. Questions in Montague Grammar. *Foundations of Language* 10, 41–53. (Reprinted in Barbara H. Partee, ed. 1976. *Montague Grammar*, 247–259. New York: Academic Press.)

Haudry, J. 1973. Parataxe, hypotaxe et correlation dans la phrase latine. *Bulletin de la Société Linguistique de Paris* 68, 147–186.

Heim, Irene. 1982. The semantics of definite and indefinite noun phrases. Doctoral dissertation, University of Massachusetts, Amherst.

Heim, Irene. 1987. Where does the definiteness restriction apply? Evidence from the definiteness of variables. In Eric Reuland and Alice G. B. ter Meulen, eds., *The representation of (in)definiteness*, 21–42. Cambridge, Mass.: MIT Press.

Hendrick, Randall, and Michael Rochemont. 1982. Complementation, multiple wh and echo questions. Ms., University of North Carolina and University of California, Irvine.

Higginbotham, James. 1980. Pronouns and bound variables. *Linguistic Inquiry* 11, 679–708.

Higginbotham, James. 1983. Logical Form, binding, and nominals. *Linguistic Inquiry* 14, 395–420.

Higginbotham, James. 1985. On semantics. *Linguistic Inquiry* 16, 547–593.

Higginbotham, James, and Robert May. 1981. Questions, quantifiers and crossing. *The Linguistic Review* 1, 41–80.

Hoji, Hajime. 1985. Logical Form constraints and configurational structures in Japanese. Doctoral dissertation, University of Washington, Seattle.

Hoji, Hajime. 1986. Weak Crossover and Japanese phrase structure. In Takashi Imai and Mamoru Saito, eds., *Issues in Japanese linguistics*, 163–201. Dordrecht: Foris.

Hoji, Hajime. To appear. Falsifiability and repeatability in generative grammar: A case study of anaphora and scope dependency. *Lingua*.

Holmberg, Anders, ed. 1992. *Papers from the Workshop on the Scandinavian Noun Phrase*. Report 32. Umeå, Sweden: Department of General Linguistics, University of Umeå.

Hornstein, Norbert. 1984. *Logic as grammar*. Cambridge, Mass.: MIT Press.

Hornstein, Norbert. 1995. *Logical Form: From GB to minimalism*. Cambridge, Mass.: Blackwell.

Hornstein, Norbert. 2001. *Move! A minimalist theory of construal*. Cambridge, Mass.: Blackwell.

Huang, Chu-Ren. 1987. Cliticization and type-lifting: A unified account of Mandarin NP. Doctoral dissertation, Cornell University, Ithaca, N.Y. (Published by Indiana University Linguistics Club Publications, 1989.)

Huang, C.-T. James. 1982. Logical relations in Chinese and the theory of grammar. Doctoral dissertation, MIT, Cambridge, Mass.

Huang, C.-T. James. 1993. Reconstruction and the structure of VP. *Linguistic Inquiry* 24, 103–138.

Iljic, Robert. 1994. Quantification in Mandarin Chinese: Two markers of plurality. *Linguistics* 32, 91–116.

Ishii, Yasuo. 1991. Operators and empty categories in Japanese. Doctoral dissertation, University of Connecticut, Storrs.

Jackendoff, Ray. 1977. *X̄ syntax: A study of phrase structure*. Cambridge, Mass.: MIT Press.

Jiang, Zixin. 1991. Some aspects of the topic and subject in Chinese. Doctoral dissertation, University of Chicago, Chicago, Ill.

Kamp, Hans. 1981. A theory of truth and semantic representation. In Jeroen Groenendijk, Theo Janssen, and Martin Stokhof, eds., *Formal methods in the study of language*, 277–321. Amsterdam: Mathematical Centre.

Karttunen, Lauri. 1977. The syntax and semantics of questions. *Linguistics and Philosophy* 1, 3–44.

Katz, Jerrold J., and Paul M. Postal. 1964. *An integrated theory of linguistic descriptions.* Cambridge, Mass.: MIT Press.

Kayne, Richard. 1975. *French syntax.* Cambridge, Mass.: MIT Press.

Kayne, Richard. 1983. Connectedness. *Linguistic Inquiry* 14, 223–249.

Kayne, Richard. 1994. *The antisymmetry of syntax.* Cambridge, Mass.: MIT Press.

Kayne, Richard. 2001. Pronouns and their antecedents. Ms., New York University.

Kester, Ellen-Petra. 1993. The inflectional properties of Scandinavian adjectives. *Studia Linguistica* 47, 139–153.

Kim, Soowon. 1991. Chain scope and quantification structure. Doctoral dissertation, Brandeis University, Waltham, Mass.

É. Kiss, Katalin. 1986. Against LF-movement and *wh*-phrases. Ms., Hungarian Academy of Sciences, Budapest.

Klima, Edward S. 1964. Negation in English. In Jerry A. Fodor and Jerrold Katz, eds., *Readings in the philosophy of language*, 246–323. Englewood Cliffs, N.J.: Prentice-Hall.

Koopman, Hilda, and Dominique Sportiche. 1982. Variables and the Bijection Principle. *The Linguistic Review* 2, 139–160.

Kuno, Susumu. 1973. *The structure of the Japanese language.* Cambridge, Mass.: MIT Press.

Kuno, Susumu, and Jane J. Robinson. 1972. Multiple *wh*-questions. *Linguistic Inquiry* 3, 463–487.

Kuroda, S.-Y. 1965. Generative grammatical studies in Japanese language. Doctoral dissertation, MIT, Cambridge, Mass. (Reprinted by Garland Press, New York, 1979.)

Kuroda, S.-Y. 1968. English relativization and certain related problems. *Language* 44, 244–266. (Reprinted in David A. Reibel and Sanford A. Schane, eds. 1969. *Modern studies in English: Readings in transformational grammar*, 264–287. Englewood Cliffs, N.J.: Prentice-Hall.)

Kuroda, S.-Y. 1992. Pivot-independent relativization in Japanese. In *Japanese syntax and semantics: Collected papers*, chap. 3. Dordrecht: Kluwer.

Kuroda, S.-Y. 1999. Notes on so-called head-internal relative clauses in Japanese. In Masatake Muraki and Enoch Iwamoto, eds., *Linguistics: In search of the human mind. A festschrift for Kazuko Inoue*, 414–429. Tokyo: Kaitaku-sha.

Laka Mugarza, Miren Itziar. 1990. Negation in syntax: On the nature of functional categories and projections. Doctoral dissertation, MIT, Cambridge, Mass.

Lappin, Shalom, Robert D. Levine, and David E. Johnson. 2000a. The structure of unscientific revolutions. *Natural Language and Linguistic Theory* 18, 665–671.

Lappin, Shalom, Robert D. Levine, and David E. Johnson. 2000b. The revolution confused: A response to our critics. *Natural Language and Linguistic Theory* 18, 873–890.

Larson, Richard. 1985. Bare-NP adverbs. *Linguistic Inquiry* 16, 595–621.

Larson, Richard, and Naoko Takahashi. 2002. Order and interpretation in Japanese relative clauses. Paper presented at the annual meeting of the Linguistic Society of America, San Francisco.

Lasnik, Howard, and Mamoru Saito. 1984. On the nature of proper government. *Linguistic Inquiry* 15, 235–289.

Lasnik, Howard, and Mamoru Saito. 1992. *Move α*. Cambridge, Mass.: MIT Press.

Lebeaux, David. 1992. Relative clauses, licensing, and the nature of the derivation. In Susan Rothstein and Margaret Speas, eds., *Perspectives on phrase structure: Heads and licensing*, 209–239. Syntax and Semantics 25. San Diego, Calif.: Academic Press.

Lee, Mina. 2001. Qualifying paper, University of Southern California, Los Angeles.

Lee, Thomas H. T. 1986. Studies on quantification in Chinese. Doctoral dissertation, University of California, Los Angeles.

Lees, Robert B. 1960. *The grammar of English nominalizations*. The Hague: Mouton.

Lees, Robert B. 1961. The constituent structures of noun phrases. *American Speech* 36, 159–168.

Legendre, Géraldine, Paul Smolensky, and Colin Wilson. 1998. When is less more? Faithfulness and minimal links in *wh*-chains. In Pilar Barbosa, Danny Fox, Paul Hagstrom, Martha McGinnis, and David Pesetsky, eds., *Is the best good enough? Optimality and competition in syntax*, 249–290. Cambridge, Mass.: MIT Press.

Lewis, David. 1975. Adverbs of quantification. In Edward Keenan, ed., *Formal semantics of natural languages*, 3–15. Cambridge: Cambridge University Press.

Li, Charles, and Sandra Thompson. 1981. *Mandarin Chinese: A functional reference grammar*. Berkeley: University of California Press.

Li, Yen-hui Audrey. 1992. Indefinite *wh* in Mandarin Chinese. *Journal of East Asian Linguistics* 1, 125–156.

Li, Yen-hui Audrey. 1998. Argument determiner phrases and number phrases. *Linguistic Inquiry* 29, 693–702.

Li, Yen-hui Audrey. 1999a. Form and function correspondence: Structures and interpretations of nominal expressions in Mandarin Chinese. In Yukinori Takubo, ed., *Comparative syntax of Japanese, Korean, Chinese and English*, 147–186. Report of the International Scientific Research Program, Ministry of Education, Science and Culture, Japan.

Li, Yen-hui Audrey. 1999b. Plurality in a classifier language. *Journal of East Asian Linguistics* 8, 75–99.

Li, Yen-hui Audrey. 2001. Universal constructions? Relativization in English and Chinese. *Concentric* 27, 81–102.

Longobardi, Giuseppe. 1994. Reference and proper names. *Linguistic Inquiry* 25, 609–666.

Mahajan, Anoop. 2000. Relative asymmetries and Hindi correlatives. In Artemis Alexiadou, Paul Law, Andre Meinunger, and Chris Wilder, eds., *The syntax of relative clauses*, 201–230. Amsterdam: John Benjamins.

May, Robert. 1977. The grammar of quantification. Doctoral dissertation, MIT, Cambridge, Mass.

May, Robert. 1985. *Logical Form: Its structure and derivation*. Cambridge, Mass.: MIT Press.

May, Robert. 1990. A note on quantifier absorption. *The Linguistic Review* 7, 121–127.

McCawley, James D. 1972. Japanese relative clauses. In Paul M. Peranteau, Judith N. Levi, and Gloria C. Phares, eds., *The Chicago which hunt: Papers from the Relative Clause Festival*, 205–214. Chicago: University of Chicago, Chicago Linguistic Society.

McCawley, James D. 1981. The syntax and semantics of English relative clauses. *Lingua* 53, 99–149.

McCawley, James D. 1982. Parentheticals and discontinuous constituent structure. *Linguistic Inquiry* 13, 91–106.

McCloskey, James. 1990. Resumptive pronouns, A′-binding, and levels of representation in Irish. In Randall Hendrick, ed., *Syntax and semantics of the modern Celtic languages*, 199–248. Syntax and Semantics 23. San Diego, Calif.: Academic Press.

McCloskey, James. To appear. Resumption, successive cylicity, and the locality of operations. In Samuel David Epstein and Daniel Seely, eds., *Derivation and explanation*. Oxford: Blackwell.

Miyagawa, Shigeru. 2001. The EPP, scrambling and *wh*-in-situ. In Michael Kenstowicz, ed., *Ken Hale: A life in language*, 293–338. Cambridge, Mass.: MIT Press.

Moltmann, Friederike, and Anna Szabolcsi. 1994. Scope interactions with pair-list quantifiers. In Mercè Gonzàlez, ed., *NELS 24*, 381–396. Amherst: University of Massachusetts, GLSA.

Montague, Richard. 1974. English as a formal language. In Richmond H. Thomason, ed., *Formal philosophy: Selected papers of Richard Montague*, 188–221. New Haven, Conn.: Yale University Press.

Munn, Alan. 1992. A null operator analysis of ATB gaps. *The Linguistic Review* 9, 1–26.

Munn, Alan. 1994. A minimalist account of reconstruction asymmetries. In Mercè Gonzàlez, ed., *NELS 24*, 397–410. Amherst: University of Massachusetts, GLSA.

Muraki, Masatake. 1970. Presupposition, pseudo-clefting, and thematization. Doctoral dissertation, University of Texas, Austin.

Murasugi, Keiko. 1991. Noun phrases in Japanese and English: A study in syntax, learnability, and acquisition. Doctoral dissertation, University of Connecticut, Storrs.

Murasugi, Keiko. 2000a. Antisymmetry analysis of Japanese relative clauses. In Artemis Alexiadou, Paul Law, Andre Meinunger, and Chris Wilder, eds., *The syntax of relative clauses*, 231–264. Amsterdam: John Benjamins.

Murasugi, Keiko. 2000b. Japanese complex noun phrases and the antisymmetry theory. In Roger Martin, David Michaels, and Juan Uriagereka, eds., *Step by step: Essays on minimalist syntax in honor of Howard Lasnik*, 211–234. Cambridge, Mass.: MIT Press.

Ning, Chun-yuan. 1993. Theory of relativization in Chinese. Doctoral dissertation, University of California, Irvine.

Nishigauchi, Taisuke. 1990. *Quantification in the theory of grammar*. Dordrecht: Kluwer.

Nishigauchi, Taisuke. 1998. "Multiple sluicing" in Japanese and the functional nature of *wh*-phrases. *Journal of East Asian Linguistics* 7, 121–152.

Nunes, Jairo. 1995. The copy theory of movement and the linearization of chains in the Minimalist Program. Doctoral dissertation, University of Maryland, College Park.

Nunes, Jairo. 2001. Sideward movement. *Linguistic Inquiry* 32, 303–344.

Oka, Toshifusa. 1993. Minimalism in syntactic derivation. Doctoral dissertation, MIT, Cambridge, Mass.

Ouhalla, Jamal. 1988. Movement in noun phrases. Paper presented at the meeting of the Linguistic Association of Great Britain, Durham, U.K., March 1988.

Ouhalla, Jamal. 1996. Remarks on the binding properties of *wh*-pronouns. *Linguistic Inquiry* 27, 676–708.

Ouhalla, Jamal. 1999. Predication and expletive determiners in definite relatives. Ms., Queen Mary-London University, London.

Ouhalla, Jamal. 2001. Parasitic gaps and resumptive pronouns. In Peter W. Culicover and Paul M. Postal, eds., *Parasitic gaps*, 128–147. Cambridge, Mass.: MIT Press.

Partee, Barbara. 1975. Montague Grammar and transformational grammar. *Linguistic Inquiry* 6, 203–300.

Pesetsky, David. 1982. Paths and categories. Doctoral dissertation, MIT, Cambridge, Mass.

Pesetsky, David. 1987. *Wh*-in situ: Movement and unselective binding. In Eric J. Reuland and Alice G. B. ter Meulen, eds., *The representation of (in)definiteness*, 98–129. Cambridge, Mass.: MIT Press.

Pesetsky, David. 1998. Some optimality principles of sentence pronunciation. In Pilar Barbosa, Danny Fox, Paul Hagstrom, Martha McGinnis, and David Pesetsky, eds., *Is the best good enough? Optimality and competition in syntax*, 337–384. Cambridge, Mass.: MIT Press.

Pesetsky, David. 2000. *Phrasal movement and its kin*. Cambridge, Mass.: MIT Press.

Platzack, Christer. 2000. A complement of N account of restrictive and non-restrictive relatives: The case of Swedish. In Artemis Alexiadou, Paul Law, Andre Meinunger, and Chris Wilder, eds., *The syntax of relative clauses*, 265–308. Amsterdam: John Benjamins.

Prince, Ellen F. 1990. Syntax and discourse: A look at resumptive pronouns. In Kira Hall, Jean-Pierre Koenig, Michael Meacham, Sondra Reinman, and Laurel A. Sutton, eds., *Proceedings of the Sixteenth Annual Meeting of the Berkeley Linguistic Society*, 482–497. Berkeley: University of California, Berkeley Linguistic Society.

Reinhart, Tanya. 1981. Definite NP anaphora and c-command domains. *Linguistic Inquiry* 12, 605–635.

Reinhart, Tanya. 1997. Quantifier scope: How labor is divided between QR and choice function. *Linguistics and Philosophy* 20, 335–397.

Reinhart, Tanya, and Eric Reuland. 1993. Reflexivity. *Linguistic Inquiry* 24, 657–720.

Richards, Norvin. 1997. What moves where when in which language? Doctoral dissertation, MIT, Cambridge, Mass.

Richards, Norvin. 1998. The Principle of Minimal Compliance. *Linguistic Inquiry* 29, 599–630.

Ritter, Elizabeth. 1986. NSO noun phrase in a VSO language. Ms., MIT, Cambridge, Mass.

Ritter, Elizabeth. 1989. A head-movement approach to construct-state noun phrases. *Linguistics* 26, 909–929.

Ritter, Elizabeth. 1991. Two functional categories in noun phrases: Evidence from modern Hebrew. In Susan Rothstein, ed., *Perspectives on phrase structure*, 37–62. Syntax and Semantics 25. San Diego, Calif.: Academic Press.

Ritter, Elizabeth. 1995. On the syntactic category of pronouns and agreement. *Natural Language and Linguistic Theory* 13, 405–443.

Rizzi, Luigi. 1990. *Relativized Minimality*. Cambridge, Mass.: MIT Press.

Rizzi, Luigi. 1997. The fine structure of the left periphery. In Liliane Haegeman, ed., *Elements of grammar*, 281–337. Dordrecht: Kluwer.

Roberts, Ian. 2000. Caricaturing dissent. *Natural Language and Linguistic Theory* 18, 849–857.

Ross, John R. 1967. Constraints on variables in syntax. Doctoral dissertation, MIT, Cambridge, Mass.

Rudin, Catherine. 1988. On multiple questions and multiple *wh*-fronting. *Natural Language and Linguistic Theory* 6, 445–501.

Rygaloff, Alexis. 1973. *Grammaire élémentaire du chinois*. Paris: Presses Universitaires de France.

Safir, Ken. 1986. Relative clauses in a theory of binding and levels. *Linguistic Inquiry* 17, 663–689.

Safir, Ken. 1999. Vehicle change and reconstruction in Ā-chains. *Linguistic Inquiry* 30, 587–620.

Saito, Mamoru. 1985. Some asymmetries in Japanese and their theoretical implications. Doctoral dissertation, MIT, Cambridge, Mass.

Saito, Mamoru. 1994. Additional-*wh* effects and the adjunction site theory. *Journal of East Asian Linguistics* 3, 195–240.

Sauerland, Uli. 1998. The meaning of chains. Doctoral dissertation, MIT, Cambridge, Mass.

Schachter, Paul. 1973. Focus and relativization. *Language* 49, 19–46.

Schmitt, Cristina. 2000. Some consequences of the complement analysis for relative clauses, demonstratives and the wrong adjectives. In Artemis Alexiadou, Paul Law, Andre Meinunger, and Chris Wilder, eds., *The syntax of relative clauses*, 309–348. Amsterdam: John Benjamins.

Sells, Peter. 1984. Syntax and semantics of resumptive pronouns. Doctoral dissertation, University of Massachusetts, Amherst.

Sells, Peter. 1985. Restrictive and non-restrictive modification. Report CSLI-85-28. Stanford, Calif.: Stanford University, Center for the Study of Language and Information.

Sharvit, Yael. 1996. The syntax and semantics of functional relative clauses. Doctoral dissertation, Rutgers University, New Brunswick, N.J.

Sharvit, Yael. 1999. Resumptive pronouns in relative clauses. *Natural Language and Linguistic Theory* 17, 587–612.

Shi, Dingxu. 1992. The nature of topic comment constructions and topic chains. Doctoral dissertation, University of Southern California, Los Angeles.

Siloni, Tali. 1989. Le syntagme nominal en hébreu. Ms., Université de Genève.

Siloni, Tali. 1990. Hebrew noun phrases: Generalized noun raising. Ms., Université de Genève.

Simpson, Andrew. 2000. Wh-*movement and the theory of feature checking*. Amsterdam: John Benjamins.

Simpson, Andrew. 2001. Definiteness agreement and the Chinese DP. *Language and Linguistics* 2, 125–156.

Simpson, Andrew. 2002. On the status of "modifying" DE and the structure of the Chinese DP. In Sze Wing Tang and Chen-Sheng Luther Liu, eds., *On the formal way to Chinese linguistics*. Stanford, Calif.: CSLI Publications.

Smith, Carlota S. 1964. Determiners and relative clauses in a generative grammar of English. *Language* 40, 37–52. (Reprinted in David A. Reibel and Sanford A. Schane, eds. 1969. *Modern studies in English*, 247–263. Englewood Cliffs, N.J.: Prentice-Hall.)

Sportiche, Dominique. 1988. A theory of floating quantifiers and its corollaries for constituent structure. *Linguistic Inquiry* 19, 425–450.

Sproat, Richard, and Chilin Shih. 1991. The cross-linguistic distribution of adjective ordering restrictions. In Carol Georgopoulos and Roberta Ishihara, eds., *Interdisciplinary approaches to language*, 565–593. Dordrecht: Kluwer.

Stockwell, Robert S., Paul Schachter, and Barbara Partee. 1973. *The major syntactic structures of English*. New York: Holt, Rinehart and Winston.

Stroik, Thomas. 1992. English *wh*-in-situ constructions. *Linguistic Analysis* 22, 133–153.

Stroik, Thomas. 1995. Some remarks on superiority effects. *Lingua* 95, 239–258.

Szabolcsi, Anna. 1997a. Variation, distributivity, and the illusion of branching. In Anna Szabolcsi, ed., *Ways of scope taking*, 29–70. Dordrecht: Kluwer.

Szabolcsi, Anna. 1997b. Strategies for scope taking. In Anna Szabolcsi, ed., *Ways of scope taking*, 109–154. Dordrecht: Kluwer.

Szabolcsi, Anna. 1997c. Quantifiers in pair-list readings. In Anna Szabolcsi, ed., *Ways of scope taking*, 311–348. Dordrecht: Kluwer.

Takano, Yuji. 1996. Movement and parametric variation in syntax. Doctoral dissertation, University of California, Irvine.

Tang, Chih-chen Jane. 1990. Chinese phrase structure and the extended X'-theory. Doctoral dissertation, Cornell University, Ithaca, N.Y.

Tang, Ting-chi. 1979. *Studies in Chinese syntax*. Taipei: Student Books.

Taraldsen, Tarald. 1981. The theoretical interpretation of a class of marked extractions. In Adriana Belletti, Luciana Brandi, and Luigi Rizzi, eds., *Theory of markedness in generative grammar*, 475–516. Pisa: Scuola Normale Superiore.

Taraldsen, Tarald. 1990. D-projections and N-projections in Norwegian. In Marina Nespor and Joan Mascaró, eds., *Grammar in progress*, 419–431. Dordrecht: Foris.

Teng, Shou-hsin. 1974. *A semantic study of transitivity relations in Chinese*. Berkeley and Los Angeles: University of California Press. (Reprinted Taipei: Student Books, 1975.)

Tsai, Wei-tien Dylan. 1994. On economizing the theory of A-bar dependency. Doctoral dissertation, MIT, Cambridge, Mass.

Tsao, Feng-fu. 1979. *A functional study of topic in Chinese: The first step towards discourse analysis*. Taipei: Student Books.

Ueyama, Ayumi. 1998. Two types of dependency. Doctoral disssertation, University of Southern California, Los Angeles.

Uriagereka, Juan. 1998. *Rhyme and reason*. Cambridge, Mass.: MIT Press.

Valois, Daniel. 1991. The internal syntax of DP and adjective placement in French and English. In Tim Sherer, ed., *NELS 21*, 367–382. Amherst: University of Massachusetts, GLSA.

Vergnaud, Jean-Roger. 1974. French relative clauses. Doctoral dissertation, MIT, Cambridge, Mass.

Watanabe, Akira. 1992. Subjacency and S-Structure movement of *wh*-in-situ. *Journal of East Asian Linguistics* 1, 255–291.

Watanabe, Shin. 1995. Aspects of questions in Japanese and their theoretical implications. Doctoral dissertation, University of Southern California, Los Angeles.

Wiltschko, Martina. 1998. Superiority in German. In Emily Curtis, James Lyle, and Gabriel Webster, eds., *The Proceedings of the Sixteenth West Coast Conference on Formal Linguistics*, 431–446. Stanford, Calif.: Stanford University, Center for the Study of Language and Information.

Wu, Xiu-zhi. 2001. Grammaticalization and the development of functional categories in Chinese. Doctoral dissertation, University of Southern California, Los Angeles.

Yorifuji, Atsushi. 1976. Men ni tsuite (A study of the suffix *-men*). *Area and Cultural Studies* 26, 73–88.

Yoshida, Keiko, and Tomoyuki Yoshida. 1997. Question marker drop in Japanese. *International Christian University Language Research Bulletin* 11, 37–54.

Zhang, Niina. 2001. The interaction between the relative D and its external D in Chinese. Ms., Zentrum für allgemeine Sprachwissenschaft, Berlin.

Index